SCIENCE FUSION

fusion [FYOO • zhuhn] a combination of two or more things that releases energy

This **Interactive Student Edition** belongs to

Teacher/Room

HOLT McDOUGAL

HOUGHTON MIFFLIN HARCOURT

Consulting Authors

Michael A. DiSpezio

Global Educator
North Falmouth, Massachusetts

Michael DiSpezio is a renaissance educator who moved from the research laboratory of a Nobel Prize winner to the K–12 science classroom. He has authored or co-authored numerous textbooks and written more than 25 trade books. For nearly a decade he worked with the JASON Project, under the auspices of the National Geographic Society, where he designed curriculum, wrote lessons, and hosted dozens of studio and location broadcasts. Over the past two decades, he has developed supplementary material for organizations and shows that include PBS *Scientific American Frontiers, Discover* magazine, and the Discovery Channel. He has extended his reach outside the United States and into topics of crucial importance today. To all his projects, he brings his extensive background in science and his expertise in classroom teaching at the elementary, middle, and high school levels.

Marjorie Frank

Science Writer and
Content-Area Reading Specialist
Brooklyn, New York

An educator and linguist by training, a writer and poet by nature, Marjorie Frank has authored and designed a generation of instructional materials in all subject areas, including past HMH Science programs. Her other credits include authoring science issues of an award-winning children's magazine; writing game-based digital assessments in math, reading, and language arts; and serving as instructional designer and co-author of pioneering school-to-work software for Classroom Inc., a nonprofit organization dedicated to improving reading and math skills for middle and high school learners. She wrote lyrics and music for *SCIENCE SONGS,* which was an American Library Association nominee for notable recording. In addition, she has served on the adjunct faculty of Hunter, Manhattan, and Brooklyn Colleges, teaching courses in science methods, literacy, and writing.

Acknowledgments for Covers

Front cover: *Skier* (bg) ©David Stoecklein/Corbis; *pacific wheel* (l) ©Geoffrey George/Getty Images; *snowboarder* (cl) ©Jonathan Nourok/Photographer's Choice/Getty Images; *water droplet* (cr) ©L. Clarke/Corbis; *molecular structure* (r) ©Stockbyte/Getty Images

Printed in the U.S.A.

ISBN 978-0-547-58947-3

15 16 17 18 19 20 0029 21 20 19 18 17 16

4500586004 DEFG

Michael R. Heithaus

Director, School of Environment and Society
Associate Professor, Department of Biological Sciences
Florida International University
North Miami, Florida

Mike Heithaus joined the Florida International University Biology Department in 2003. He has served as Director of the Marine Sciences Program and is now Director of the School of Environment and Society, which brings together the natural and social sciences and humanities to develop solutions to today's environmental challenges. While earning his doctorate, he began the research that grew into the Shark Bay Ecosystem Project in Western Australia, with which he still works. Back in the United States, he served as a Research Fellow with National Geographic, using remote imaging in his research and hosting a 13-part *Crittercam* television series on the National Geographic Channel. His current research centers on predator-prey interactions among vertebrates, such as tiger sharks, dolphins, dugongs, sea turtles, and cormorants.

Donna M. Ogle

Professor of Reading and Language
National-Louis University
Chicago, Illinois

Creator of the well-known KWL strategy, Donna Ogle has directed many staff development projects translating theory and research into school practice in middle and secondary schools throughout the United States. She is a past president of the International Reading Association and has served as a consultant on literacy projects worldwide. Her extensive international experience includes coordinating the Reading and Writing for Critical Thinking Project in Eastern Europe, developing an integrated curriculum for a USAID Afghan Education Project, and speaking and consulting on projects in several Latin American countries and in Asia. Her books include *Coming Together as Readers; Reading Comprehension: Strategies for Independent Learners; All Children Read;* and *Literacy for a Democratic Society.*

Program Reviewers

Content Reviewers

Paul D. Asimow, PhD
Professor of Geology and Geochemistry
Division of Geological and Planetary Sciences
California Institute of Technology
Pasadena, CA

Laura K. Baumgartner, PhD
Postdoctoral Researcher
Molecular, Cellular, and Developmental Biology
University of Colorado
Boulder, CO

Eileen Cashman, PhD
Professor
Department of Environmental Resources Engineering
Humboldt State University
Arcata, CA

Hilary Clement Olson, PhD
Research Scientist Associate V
Institute for Geophysics, Jackson School of Geosciences
The University of Texas at Austin
Austin, TX

Joe W. Crim, PhD
Professor Emeritus
Department of Cellular Biology
The University of Georgia
Athens, GA

Elizabeth A. De Stasio, PhD
Raymond H. Herzog Professor of Science
Professor of Biology
Department of Biology
Lawrence University
Appleton, WI

Dan Franck, PhD
Botany Education Consultant
Chatham, NY

Julia R. Greer, PhD
Assistant Professor of Materials Science and Mechanics
Division of Engineering and Applied Science
California Institute of Technology
Pasadena, CA

John E. Hoover, PhD
Professor
Department of Biology
Millersville University
Millersville, PA

William H. Ingham, PhD
Professor (Emeritus)
Department of Physics and Astronomy
James Madison University
Harrisonburg, VA

Charles W. Johnson, PhD
Chairman, Division of Natural Sciences, Mathematics, and Physical Education
Associate Professor of Physics
South Georgia College
Douglas, GA

Program Reviewers *(continued)*

Tatiana A. Krivosheev, PhD
Associate Professor of Physics
Department of Natural Sciences
Clayton State University
Morrow, GA

Joseph A. McClure, PhD
Associate Professor Emeritus
Department of Physics
Georgetown University
Washington, DC

Mark Moldwin, PhD
Professor of Space Sciences
Atmospheric, Oceanic, and Space Sciences
University of Michigan
Ann Arbor, MI

Russell Patrick, PhD
Professor of Physics
Department of Biology, Chemistry, and Physics
Southern Polytechnic State University
Marietta, GA

Patricia M. Pauley, PhD
Meteorologist, Data Assimilation Group
Naval Research Laboratory
Monterey, CA

Stephen F. Pavkovic, PhD
Professor Emeritus
Department of Chemistry
Loyola University of Chicago
Chicago, IL

L. Jeanne Perry, PhD
Director (Retired)
Protein Expression Technology Center
Institute for Genomics and Proteomics
University of California, Los Angeles
Los Angeles, CA

Kenneth H. Rubin, PhD
Professor
Department of Geology and Geophysics
University of Hawaii
Honolulu, HI

Brandon E. Schwab, PhD
Associate Professor
Department of Geology
Humboldt State University
Arcata, CA

Marllin L. Simon, Ph.D.
Associate Professor
Department of Physics
Auburn University
Auburn, AL

Larry Stookey, PE
Upper Iowa University
Wausau, WI

Kim Withers, PhD
Associate Research Scientist
Center for Coastal Studies
Texas A&M University-Corpus Christi
Corpus Christi, TX

Matthew A. Wood, PhD
Professor
Department of Physics & Space Sciences
Florida Institute of Technology
Melbourne, FL

Adam D. Woods, PhD
Associate Professor
Department of Geological Sciences
California State University, Fullerton
Fullerton, CA

Natalie Zayas, MS, EdD
Lecturer
Division of Science and Environmental Policy
California State University, Monterey Bay
Seaside, CA

Teacher Reviewers

Ann Barrette, MST
Whitman Middle School
Wauwatosa, WI

Barbara Brege
Crestwood Middle School
Kentwood, MI

Katherine Eaton Campbell, M Ed
Chicago Public Schools-Area 2 Office
Chicago, IL

Karen Cavalluzzi, M Ed, NBCT
Sunny Vale Middle School
Blue Springs, MO

Katie Demorest, MA Ed Tech
Marshall Middle School
Marshall, MI

Jennifer Eddy, M Ed
Lindale Middle School
Linthicum, MD

Tully Fenner
George Fox Middle School
Pasadena, MD

Dave Grabski, MS Ed
PJ Jacobs Junior High School
Stevens Point, WI

Amelia C. Holm, M Ed
McKinley Middle School
Kenosha, WI

Ben Hondorp
Creekside Middle School
Zeeland, MI

George E. Hunkele, M Ed
Harborside Middle School
Milford, CT

Jude Kesl
Science Teaching Specialist 6–8
Milwaukee Public Schools
Milwaukee, WI

Joe Kubasta, M Ed
Rockwood Valley Middle School
St. Louis, MO

Mary Larsen
Science Instructional Coach
Helena Public Schools
Helena, MT

Angie Larson
Bernard Campbell Middle School
Lee's Summit, MO

Christy Leier
Horizon Middle School
Moorhead, MN

Helen Mihm, NBCT
Crofton Middle School
Crofton, MD

Jeff Moravec, Sr., MS Ed
Teaching Specialist
Milwaukee Public Schools
Milwaukee, WI

Nancy Kawecki Nega, MST, NBCT, PAESMT
Churchville Middle School
Elmhurst, IL

Mark E. Poggensee, MS Ed
Elkhorn Middle School
Elkhorn, WI

Sherry Rich
Bernard Campbell Middle School
Lee's Summit, MO

Mike Szydlowski, M Ed
Science Coordinator
Columbia Public Schools
Columbia, MO

Nichole Trzasko, M Ed
Clarkston Junior High School
Clarkston, MI

Heather Wares, M Ed
Traverse City West Middle School
Traverse City, MI

Contents in Brief

SMT
Shanghai Transrapid

This maglev train uses electromagnets to move. A maglev train can travel at speeds over 300 mph!

Contents

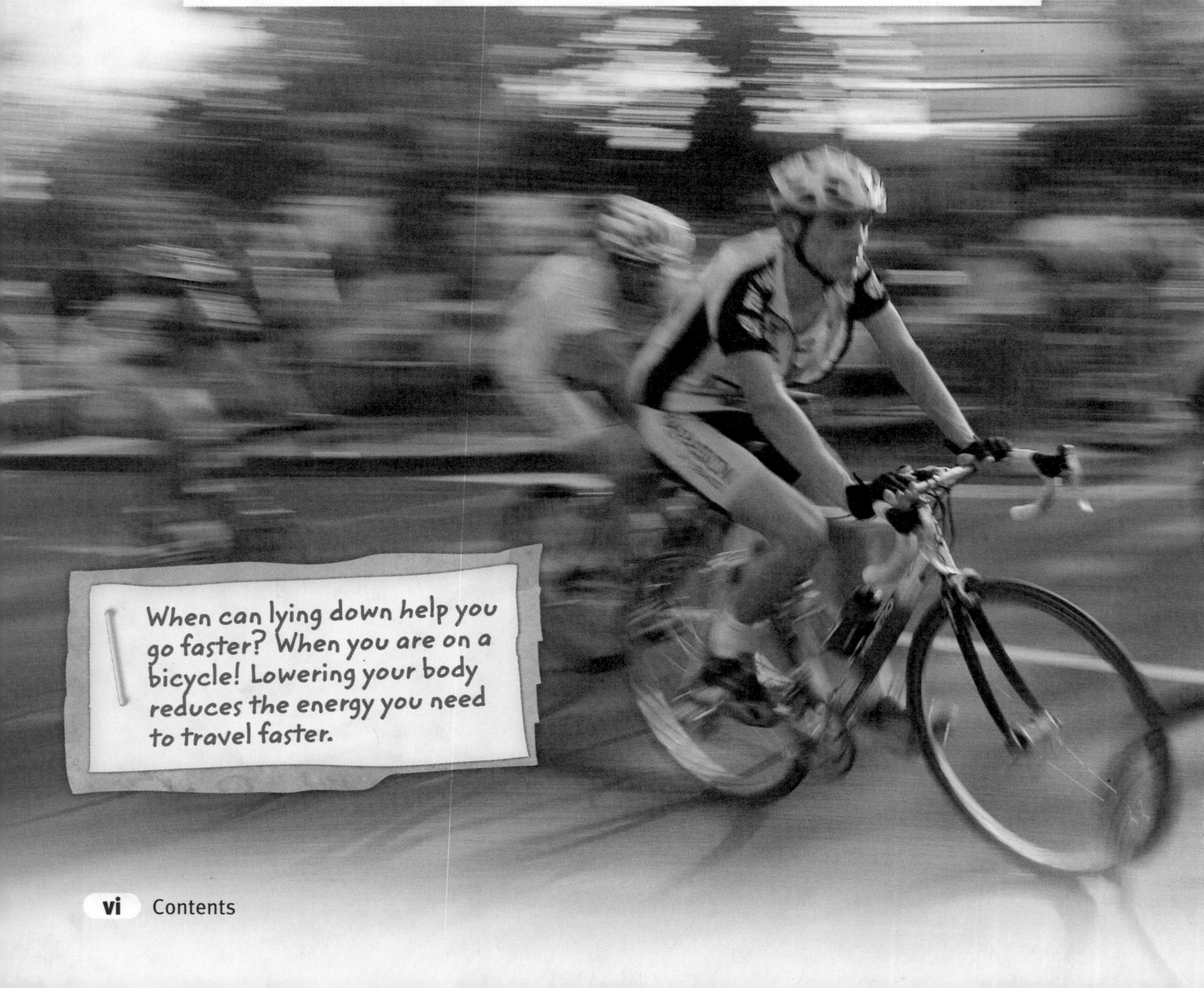

When can lying down help you go faster? When you are on a bicycle! Lowering your body reduces the energy you need to travel faster.

Probably invented more than 40,000 years ago, the bow is a complex machine that is still used today.

Assignments:

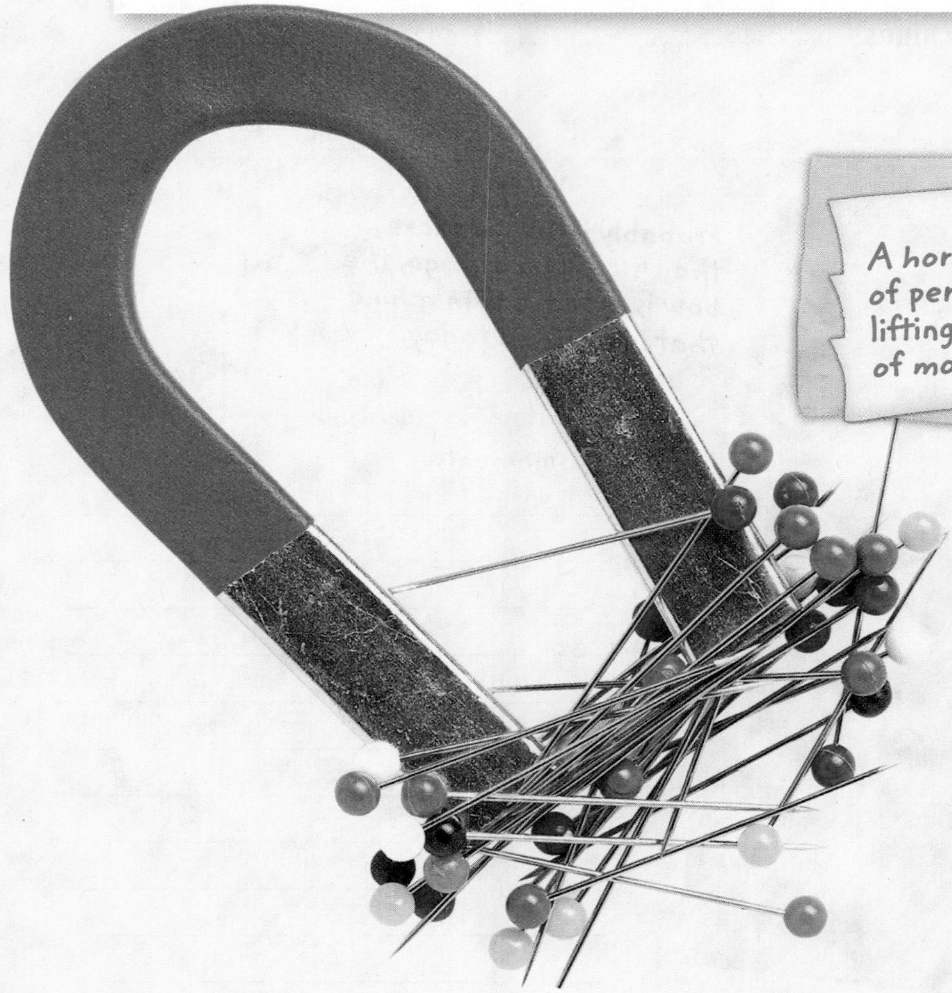

A horseshoe magnet is a type of permanent magnet. Its lifting strength is double that of most bar magnets.

Assignments:

Power up with Science Fusion!

Your program fuses . . .

Labs and Activities
e-Learning and Virtual Labs
Write-In Student Edition

. . . to generate energy for today's science learner — you.

S.T.E.M. **Engineering & Technology**

S.T.E.M. activities throughout the program!

Write-In Student Edition

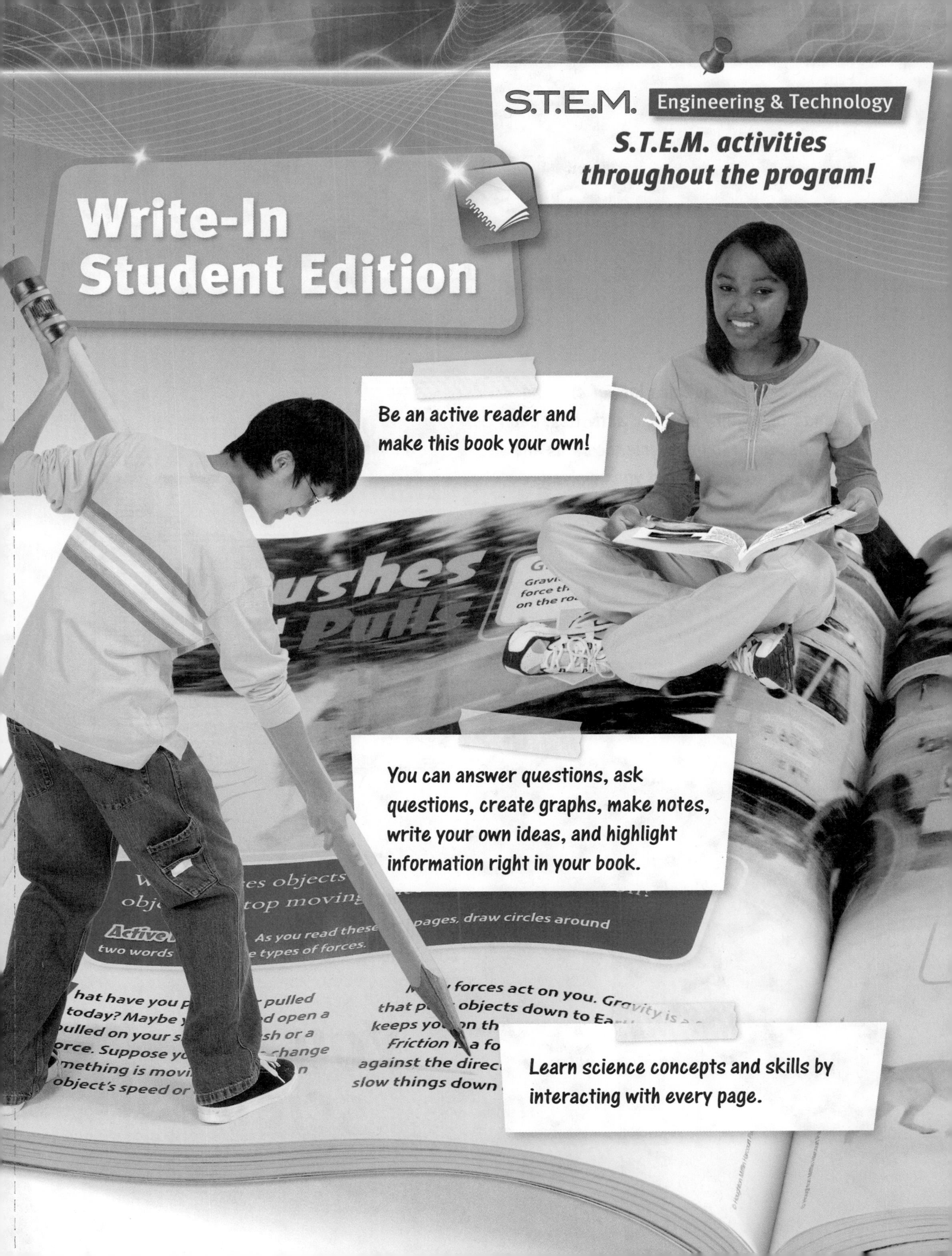

Be an active reader and make this book your own!

You can answer questions, ask questions, create graphs, make notes, write your own ideas, and highlight information right in your book.

Learn science concepts and skills by interacting with every page.

Labs and Activities

ScienceFusion includes lots of exciting hands-on inquiry labs and activities, each one designed to bring science skills and concepts to life and get you involved.

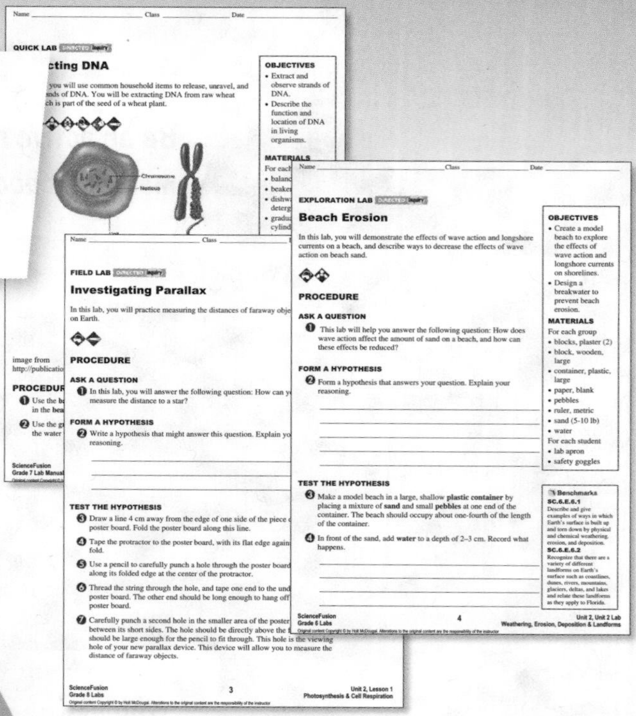

QUICK LAB
OBJECTIVES
MATERIALS
FIELD LAB
Investigating Parallax
PROCEDURE
ASK A QUESTION
FORM A HYPOTHESIS
TEST THE HYPOTHESIS
EXPLORATION LAB
Beach Erosion
In this lab, you will demonstrate the effects of wave action and longshore currents on a beach, and describe ways to decrease the effects of wave action on beach sand.
PROCEDURE
ASK A QUESTION
This lab will help you answer the following question: How does wave action affect the amount of sand on a beach, and how can these effects be reduced?
FORM A HYPOTHESIS
Form a hypothesis that answers your question. Explain your reasoning.
TEST THE HYPOTHESIS
Make a model beach in a large, shallow plastic container by placing a mixture of sand and small pebbles at one end of the container. The beach should occupy about one-fourth of the length of the container.
In front of the sand, add water to a depth of 2–3 cm. Record what happens.
OBJECTIVES
MATERIALS

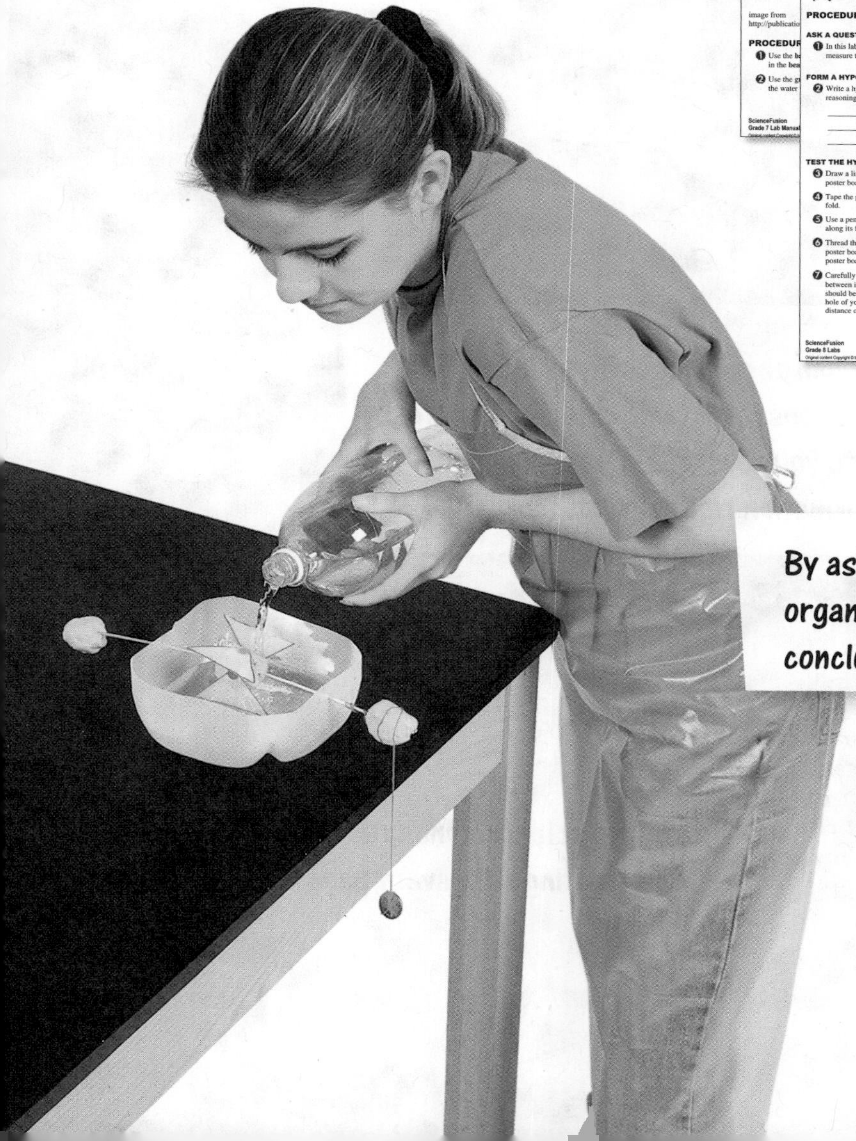

By asking questions, testing your ideas, organizing and analyzing data, drawing conclusions, and sharing what you learn...

You are the scientist!

e-Learning and Virtual Labs

Digital lessons and virtual labs provide e-learning options for every lesson of Science Fusion.

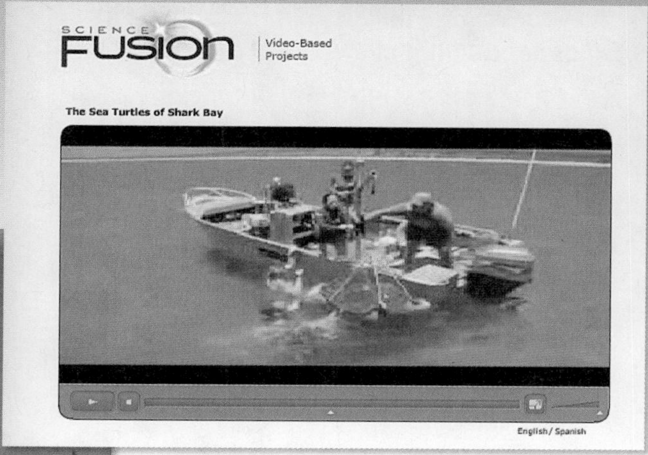

SCIENCE FUSION
Video-Based Projects
The Sea Turtles of Shark Bay
English / Spanish

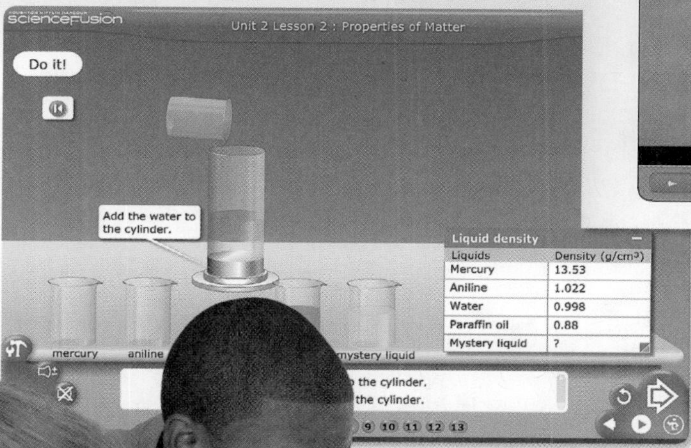

sciencefusion
Unit 2 Lesson 2 : Properties of Matter
Do it!
Add the water to the cylinder.
Liquid density
Liquids
Density (g/cm³)
Mercury
13.53
Aniline
1.022
Water
0.998
Paraffin oil
0.88
Mystery liquid
?
mercury
aniline
mystery liquid
the cylinder.
the cylinder.
9 10 11 12 13

On your own or with a group, explore science concepts in a digital world.

360° of Inquiry

UNIT 1

Motion and Forces

Big Idea

Unbalanced forces cause changes in the motion of objects, and these changes can be predicted and described.

The parachute helps slow the shuttle down.
Discovery
United States

What do you think?

How do you change the direction in which an object is moving? By applying force, of course. Can you tell what force helps the shuttle slow down? What allows the rocket in the photo to lift off?

Unit 1

Motion and Forces

CITIZEN SCIENCE

What's in a Vane?

For hundreds of years, people have used the wind to do work, such as grind flour and pump water.

1 Define The Problem

We need electricity to do work, such as power the lights and appliances that we use daily. As our need for electricity grows, many people are becoming more interested in new ways to generate electricity. Have you heard of using windmills to generate electricity?

A windmill vane, or sail, is a large structure that is attached to a rotating axle. The vane catches the wind and turns around. This turning motion can be used to generate electricity.

2 Think About It

Designing a windmill vane

What characteristics of a windmill vane help it to catch the most wind? Create two different designs for windmill vanes that you can test to see which characteristics are the most beneficial.

Consider these factors as you design your vanes.

- ☐ the size of the vanes
- ☐ the shape of the vanes
- ☐ materials used to build the vanes

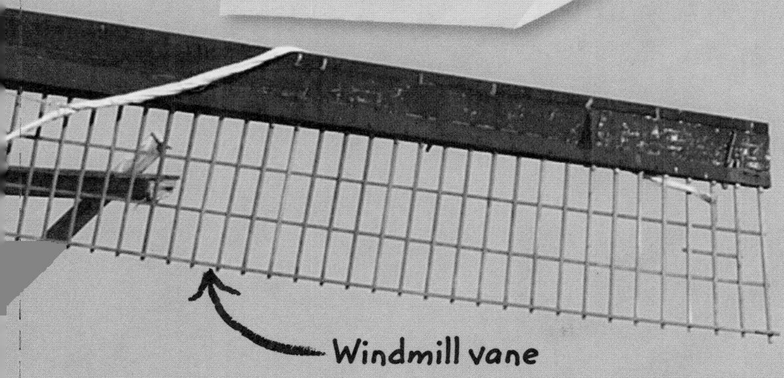
Windmill vane

Take It Home

With the help of an adult, research windmills that are used to generate electricity for homes. Study the different designs and decide which would be best for your family.

3 Plan and Test Your Design

A Your windmill designs should feature four windmill vanes attached to a straw or wooden spindle. The straw or spindle will be the axle. You should mount your axle so that it can spin freely. In the space below, sketch two designs that you would like to test.

B In the space below, identify what you will use as a wind source and the variables you must control.

____

____

____

____

____

C Conduct your test and briefly state your findings below.

____

____

____

____

____

Lesson 1

Motion and Speed

ESSENTIAL QUESTION

How are distance, time, and speed related?

By the end of this lesson, you should be able to analyze how distance, time, and speed are related.

The personal watercraft in this photo is going fast. How can we measure how fast it is going?

Lesson Labs

Quick Labs
- Investigate Changing Positions
- Create a Distance-Time Graph

S.T.E.M. Lab
- Investigate Average Speed

Engage Your Brain

1 Predict Circle the correct words in the paragraph below to make true statements.

A dog usually moves faster than a bug. That means that if I watch them move for one minute, then the dog would have traveled a *greater/ smaller* distance than the bug. However, a car usually goes *faster/slower* than a dog. If the car and the dog both traveled to the end of the road, then the *car/dog* would get there first.

2 Explain Draw or sketch something that you might see move. Write a caption that answers the following questions: How would you describe its motion? Is it moving at a constant speed, or does it speed up and slow down?

Active Reading

3 Define Fill in the blank with the word that best completes the following sentences.

If an object changes its position, then it is

____

The speed of a car describes

____

____

Vocabulary Terms

- **position**
- **reference point**
- **motion**
- **speed**
- **vector**
- **velocity**

4 Apply As you learn the definition of each vocabulary term in this lesson, make your own definition or sketch to help you remember the meaning of the term.

Location, location,

How can you describe the location of an object?

Have you ever gotten lost while looking for a specific place? If so, you probably know that the description of the location can be very important. Imagine that you are trying to describe your location to a friend. How would you explain where you are? You need two pieces of information: a position and a reference point.

With a Position

Position describes the location of an object. Often, you describe where something is by comparing its position with where you currently are. For example, you might say that a classmate sitting next to you is two desks to your right, or that a mailbox is two blocks south of where you live. Each time you identify the position of an object, you are comparing the location of the object with the location of another object or place.

With a Reference Point

When you describe a position by comparing it to the location of another object or place, you are using a reference point. A **reference point** is a location to which you compare other locations. In the example above of a mailbox that is two blocks south of where you live, the reference point is "where you live."

Imagine that you are at a zoo with some friends. If you are using the map to the right, you could describe your destination using different reference points. Using yourself as the reference point, you might say that the red panda house is one block east and three blocks north of your current location. Or you might say the red panda house is one block north and one block east of the fountain. In this example, the fountain is your reference point.

Active Reading **5 Apply** How would you describe where this question is located on the page? Give two different answers using two different reference points.

location

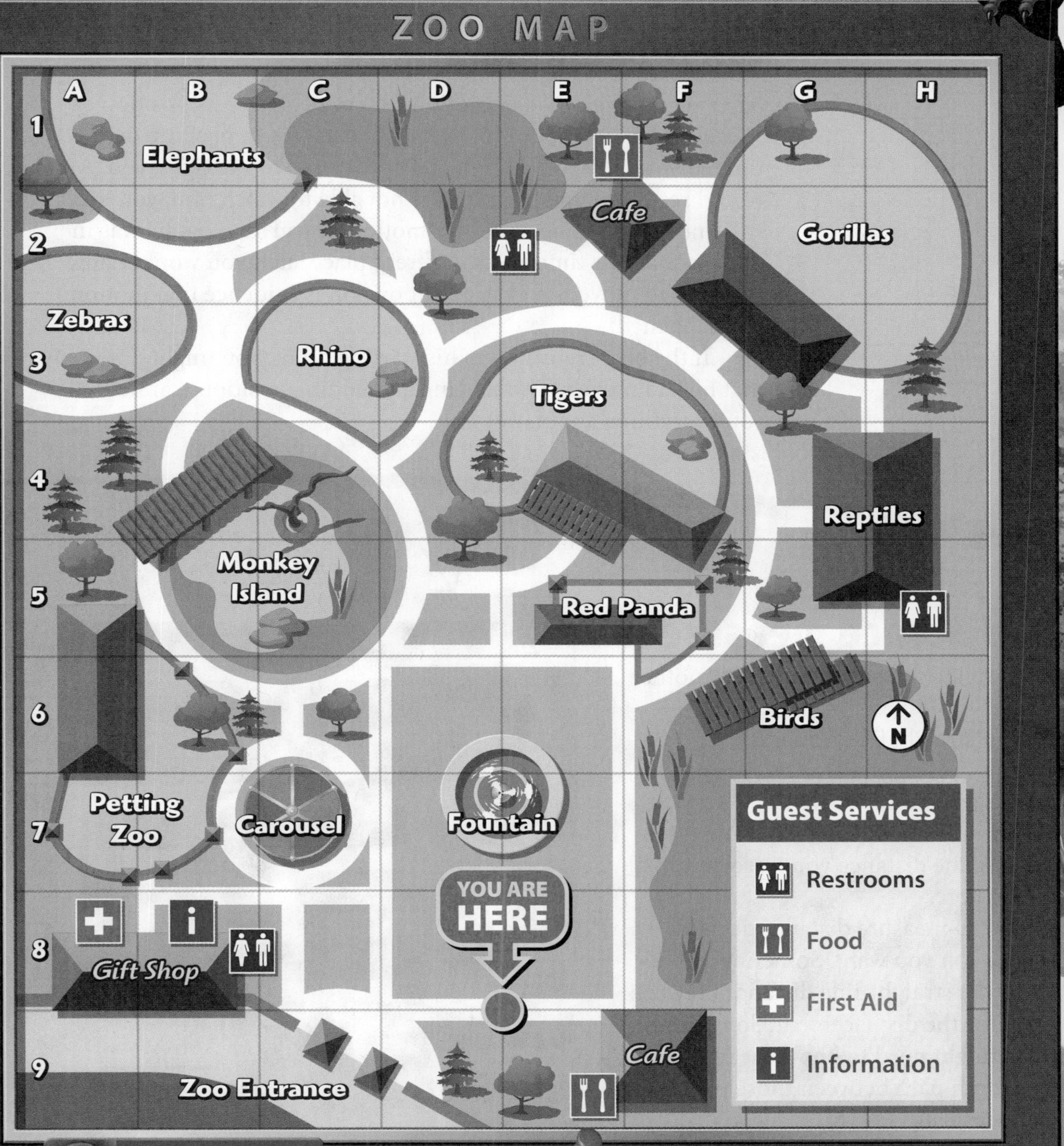
ZOO MAP
A B C D E F G H
1 2 3 4 5 6 7 8 9
Elephants
Cafe
Gorillas
Zebras
Rhino
Tigers
Reptiles
Monkey Island
Red Panda
Birds
N
Petting Zoo
Carousel
Fountain
YOU ARE HERE
Gift Shop
Zoo Entrance
Cafe
Guest Services
Restrooms
Food
First Aid
Information

Visualize It!

6 Apply One of your friends is at the southeast corner of Monkey Island. He would like to meet you. How would you describe your location to him?

____

____

____

7 Apply You need to go visit the first aid station. How would you describe how to get there?

____

____

____

MOVE It!

What is motion?

An object moves, or is in motion, when it changes its position relative to a reference point. **Motion** is a change in position over time. If you were to watch the biker pictured to the right, you would see him move. If you were not able to watch him, you might still know something about his motion. If you saw that he was in one place at one time and a different place later, you would know that he had moved. A change in position is evidence that motion has happened.

If the biker returned to his starting point, you might not know that he had moved. The starting and ending positions cannot tell you everything about motion.

How is distance measured?

Suppose you walk from one building to another building that is several blocks away. If you could walk in a straight line, you might end up 500 meters from where you started. The actual distance you travel, however, would depend on the exact path you take. If you take a route that has many turns, the distance you travel might be 900 meters or more.

The way you measure distance depends on the information you want. Sometimes you want to know the straight-line distance between two positions, or the displacement. Sometimes, however, you might need to know the total length of a certain path between those positions.

When measuring any distances, scientists use a standard unit of measurement. The standard unit of length is the meter (m), which is about 3.3 feet. Longer distances can be measured in kilometers (km), and shorter distances in centimeters (cm). In the United States, distance is often measured in miles (mi), feet (ft), or inches (in).

The distance from point A to point B depends on the path you take.

A
B

Visualize It!

8 Illustrate Draw a sample path on the maze that is a different distance than the one in red but still goes from the start point, "A," to the finish point, "B."

petrles
AZONIC

This biker is in motion.

What is speed?

A change in an object's position tells you that motion took place, but it does not tell you how quickly the object changed position. The **speed** of an object is a measure of how far something moves in a given amount of time. In other words, speed measures how quickly or slowly the object changes position. In the same amount of time, a faster object would move farther than a slower moving object would.

What is average speed?

The speed of an object is rarely constant. For example, the biker in the photo above may travel quickly when he begins a race but may slow down as he gets tired at the end of the race. *Average speed* is a way to calculate the speed of an object that may not always be moving at a constant speed. Instead of describing the speed of an object at an exact moment in time, average speed describes the speed over a stretch of time.

Active Reading **9 Compare** What is the difference between speed and average speed?

____

____

____

Think Outside the Book **Inquiry**

10 Analyze Research the top speeds of a cheetah, a race car, and a speed boat. How do they rank in order of speed? Make a poster showing which is fastest and which is slowest. How do the speeds of the fastest human runners compare to the speeds you found?

Speed It Up!

How is average speed calculated?

Active Reading

11 Identify As you read, underline sentences that relate distance and time.

Speed can be calculated by dividing the distance an object travels by the time it takes to cover the distance. Speed is shown in the formula as the letter *s*, distance as the letter *d*, and time as the letter *t*. The formula shows how distance, time, and speed are related. If two objects travel the same distance, the object that took a shorter amount of time will have the greater speed. An object with a greater speed will travel a longer distance in the same amount of time than an object with a lower speed will.

The following equation can be used to find average speed:

$$\text{average speed} = \frac{\text{distance}}{\text{time}}$$

$$s = \frac{d}{t}$$

The standard unit for speed is meters per second (m/s). Speed can also be given in kilometers per hour (km/h). In the United States, speeds are often given in miles per hour (mi/h or mph). One mile per hour is equal to 0.45 m/s.

Do the Math **Sample Problem**

A penguin swimming underwater goes 20 meters in 8 seconds. What is its average speed?

Identify

A. What do you know? $d = 20$ m, $t = 8$ s

B. What do you want to find out? average speed

Plan

C. Draw and label a sketch: 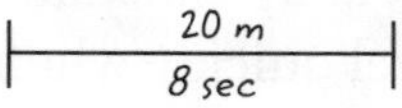
20 m
8 sec

D. Write the formula: $s = d/t$

E. Substitute into the formula: $s = \frac{20\text{ m}}{8\text{ s}}$

Solve

F. Calculate and simplify: $s = \frac{20\text{ m}}{8\text{ s}} = 2.5\text{ m/s}$

G. Check that your units agree: Unit is m/s. Unit of speed is distance/time. Units agree.

Answer: 2.5 m/s

1702

Do the Math You Try It

12 Calculate This runner completed a 100-meter race with a time of 13.75 seconds. What was her average speed?

Identify

A. What do you know?

B. What do you want to find out?

Plan

C. Draw and label a sketch:

D. Write the formula:

E. Substitute into the formula:

Solve

F. Calculate and simplify:

G. Check that your units agree:

Answer:

Fast Graphs

How is constant speed graphed?

A convenient way to show the motion of an object is by using a graph that plots the distance the object has traveled against time. This type of graph is called a distance-time graph. You can use it to see how both distance and speed change with time.

How far away the object is from a reference point is plotted on the *y*-axis. So the *y*-axis expresses distance in units such as meters, centimeters, or kilometers. Time is plotted on the *x*-axis, and can display units such as seconds, minutes, or hours. If an object moves at a constant speed, the graph is a straight line.

You can use a distance-time graph to determine the average speed of an object. The slope, or steepness, of the line is equal to the average speed of the object. You calculate the average speed for a time interval by dividing the change in distance by the change in time for that time interval.

Suppose that an ostrich is running at a constant speed. The distance-time graph of its motion is shown below. To calculate the speed of the ostrich, choose two data points from the graph below and calculate the slope of the line. The calculation of the slope is shown below. Since we know that the slope of a line on a distance-time graph is its average speed, then we know that the ostrich's speed is 14 m/s.

How can you calculate slope?

$$\text{slope} = \frac{\text{change in } y}{\text{change in } x}$$

$$= \frac{140\ m - 70\ m}{10\ s - 5\ s}$$

$$= \frac{70\ m}{5\ s}$$

$$= 14\ m/s$$

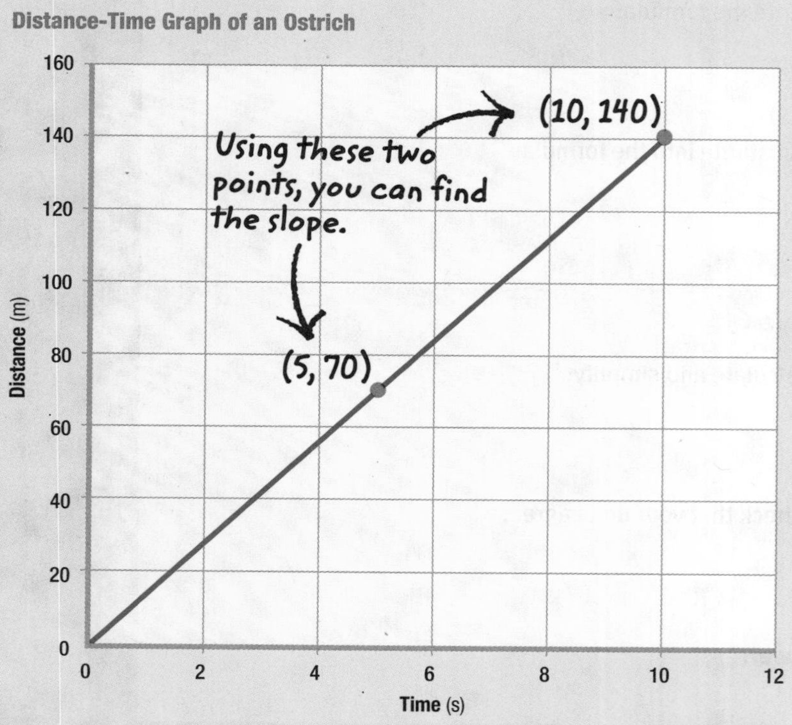

Distance-Time Graph of an Ostrich
Distance (m)
Time (s)
160
140
120
100
80
60
40
20
0
2
4
6
8
10
12
Using these two points, you can find the slope.
(10, 140)
(5, 70)

Visualize It!

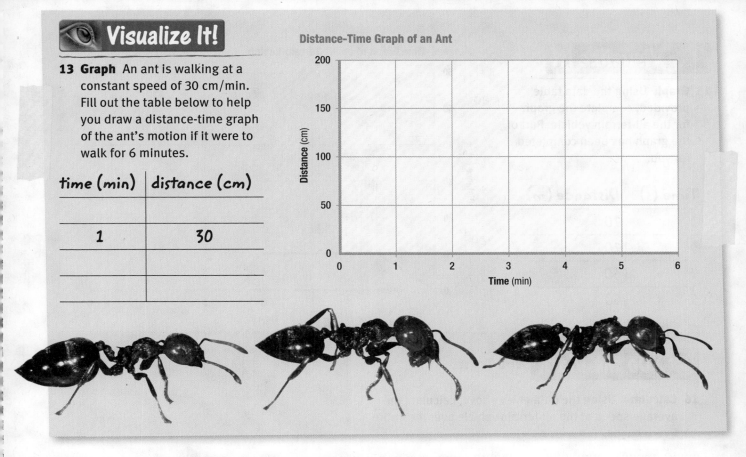

13 Graph An ant is walking at a constant speed of 30 cm/min. Fill out the table below to help you draw a distance-time graph of the ant's motion if it were to walk for 6 minutes.

time (min)	distance (cm)
1	30

Distance-Time Graph of an Ant

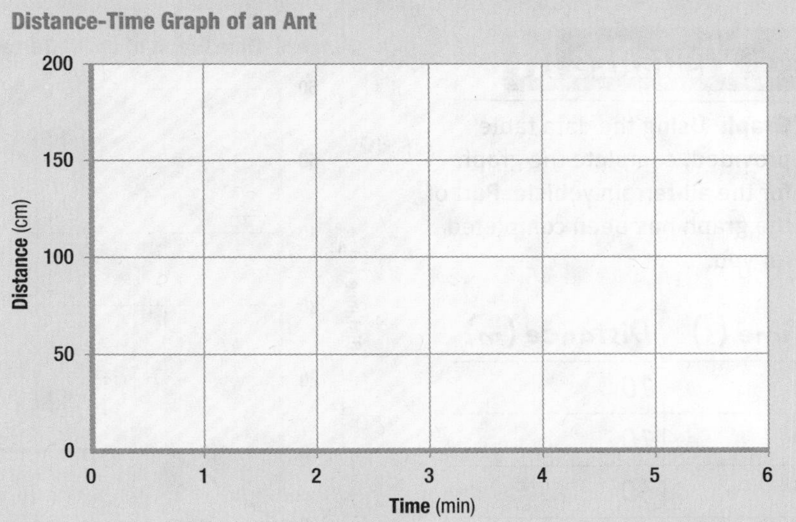
Distance (cm)
200
150
100
50
0
0
1
2
3
4
5
6
Time (min)

How are changing speeds graphed?

Some distance-time graphs show the motion of an object with a changing speed. In these distance-time graphs, the change in the slope of a line indicates that the object has either sped up, slowed down, or stopped.

As an object moves, the distance it travels increases with time. The motion can be seen as a climbing line on the graph. The slope of the line indicates speed. Steeper lines show intervals where the speed is greater than intervals with less steep lines. If the line gets steeper, the object is speeding up. If the line gets less steep, the object is slowing. If the line becomes flat, or horizontal, the object is not moving. In this interval, the speed is zero meters per second.

For objects that change speed, you can calculate speed for a specific interval of time. You would choose two points close together on the graph. Or, you can calculate the average speed over a long interval of time. You would choose two points far apart on the graph to calculate an average over a long interval of time.

Active Reading **14 Analyze** If a line on a distance-time graph becomes steeper, what has happened to the speed of the object? What if it becomes a flat horizontal line?

Visualize It!

15 Graph Using the data table provided, complete the graph for the all-terrain vehicle. Part of the graph has been completed for you.

Time (s)	Distance (m)
1	10
3	10
4	30
5	50

Distance-Time Graph of an All-Terrain Vehicle

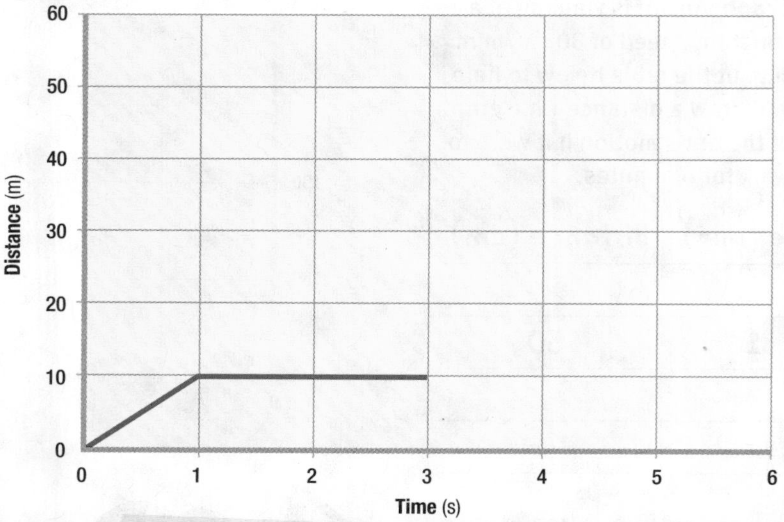
Distance (m)
0
10
20
30
40
50
60
Time (s)
0
1
2
3
4
5
6

Do the Math

You Try It

16 Calculate Using the data given above, calculate the average speed of the all-terrain vehicle over the entire five seconds.

Identify

A. What do you know?

B. What do you want to find out?

Plan

C. Draw and label a sketch:

D. Write the formula:

E. Substitute into the formula:

Solve

F. Calculate and simplify:

G. Check that your units agree:

Answer:

What would the distance-time graph of this ATV's motion look like?

Follow Directions

What is velocity?

Suppose that two birds start from the same place and fly at 10 km/h for 5 minutes. Why might they not end up at the same place? Because the birds were flying in different directions! There are times when the direction of motion must be included in a measurement. A **vector** is a quantity that has both size and direction.

In the example above, the birds' speeds were the same, but their velocities were different. **Velocity** [vuh•LAHS•ih•tee] is speed in a specific direction. If a police officer gives a speeding ticket for a car traveling 100 km/h, the ticket does not list a velocity. But it would list a velocity if it described the car traveling south at 100 km/h.

Because velocity includes direction, it is possible for two objects to have the same speed but different velocities. In the picture to the right, the chair lifts are going the same speed but in opposite directions: some people are going up the mountain while others are going down the mountain.

Average velocity is calculated in a different way than average speed. Average speed depends on the total distance traveled along a path. Average velocity depends on the straight-line distance from the starting point to the final point, or the displacement. A chair lift might carry you up the mountain at an average speed of 5 km/h, giving you an average velocity of 5 km/h north. After a round-trip ride, your average traveling speed would still be 5 km/h. Your average velocity, however, would be 0 km/h because you ended up exactly where you started.

These chair lifts have opposite velocities because they are going at the same speed but in opposite directions.

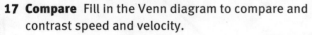

17 Compare Fill in the Venn diagram to compare and contrast speed and velocity.

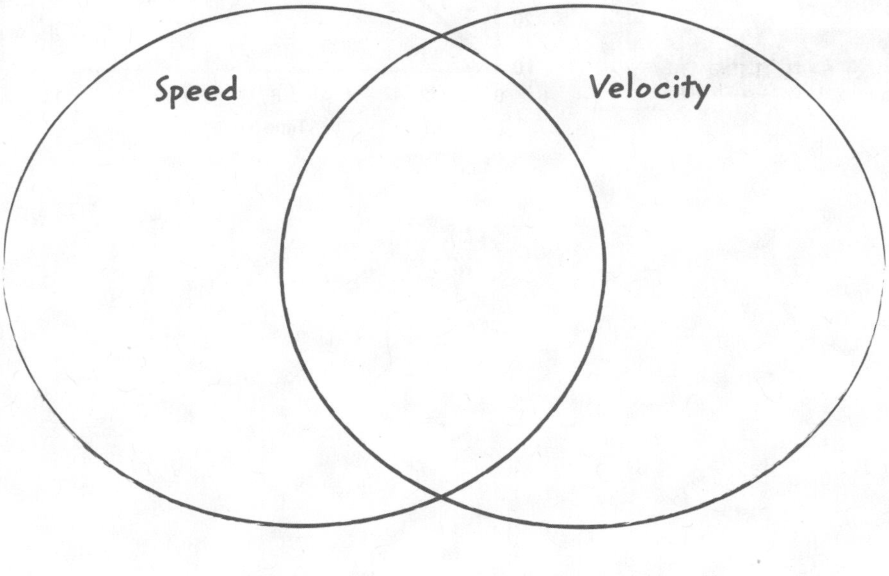
Speed
Velocity

Visual Summary

To complete this summary, check the box that indicates true or false. Then use the key below to check your answers. You can use this page to review the main concepts of the lesson.

Motion and Speed

Motion is a change in position over time.

YOU ARE
HERE

	T	F	
18	☐	☐	A reference point is a location to which you compare other locations.
19	☐	☐	Distance traveled does not depend on the path you take.

Speed measures how far something moves in a given amount of time.

$$s = \frac{d}{t}$$

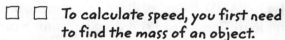

	T	F	
20	☐	☐	To calculate speed, you first need to find the mass of an object.
21	☐	☐	Average speed is a way to describe the speed of an object that may not always be moving at a constant speed.

A distance-time graph plots the distance traveled by an object and the time it takes to travel that distance.

	T	F	
22	☐	☐	In the graph at the right, the object is moving at a constant speed.

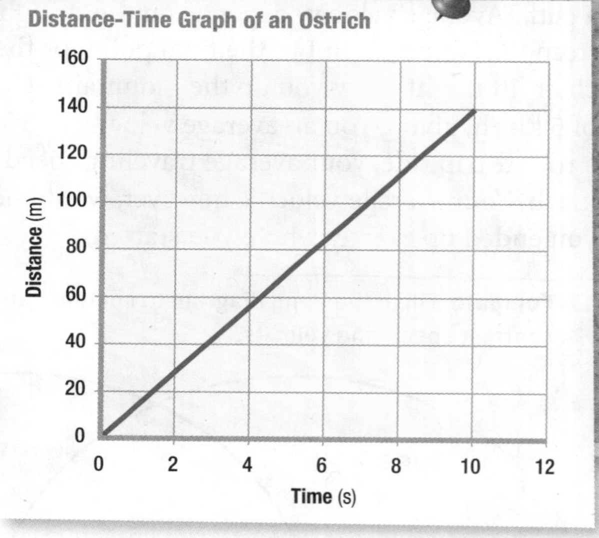

Distance-Time Graph of an Ostrich
Distance (m)
0
20
40
60
80
100
120
140
160
Time (s)
0
2
4
6
8
10
12

Answers: 18 T; 19 F; 20 F; 21 T; 22 T

23 Predict Amy and Ellie left school at the same time. Amy lives farther away than Ellie, but she and Ellie arrived at their homes at the same time. Compare the girls' speeds.

Lesson Review

Vocabulary

Draw a line to connect the following terms to their definitions.

1 velocity
2 reference point
3 speed
4 position

A describes the location of an object
B speed in a specific direction
C a location to which you compare other locations
D a measure of how far something moves in a given amount of time

Key Concepts

5 Describe What information do you need to describe an object's location?

6 Predict How would decreasing the time it takes you to run a certain distance affect your speed?

7 Calculate Juan lives 100 m away from Bill. What is Juan's average speed if he reaches Bill's home in 50 s?

8 Describe What do you need to know to describe the velocity of an object?

Use this graph to answer the following questions.

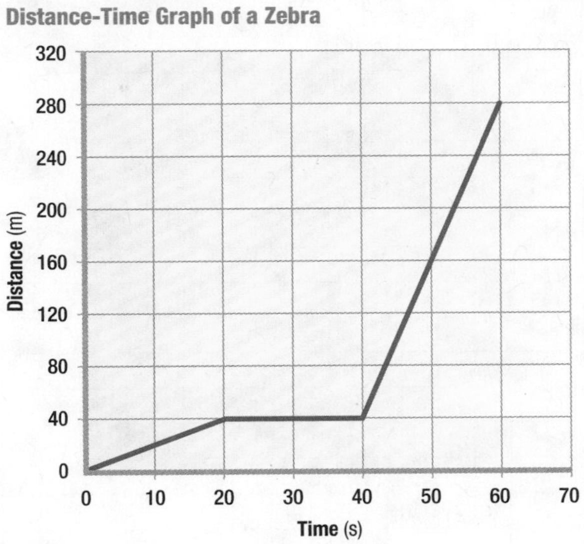
Distance-Time Graph of a Zebra
Distance (m)
320
280
240
200
160
120
80
40
0
0
10
20
30
40
50
60
70
Time (s)

9 Analyze When is the zebra in motion? When is it not moving?

In motion: ____________

Not moving: ____________

10 Calculate What is the average speed of the zebra during the time between 0 s and 40 s?

Critical Thinking

11 Apply Look around you to find an object in motion. Describe the object's motion by discussing its position and direction of motion in relation to a reference point. Then explain how you could determine the object's speed.

My Notes

Think Science

Interpreting Graphs

A visual display, such as a graph or table, is a useful way to show data that you have collected in an experiment. The ability to interpret graphs is a necessary skill in science, and it is also important in everyday life. You will come across various types of graphs in newspaper articles, medical reports, and, of course, textbooks. Understanding a report or article's message often depends heavily on your ability to read and interpret different types of graphs.

Tutorial

Ask yourself the following questions when studying a graph.

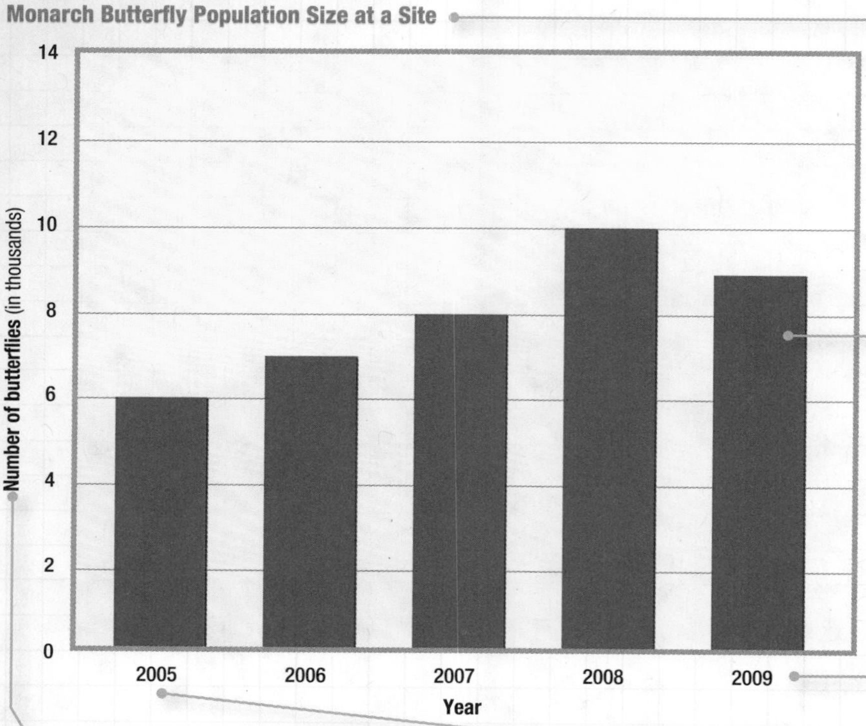

Monarch Butterfly Population Size at a Site
Number of butterflies (in thousands)
14
12
10
8
6
4
2
0
2005
2006
2007
2008
2009
Year

What is the title of the graph? Reading the title can tell you the subject or main idea of the graph. The subject here is monarch butterfly population.

What type of graph is it? Bar graphs, like the one here, are useful for comparing categories or total values. The lengths of the bars are proportional to the value they represent.

Do you notice any trends in the graph? After you understand what the graph is about, look for patterns. For example, here the monarch butterfly population increased each year from 2005 to 2008. But in 2009, the monarch butterfly population decreased.

What are the labels and headings in the graph? What is on each axis of the graph? Here, the vertical axis shows the population in thousands. Each bar represents a different year from 2005 to 2009. So from 2005 to 2009, the monarch butterfly population ranged from 6,000 to 10,000.

Can you describe the data in the graph? Data can be numbers or text. Analyze the information you read at specific data points. For example, the graph here tells us that there were 6,000 monarch butterflies in 2005.

You Try It!

A member of your research group has made the graph shown below about an object in motion. Study the graph, then answer the questions that follow.

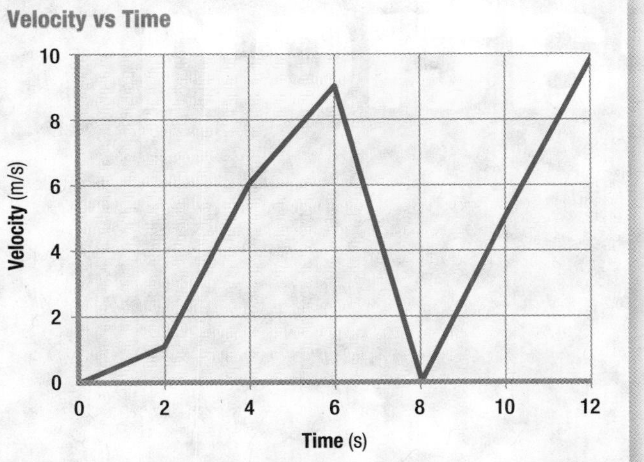

Velocity vs Time
Velocity (m/s)
10
8
6
4
2
0
0
2
4
6
8
10
12
Time (s)

1 Interpreting Graphs Study the graph shown above. Identify the title of this graph, the *x*-axis, the *y*-axis, and the type of graph.

A title of graph ______________________

B *x*-axis ______________________

C *y*-axis ______________________

D type of graph ______________________

2 Identify Study the graph shown above and record the velocity at the indicated times.

Time (s)	Velocity (m/s)
2	
4	
6	
8	
10	

3 Using Graphs Use the graph to answer the following questions.

A What is the approximate velocity of the object at 5 seconds?

____

B During what time interval is the object slowing down? Explain how you can tell.

____

C At what time or times was the velocity of the object about 40 m/s?

____

4 Communicating Results In a short paragraph, describe the motion of the object.

____

Take It Home

Find a newspaper or magazine article that has a graph. What type of graph is it? Study the graph and determine its main message. Bring the graph to class and be prepared to discuss your interpretation of the graph.

Acceleration

ESSENTIAL QUESTION

How does motion change?

By the end of this lesson, you should be able to analyze how acceleration is related to time and velocity.

The riders on this roller coaster are constantly changing direction and speed.

Lesson Labs

Quick Labs
- Acceleration and Slope
- Mass and Acceleration

S.T.E.M. Lab
- Investigate Acceleration

Engage Your Brain

1 Predict Check T or F to show whether you think each statement is true or false.

T	F	
☐	☐	A car taking a turn at a constant speed is accelerating.
☐	☐	If an object has low acceleration, it isn't moving very fast.
☐	☐	An accelerating car is always gaining speed.

2 Identify The names of the two things that can change when something accelerates are scrambled together below. Unscramble them!

PEDSE

____

CDEIINORT

____

Active Reading

3 Synthesize You can often define an unknown word if you know the meaning of its word parts. Use the word parts and sentence below to make an educated guess about the meaning of the word *centripetal*.

Word part	Meaning
centri-	center
pet-	tend toward

Example Sentence:
Josephina felt the centripetal force as she spun around on the carnival ride.

centripetal:

____

____

____

Vocabulary Terms

- **acceleration**
- **centripetal acceleration**

4 Distinguish As you read, draw pictures or make a chart to help remember the relationship between distance, velocity, and acceleration.

Getting up to

How do we measure changing velocity?

Imagine riding a bike as in the images below. You start off not moving at all, then move slowly, and then faster and faster each second. Your velocity is changing. You are accelerating.

Active Reading **5 Identify** Underline the two components of a vector.

Acceleration Measures a Change in Velocity

Just as velocity measures a rate of change in position, acceleration measures a rate of change in velocity. **Acceleration** (ack•SELL•uh•ray•shuhn) is the rate at which velocity changes. Velocity is a vector, having both a magnitude and direction, and if either of these change, then the velocity changes. So, an object accelerates if its speed, its direction of motion, or both change.

Keep in mind that acceleration depends not only on how much velocity changes, but also on how much time that change takes. A small change in velocity can still be a large acceleration if the change happens quickly, and a large change in velocity can be a small acceleration if it happens slowly. Increasing your speed by 5 m/s in 5 s is a smaller acceleration than to do the same in 1 s.

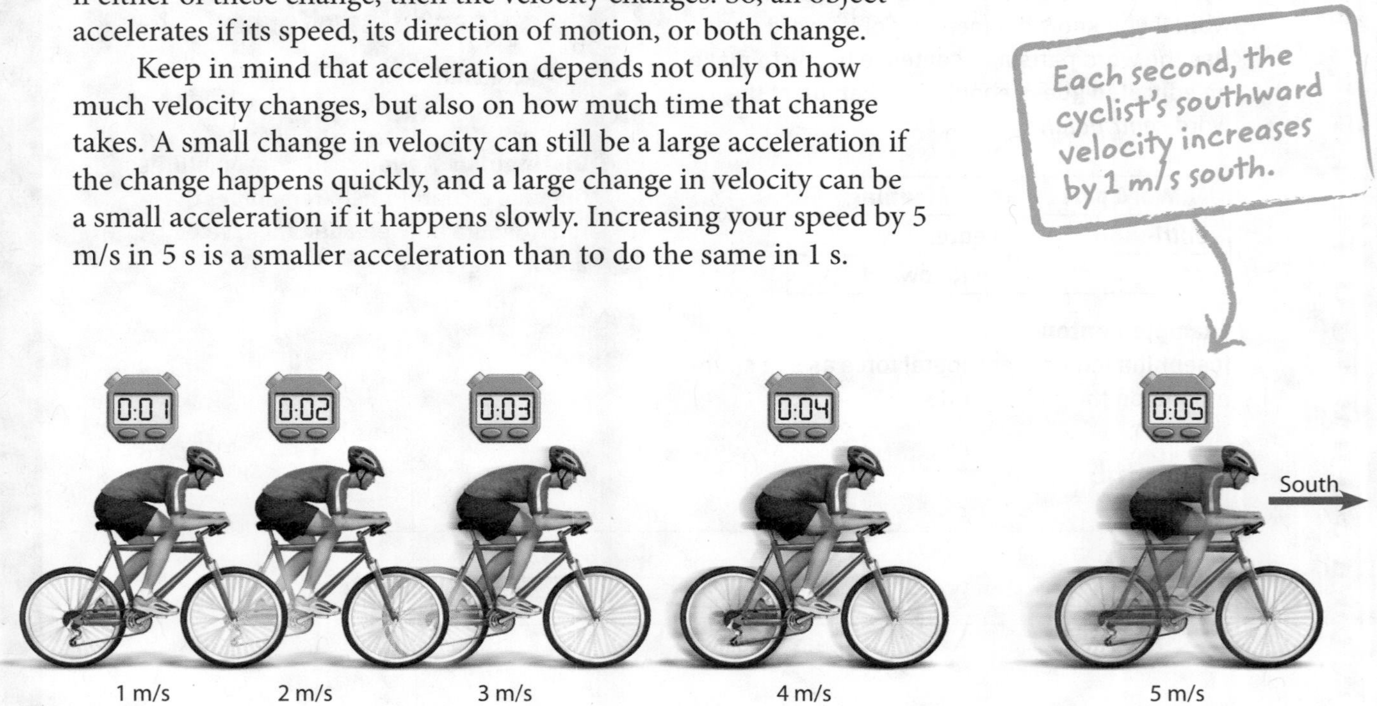

Each second, the cyclist's southward velocity increases by 1 m/s south.
0:01
0:02
0:03
0:04
0:05
South
1 m/s
2 m/s
3 m/s
4 m/s
5 m/s

Speed

How is average acceleration calculated?

Acceleration is a change in velocity as compared with the time it takes to make the change. You can find the average acceleration experienced by an accelerating object using the following equation.

$$\text{average acceleration} = \frac{(\text{final velocity} - \text{starting velocity})}{\text{time}}$$

Velocity is expressed in meters per second (m/s) and time is measured in seconds (s). So acceleration is measured in meters per second per second, or meters per second squared (m/s^2).

As an example, consider an object that starts off moving at 8 m/s west, and then 16 s later is moving at 48 m/s west. The average acceleration of this object is found by in the following equation.

$$a = \frac{(48 \text{ m/s} - 8 \text{ m/s})}{16 \text{ s}}$$
$$a = 2.5 \text{ m/s}^2 \text{ west}$$

Active Reading

6 Identify Underline the units of acceleration.

This formula is often abbreviated as

$$a = \frac{(v_2 - v_1)}{t}$$

Visualize It!

7 Analyze What is the change in velocity of the biker below as he travels from point *B* to point *C*? What is his acceleration from point *B* to point *C*?

____

____

8 Calculate Find the average acceleration of the cyclist moving from point *A* to point *B*, and over the whole trip (from point *A* to point *D*).

A 4 m/s
t = 0 s
B 8 m/s
t = 1 s
C 8 m/s
t = 2 s
D 7 m/s
t = 3 s
The cyclist is riding at 4 m/s. One second later, at the bottom of the hill, he is riding at 8 m/s. After going up a small incline, he has slowed to 7 m/s.

What a Drag!

How can accelerating objects change velocity?

Like velocity, acceleration is a vector, with a magnitude and a direction.

Accelerating Objects Change Speed

Although the word *acceleration* is commonly used to mean an increasing speed, in scientific use, the word applies to both increases and decreases in speed.

When you slide down a hill, you go from a small velocity to a large one. An increase in velocity like this is called *positive acceleration*. When a race car slows down, it goes from a high velocity to a low velocity. A decrease in velocity like this is called *negative acceleration*.

What is the acceleration when an object decreases speed? Because the initial velocity is larger than the final velocity, the term $(v_2 - v_1)$ will be negative. So the acceleration $a = \frac{(v_2 - v_1)}{t}$ will be a negative.

When acceleration and velocity (rate of motion) are in the same direction, the speed will increase. When acceleration and velocity are in opposing directions, the acceleration works against the initial motion in that direction, and the speed will decrease.

Active Reading

9 Identify Underline the term for an increase in velocity and the term for a decrease in velocity.

Sliding down a hill causes a positive acceleration.

The parachute dragging on the air slows the car down, causing a negative acceleration.

Accelerating Objects Change Direction

An object changing direction of motion experiences acceleration even when it does not speed up or slow down. Think about a car that makes a sharp left turn. The direction of velocity changes from "forward" to "left." This change in velocity is an acceleration, even if the speed does not change. As the car finishes the turn, the acceleration drops to zero.

What happens, however, when an object is *always* turning? An object traveling in a circular motion is always changing its direction, so it always experiences acceleration. Acceleration in circular motion is known as **centripetal acceleration**. (sehn•TRIP•ih•tahl ack•SELL•uh•ray•shuhn)

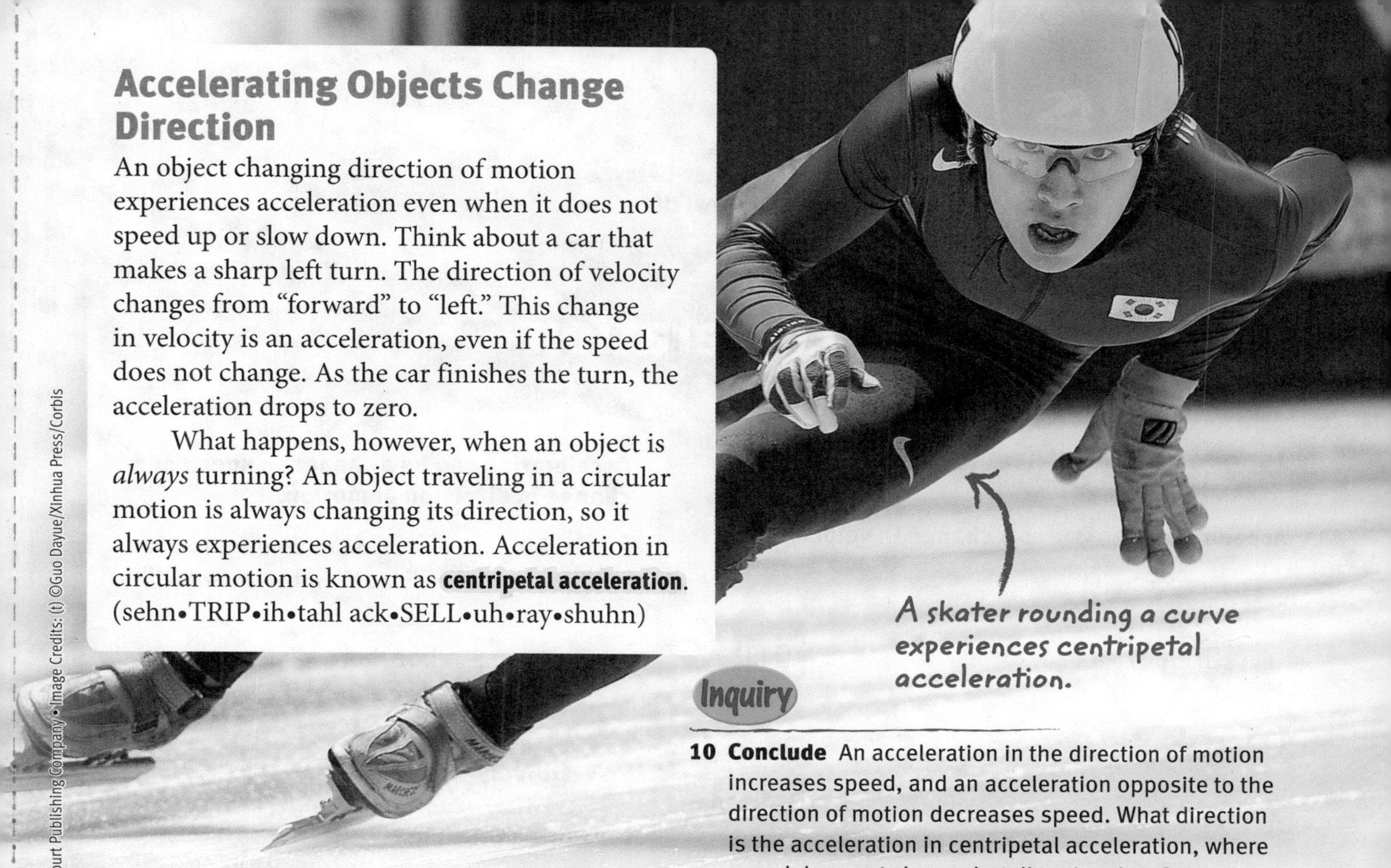

A skater rounding a curve experiences centripetal acceleration.

Inquiry

10 Conclude An acceleration in the direction of motion increases speed, and an acceleration opposite to the direction of motion decreases speed. What direction is the acceleration in centripetal acceleration, where speed does not change but direction does?

____

____

____

Do the Math

11 Calculate The horse is galloping at 13 m/s. Five seconds later, after climbing the hill, the horse is moving at 5.5 m/s. Find the acceleration that describes this change in velocity.

$$a = \frac{(v_2 - v_1)}{t}$$

5.5 m/s
5 seconds
Running uphill is tough to do without slowing down!
13 m/s
0 seconds

Visual Summary

To complete this summary, complete the statements below by filling in the blanks. You can use this page to review the main concepts of the lesson.

Acceleration

Acceleration measures a change in velocity.

0:03
0:11
1 m/s
5 m/s

12 *The formula for calculating average acceleration is*

____

Acceleration can be a change in speed or a change in direction of motion.

13 *When acceleration and velocity are in the same direction, the speed will* _______________

14 *When acceleration and velocity are in opposing directions, the speed will* _______________

15 *Objects traveling in* _______________ *motion experience centripetal acceleration.*

Answers: 12 $a = \frac{(v_2 - v_1)}{t}$; 13 increase; 14 decrease; 15 circular

16 Synthesize Explain why a moving object cannot come to a stop instantaneously (in zero seconds). Hint: Think about the acceleration that would be required.

Lesson Review

Vocabulary

Fill in the blank with the term that best completes the following sentences.

1 Acceleration is a change in ______________

2 ____________________ occurs when an object travels in a curved path.

3 A decrease in the magnitude of velocity is called ____________________

4 An increase in the magnitude of velocity is called ____________________

Key Concepts

5 State The units for acceleration are

____

6 Label In the equation $a = \frac{(v_2 - v_1)}{t}$, what do v_1 and v_2 represent?

____

____

7 Calculate What is the acceleration experienced by a car that takes 10 s to reach 27 m/s from rest?

8 Identify Acceleration can be a change in speed or ________________

9 Identify A helicopter flying west begins experiencing an acceleration of 3 m/s^2 east. Will the magnitude of its velocity increase or decrease?

____

Critical Thinking

10 Model Describe a situation when you might travel at a high velocity, but with low acceleration.

____

____

____

Use this graph to answer the following questions. Assume Jenny's direction did not change.

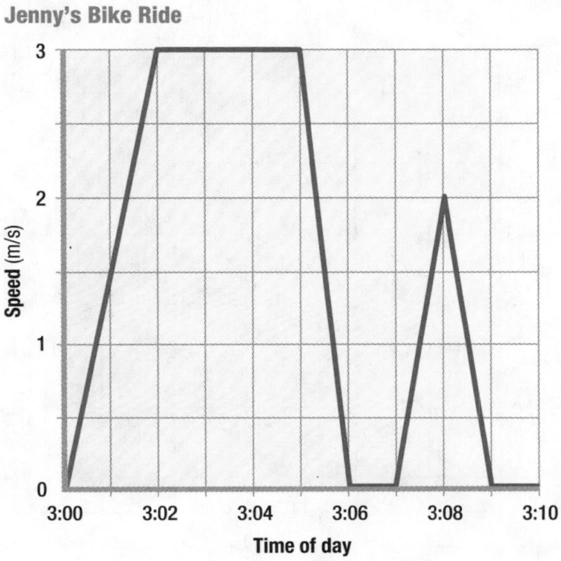

Jenny's Bike Ride
Speed (m/s)
0
1
2
3
3:00
3:02
3:04
3:06
3:08
3:10
Time of day

11 Analyze During what intervals was Jenny negatively accelerating?

____

____

12 Analyze During what intervals was Jenny positively accelerating?

____

____

13 Analyze During what intervals was Jenny not accelerating at all?

____

____

____

My Notes

Lesson 3

Forces

ESSENTIAL QUESTION

How do forces affect motion?

By the end of this lesson, you should be able to describe different types of forces and explain the effect force has on motion.

Even though this skydiver is not touching the ground, a force is still being exerted on him by Earth.

Lesson Labs

Quick Labs
- Net Force
- First Law of Skateboarding

S.T.E.M. Lab
- Newton's Laws of Motion

Engage Your Brain

1 Illustrate Draw a diagram showing how forces act on a ball tossed into the air.

2 Describe Write a caption for this photo.

Active Reading

3 Apply Many scientific words, such as *net*, also have everyday meanings. Use context clues to write your own definition for each meaning of the word *net*.

Example sentence
The fisherman scooped his catch out of the water with a net.

net:

Example sentence
Subtract the mass of the container from the total mass of the substance and the container to determine the net mass of the substance.

net:

Vocabulary Terms

- **force**
- **net force**
- **inertia**

4 Apply As you learn the definition of each vocabulary term in this lesson, create your own definition or sketch to help you remember the meaning of the term.

A Tour de Forces

What is a force, and how does it act on an object?

You have probably heard the word *force* used in conversation. People say, "Don't force the issue," or "Our team is a force to be reckoned with." Scientists also use the word *force*. What exactly is a force, as it is used in science?

A Force Is a Push or a Pull

Active Reading **5 Identify** As you read, underline the unit that is used to express force.

In science, a **force** is simply a push or a pull. All forces have both a size and a direction. A force can cause an object to change its speed or direction. When you see a change in an object's motion, one or more forces caused the change. The unit used to express force is the newton (N). You will learn how to calculate force a little later in this lesson.

Forces exist only when there is an object for them to act on. However, forces do not always cause an object to move. When you sit in a chair, the chair does not move. Your downward force on the chair is balanced by the upward force from the floor.

Visualize It!

6 Identify Draw arrows to represent the pushing forces in the image at left and the pulling forces in the image at right.

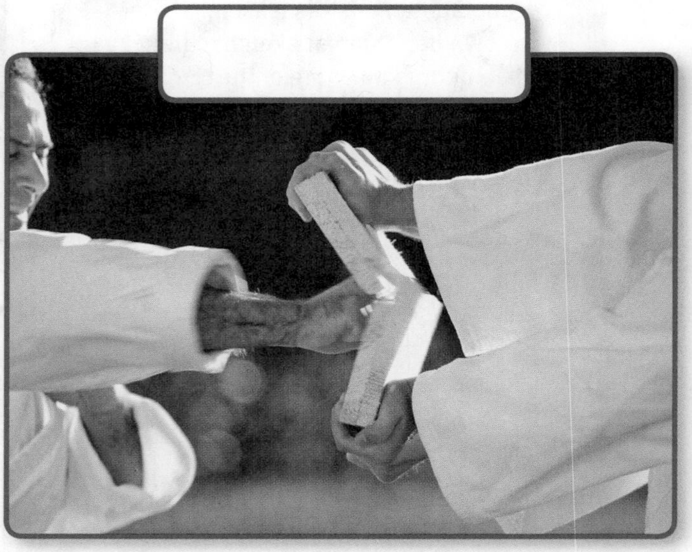

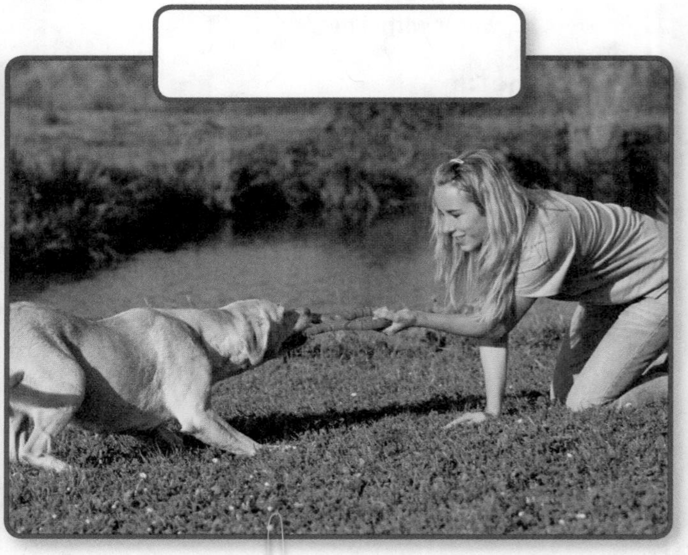

A Force Can Act Directly on an Object

It is not always easy to tell what is exerting a force or what is being acted on by a force. When one object touches or bumps into another object, we say that the objects are in contact with each other. A force exerted during contact between objects is a contact force. Friction is an example of a contact force between two surfaces. Suppose you slide a book across your desk. The amount of friction between the surface of the desk and the book cover determines how easily the book moves. Car tires rely on friction to keep a moving car from sliding off a road. Cars may slide on icy roads because ice lowers the force of friction on the tires.

A Force Can Act on an Object from a Distance

Forces can also act at a distance. One force that acts at a distance is called gravity. When you jump, gravity pulls you back to the ground even though you are not touching Earth. Magnetic force is another example of a force that can act at a distance. Magnetic force can be a push or a pull. A magnet can hold paper to a metal refrigerator door. The magnet touches the paper, not the metal, so the magnetic force is acting on the refrigerator door at a distance. Magnetic force also acts at a distance when the like poles of two magnets push each other apart. A magnetic levitation train floats because magnetic forces push the train away from its track.

Visualize It!

7 Identify The arrows in the picture below represent contact and distance forces. Label each arrow with a "C" if it is a contact force or "D" if it is a distance force.

In the Balance

What happens when multiple forces act on an object?

Active Reading

8 Identify As you read, underline how one determines net force.

Usually, more than one force is acting on an object. The combination of all the forces acting on an object is called the **net force**. How do you determine net force? The answer depends on the directions of the forces involved.

When forces act in the same direction, you simply add them together to determine the net force. For example, when forces of 1 N and 2 N act in the same direction on an object, the net force is 1 N + 2 N = 3 N. When forces act in opposite directions, you subtract the smaller force from the larger force to determine the net force: 2 N – 1 N = 1 N.

Visualize It!

9 Calculate Calculate the net force acting on the appliance box and use it to determine if the box will move.

____

____

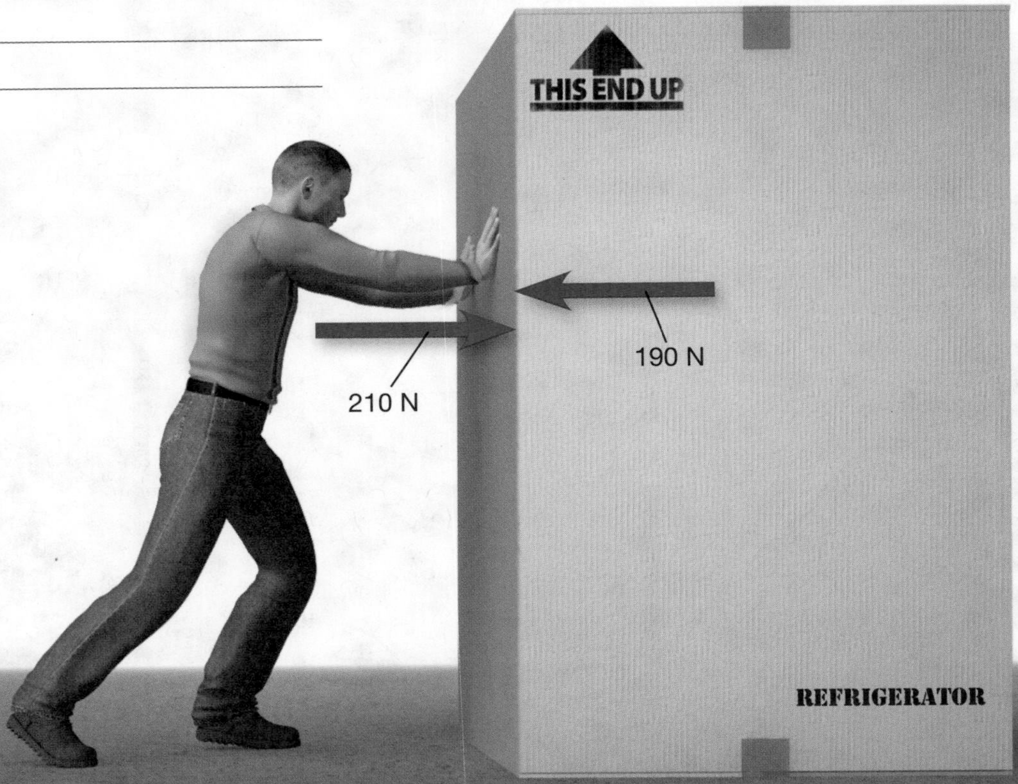

THIS END UP
190 N
210 N
REFRIGERATOR

The Forces Can Be Balanced

When the forces on an object produce a net force of 0 N, the forces are balanced. Balanced forces will not cause a change in the motion of a moving object or cause a nonmoving object to start moving. Many objects around you have only balanced forces acting on them. A light hanging from the ceiling does not move, because the force of gravity pulling downward on the light is balanced by the force of the chain pulling the light upward.

The Forces Can Be Unbalanced

When the net force on an object is not 0 N, the forces are unbalanced. Unbalanced forces produce a change in the object's motion. It could be a change in its speed or direction or both. This change in motion is called acceleration. The acceleration is always in the direction of the net force. For example, when a big dog and a small dog play with a tug toy, the bigger dog pulls with greater force, so the acceleration is in the direction of the bigger dog.

Visualize It!

10 Apply The arrows in the first image show that the forces on the rope are balanced. Draw arrows on the second image to show how the forces on the rope are unbalanced.

These two tug-of-war teams are pulling on the rope with equal force to produce a net force of 0 N. The rope does not move.

One of these teams is pulling on the rope with more force. The rope moves in the direction of the stronger team.

It's the Law

What is Newton's First Law of Motion?

Force and motion are related. In the 1680s, British scientist Sir Isaac Newton explained this relationship between force and motion with three laws of motion.

Newton's first law describes the motion of an object that has a net force of 0 N acting on it. The law states: *An object at rest stays at rest, and an object in motion stays in motion at the same speed and direction, unless it experiences an unbalanced force.* Let's look at the two parts of this law more closely.

An Object at Rest Stays at Rest

Active Reading **11 Identify** As you read, underline examples of objects affected by inertia.

Newton's first law is also called the law of inertia. **Inertia** (ih•NER•shuh) is the tendency of all objects to resist a change in motion. An object will not move until a force makes it move. So a chair will not slide across the floor unless a force pushes the chair, and a golf ball will not leave the tee until a force pushes it off.

Visualize It!

12 Explain In your own words, explain why the dishes remain in place when the magician pulls the cloth out from under them.

____

____

____

An Object in Motion Stays in Motion

Now let's look at the second part of Newton's first law of motion. It states that an object in motion stays in motion at the same speed and direction, or velocity, unless it experiences an unbalanced force. Think about coming to a sudden stop while riding in a car. The car stops because the brakes apply friction to the wheel, making the forces acting on the car unbalanced. You keep moving forward until your seat belt applies an unbalanced force on you. This force stops your forward motion.

Both parts of the law are really stating the same thing. After all, an object at rest has a velocity—its velocity is zero!

Think Outside the Book *Inquiry*

13 Apply Create a model that demonstrates the concept of inertia. Share your results with the class.

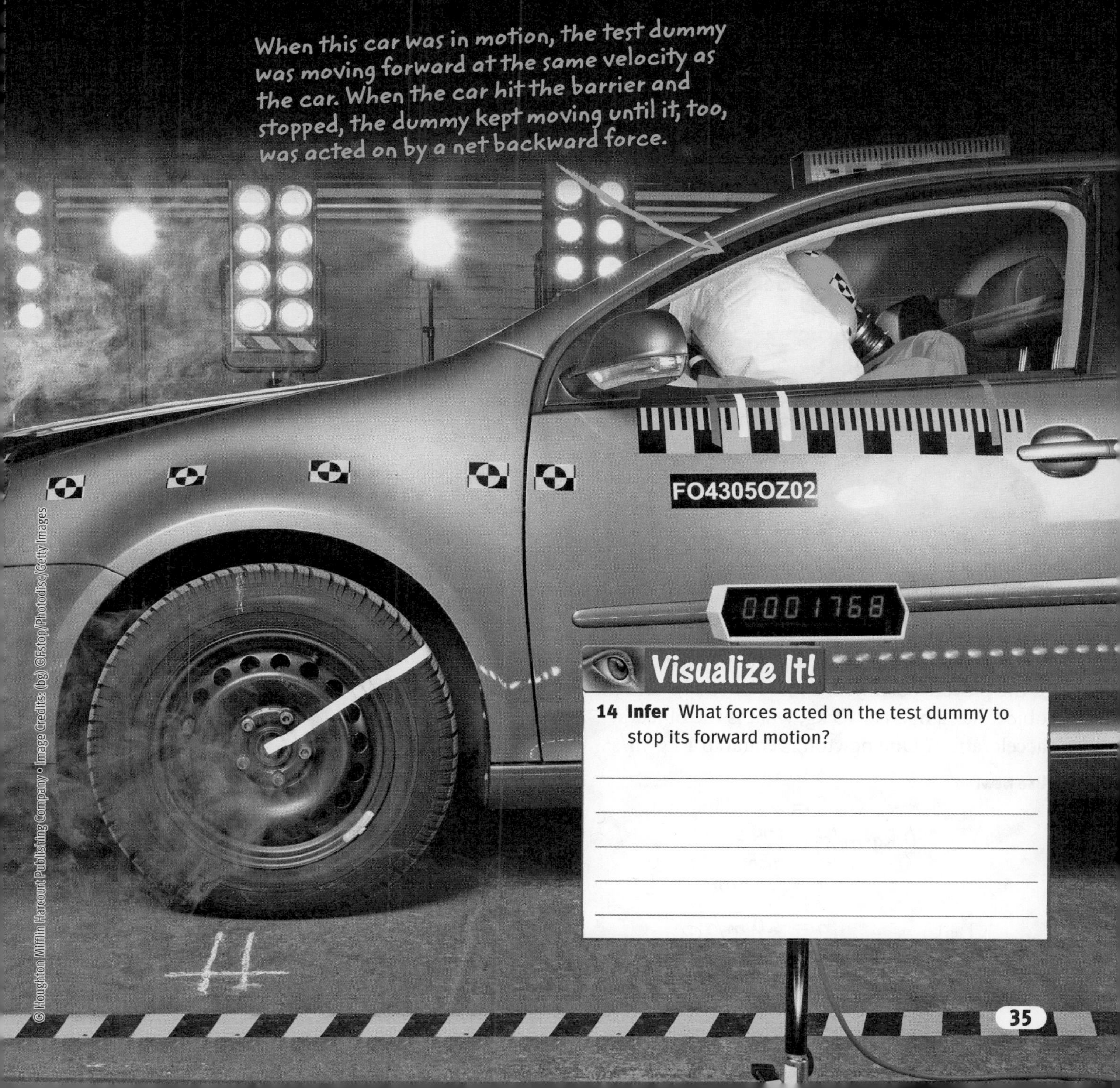
FO4305OZ02
0001768

When this car was in motion, the test dummy was moving forward at the same velocity as the car. When the car hit the barrier and stopped, the dummy kept moving until it, too, was acted on by a net backward force.

Visualize It!

14 Infer What forces acted on the test dummy to stop its forward motion?

____

____

____

____

____

What is Newton's Second Law of Motion?

Active Reading

15 Identify As you read, underline Newton's second law of motion.

When an unbalanced force acts on an object, the object accelerates. Newton's second law describes this motion. The law states: *The acceleration of an object depends on the mass of the object and the amount of force applied.*

In other words, objects that have different masses will have different accelerations if the same amount of force is used. Imagine pushing a shopping cart. When the cart is empty, you need only a small force to accelerate it. But if the cart is full of groceries, the same amount of force causes a much smaller acceleration.

Force Equals Mass Times Acceleration

Newton's second law links force, mass, and acceleration. We can express this relationship using the equation $F = ma$, where F stands for applied force, m stands for mass, and a stands for acceleration. This equation tells us that a given force applied to a large mass will result in a small acceleration. When the same force is applied to a smaller mass, the acceleration will be larger.

Do the Math

Sample Problem

These players train by pushing a massive object. If the players push with a force of 150 N, and the object has a mass of 75 kg, what is the object's acceleration? One newton is equal to 1 kg•m/s².

Use Newton's law:

$$F = ma$$

$$150\ \text{kg}\cdot\text{m/s}^2 = (75\ \text{kg})(a)$$

$$a = \frac{150}{75}\ \text{m/s}^2$$

$$a = 2.0\ \text{m/s}^2$$

You Try It

16 Calculate For a more difficult training session, the mass to be pushed is increased to 160 kg. If the players still push with a force of 150 N, what is the acceleration of the object?

Use Newton's law:

$$F = ma$$

$$150\ \text{N} =$$

Why It Matters

WEIRD SCIENCE

Newton's Second Law and You

Think about the last time you rode on a roller coaster or in a car on a hilly road. Did you feel like you were going to float out of your seat when you went over a big hill? Newton's second law can explain that feeling.

Going Up

When the roller coaster is going up a hill, you have two important forces acting on you—the force of gravity and the upward force exerted by the roller coaster seat.

Coming Down

Once the roller coaster starts down the other side, it accelerates downward, and your seat does not support your full weight.

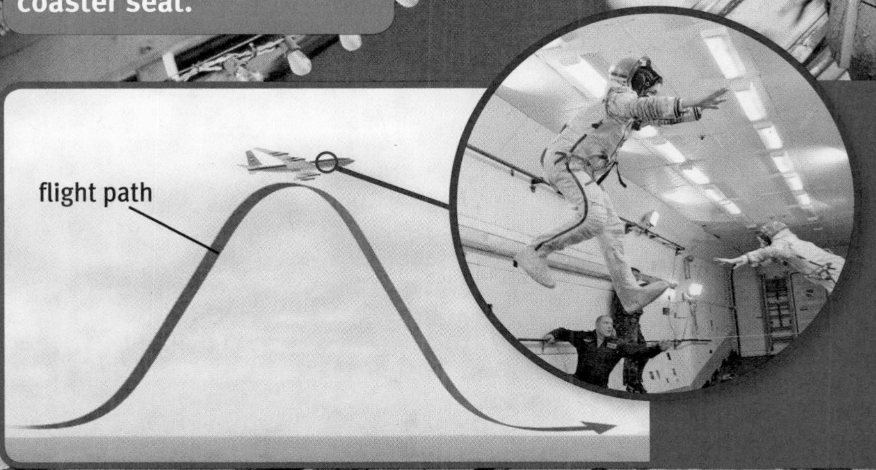
flight path

Practicing for Space

Astronauts take special flights to train for space missions. The airplane's path looks like a roller coaster hill. As the plane accelerates downward, the astronauts lose contact with the plane and fall toward Earth. This condition is called free fall.

Extend

Inquiry

17 Infer Suppose you were standing on a scale in an elevator in free fall. What would the scale read?

18 Synthesize Explain why the feeling of weightlessness in free fall is not the same as truly being weightless.

19 Compare In what ways are roller coaster rides similar to and different from training simulations in a NASA plane?

What is Newton's Third Law of Motion?

Newton also devised a third law of motion. The law states: *Whenever one object exerts a force on a second object, the second object exerts an equal and opposite force on the first.*

So when you push against a wall, Newton's law tells you that the wall is actually pushing back against you.

Objects Exert Force on Each Other

Newton's third law also can be stated as: All forces act in pairs. Whenever one object exerts a force on a second object, the second object exerts an equal and opposite force on the first. There are action forces and reaction forces. Action and reaction forces are present even when there is no motion. For example, you exert a force on a chair when you sit on it. Your weight pushing down on the chair is the action force. The reaction force is the force exerted by the chair that pushes up on your body.

Forces in Pairs Have Equal Size but Opposite Directions

When an object pushes against another object, that object pushes back equally hard. But the second object pushes back in the opposite direction. In the pool below, the swimmer's feet push against the wall as he moves forward. This push is the action force. The wall also exerts a force on the swimmer. This is the reaction force, and it moves the swimmer forward. The forces do not act on the same object. Read on to find out why the swimmer moves but the wall does not!

Visualize It!

20 Apply The arrow below represents the action force exerted by the swimmer. Draw an arrow that represents the reaction force.

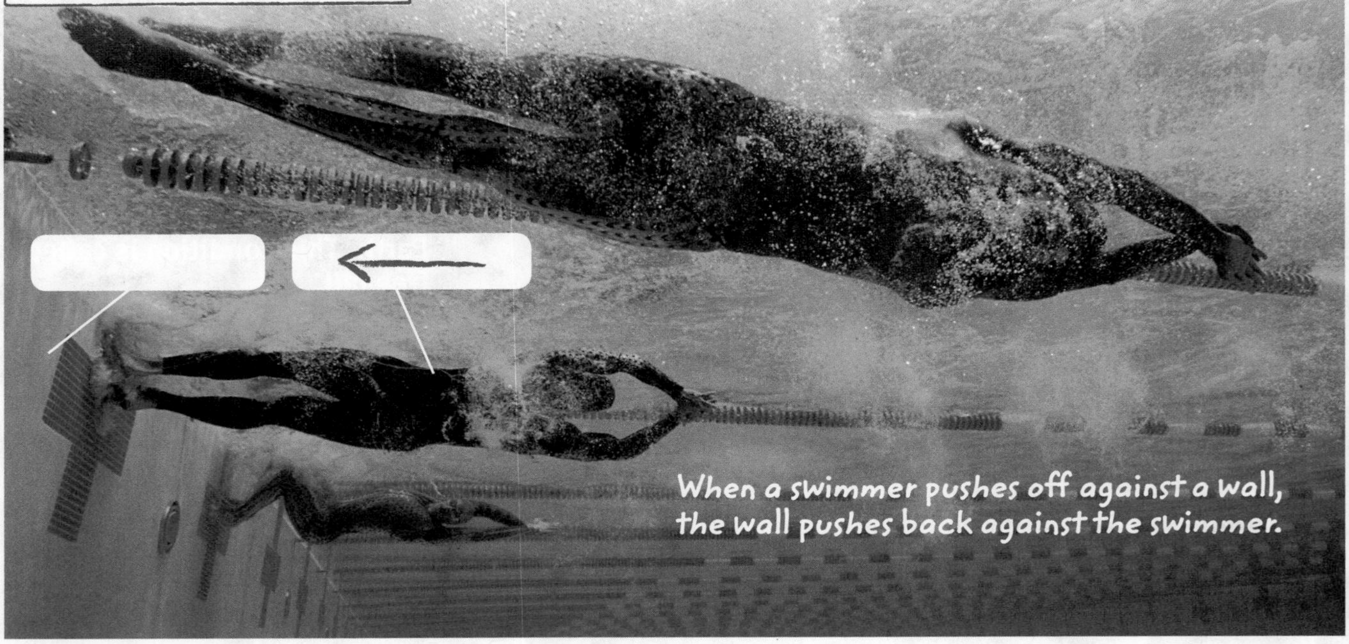

When a swimmer pushes off against a wall, the wall pushes back against the swimmer.

Forces Acting in Pairs Can Have Unequal Effects

Even though action and reaction forces are equal in size, their effects are often different. Gravitation is a force pair between two objects. If you drop a ball, gravity in an action force pulls the ball toward Earth. But the reaction force pulls Earth toward the ball! It's easy to see the effect of the action force. Why don't you see the effect of the reaction force—Earth being pulled upward? Newton's second law answers this question. The force on the ball is the same size as the force on Earth. However, Earth has much more mass than the ball. So Earth's acceleration is much smaller than that of the ball!

Visualize It!

21 Identify Label the action force and reaction force in the image below.

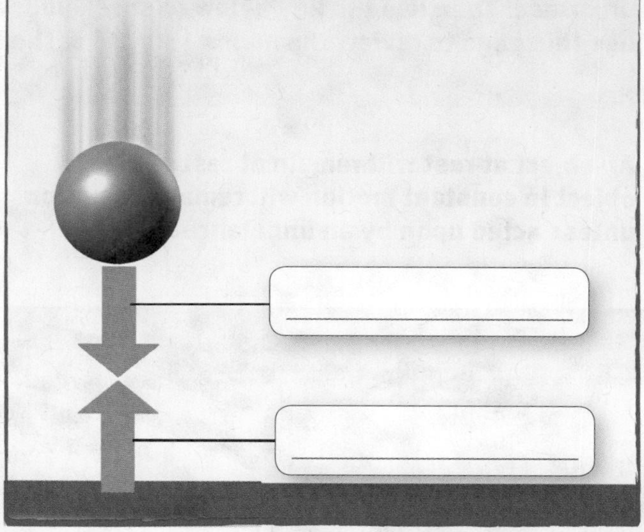

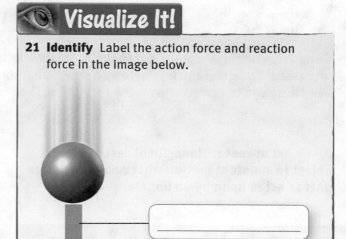

Forces Can Act in Multiple Pairs

An object can have multiple forces acting on it at once. When this happens, each force is part of a force pair. For example, when a baseball bat hits a baseball, the bat does not fly backward. A force is exerted on the ball by the bat. The bat does not fly backward, because the player's hands are exerting another force on the bat. What then keeps the player's hands from flying backward when the bat hits the ball? The bones and muscles in the player's arms exert a force on the hands. As you can see, a simple activity such as playing baseball involves the action of many forces at the same time.

22 Describe In your own words, explain Newton's third law of motion.

____

____

____

Visual Summary

To complete this summary, fill in the blanks with the correct word or phrase. Then use the key below to check your answers. You can use this page to review the main concepts of the lesson.

Forces

An object at rest will remain at rest and an object in constant motion will remain in motion unless acted upon by an unbalanced force.

23 *Newton's first law is also called the law of* ______________________

When an unbalanced force acts on an object, the object moves with accelerated motion.

24 *In the formula F = ma, m stands for* ______________________

Whenever one object exerts a force on a second object, the second object exerts an equal and opposite force on the first.

25 *Forces in the same pair have equal size but opposite* ______________________

Answers: 23: inertia; 24: mass; 25: direction

26 Synthesize A car designer is designing a new model of a popular car. He wants to use the same engine as in the old model, but improve the new car's acceleration. Use Newton's second law to explain how to improve the car's acceleration without redesigning the engine.

Lesson Review

Vocabulary

Draw a line to connect the following terms to their definitions.

1 force	**A** resistance of an object to a change in motion
2 inertia	**B** the unit that expresses force
3 newton	**C** a push or a pull

Key Concepts

4 Describe What is the action force and the reaction force when you sit down on a chair?

5 Summarize How do you determine net force?

6 Explain How do tests with crash dummies, seat belts, and air bags illustrate Newton's first law of motion?

Critical Thinking

Use this photo to answer the following questions.

7 Identify This rock, known as Balanced Rock, sits on a thin spike of rock in a canyon in Idaho. Explain the forces that keep the rock balanced on its tiny pedestal.

8 Calculate Balanced Rock has a mass of about 36,000 kg. If the acceleration due to gravity is 9.8 m/s^2, what is the force that the rock is exerting on its pedestal?

9 Infer What would happen to the moon if Earth stopped exerting the force of gravity on it?

My Notes

Lesson 4

Gravity and Motion

ESSENTIAL QUESTION

How do objects move under the influence of gravity?

By the end of this lesson, you should be able to describe the effect that gravity, including Earth's gravity, has on matter.

Overcoming the force of gravity is hard to do for very long!

Lesson Labs

Quick Labs
- Falling Water
- Gravity and Distance
- Free Fall Distances

Engage Your Brain

1 Predict Check *T* or *F* to show whether you think each statement is true or false.

T	F	
☐	☐	Earth's gravity makes heavy objects fall faster than light objects.
☐	☐	A person would weigh the same on other planets as on Earth.
☐	☐	Planets are round because of gravity.

2 Infer List some ways houses would be built differently if gravity were much stronger or much weaker.

Active Reading

3 Predict What do you think the phrase *free fall* might mean? Write your own definition. After reading the lesson, see how close you were!

Vocabulary Terms

- **gravity**
- **free fall**
- **orbit**

4 Apply This list contains the key terms you'll learn in this section. As you read, underline the definition of each term.

Down to EARTH

Gravity pulls the skydiver, his clothes, and his parachute toward the Earth, all with the same acceleration.

This stop-action photo shows that when there is no air resistance, a feather and a billiard ball fall at the same rate.

Active Reading

5 Analyze What has to happen for a feather and a ball to fall at the same rate?

____

____

____

What is gravity?

If you watch video of astronauts on the moon, you see them wearing big, bulky spacesuits and yet jumping lightly. Why is leaping on the moon easier than on Earth? The answer is gravity. **Gravity** is a force of attraction between objects due to their mass. Gravity is a noncontact force that acts between two objects at any distance apart. Even when a skydiver is far above the ground, Earth's gravity acts to pull him downward.

Gravity Is An Attractive Force

Earth's gravity pulls everything toward Earth's center. It pulls, but it does not push, so it is called an attractive force.

You feel the force due to Earth's gravity as the heaviness of your body, or your weight. Weight is a force, and it depends on mass. Greater mass results in greater weight. This force of gravity between Earth and an object is equal to the mass of the object *m* multiplied by a factor due to gravity *g*.

$$F = mg$$

On Earth, *g* is about 9.8 m/s^2. The units are the same as the units for acceleration. Does this mean that Earth's gravity accelerates all objects in the same way? The surprising answer is yes.

Suppose you dropped a heavy object and a light object at the same time. Which would hit the ground first? Sometimes an object experiences a lot of air resistance and falls slowly or flutters to the ground. But if you could take away air resistance, all objects would fall with the same acceleration. When gravity is the only force affecting the fall, a light object and a heavy object hit the ground at the same time.

Acceleration depends on both force and mass. The heavier object experiences a greater force, or weight. But the heavier object is also harder to accelerate, because it has more mass. The two effects cancel, and the acceleration due to gravity is the same for all masses.

Gravity Affects Mass Equally

All matter has mass. Gravity is a result of mass, so all matter is affected by gravity. Every object exerts a gravitational pull on every other object. Your pencil and shoes are gravitationally attracted to each other, each to your textbook, all three to your chair, and so on. So why don't objects pull each other into a big pile? The gravitational forces between these objects are too small. Other forces, such as friction, are strong enough to balance the gravitational pulls and prevent changes in motion. Gravity is not a very powerful force—you overcome the attraction of Earth's entire mass on your body every time you stand up!

However, when enough mass gathers together, its effect can be large. Gravity caused Earth and other planets to become round. All parts of the planet pulled each other toward the center of mass, resulting in a sphere.

Some astronomical bodies do not have enough mass to pull themselves into spheres. Small moons and asteroids can maintain a lumpy shape, but larger moons such as Earth's have enough mass to form a sphere.

Gravity also acts over great distances. It determines the motion of celestial bodies. The paths of planets, the sun, and other stars are determined by gravity. Even the motion of our galaxy through the universe is due to gravity.

Galaxies, made up of billions of stars, have characteristic shapes and motions that are due to gravity.

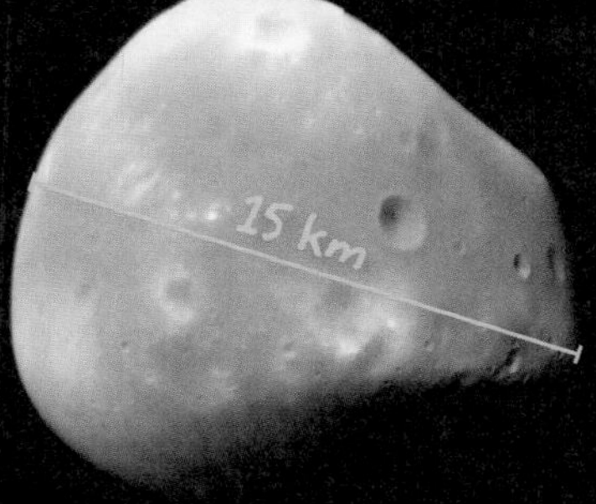
15 km

Deimos, one of the moons of Mars, is only about 15 km at its longest stretch. Deimos does not have enough mass to form a sphere.

Earth's moon has a diameter of more than 3,400 km. It has more than enough mass to pull itself into a sphere.

3,400 km

Think Outside the Book

6 Incorporate Write a short story about a time when you had to overcome the force of gravity to get something done.

A WEIGHTY Issue

What determines the force of gravity?

The law of universal gravitation relates gravitational force, mass, and distance. It states that all objects attract each other through gravitational force. The strength of the force depends on the masses involved and distance between them.

Gravity Depends on Distance

The gravitational force between two objects increases as the distance between their centers decreases. This means that objects far apart have a weaker attraction than objects close together. If two objects move closer, the attraction between them increases. For example, you can't feel the sun's gravity because it is so far away, but if you were able to stand on the surface of the sun, you would find it impossible to move due to the gravity!

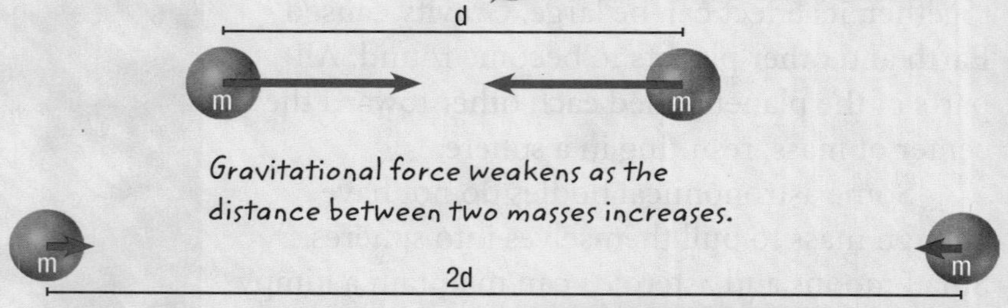
d
m
m
2d
m
m

Gravitational force weakens as the distance between two masses increases.

Active Reading **7 Explain** How does distance affect gravitational force?

____

____

Gravity Depends on Mass

The gravitational force between two objects increases with the mass of each object. This means that objects with greater mass have more attraction between them. A cow has more mass than a cat, so there is more attraction between the Earth and the cow, and the cow weighs more.

This part of the law of universal gravitation explains why astronauts on the moon bounce when they walk. The moon has less mass than Earth, so the astronauts weigh less. The force of each step pushes an astronaut higher than it would on Earth.

m
m

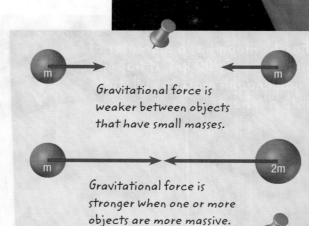

Gravitational force is weaker between objects that have small masses.

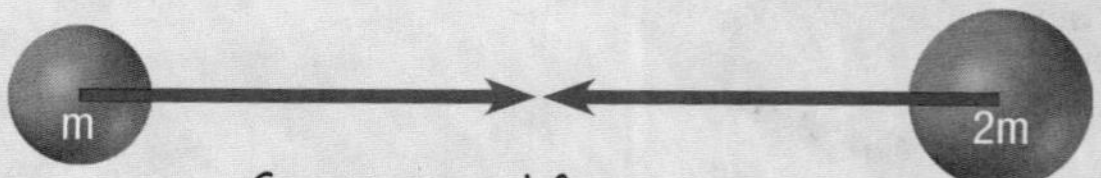
m
2m

Gravitational force is stronger when one or more objects are more massive.

Notice that the force that each object experiences is of equal strength.

Active Reading **8 Explain** How does mass affect gravitational force?

____

____

Visualize It! *Inquiry*

Finding Gravity in Strange Places

The gravity of the moon is less than that of Earth, because the moon has much less mass than Earth.

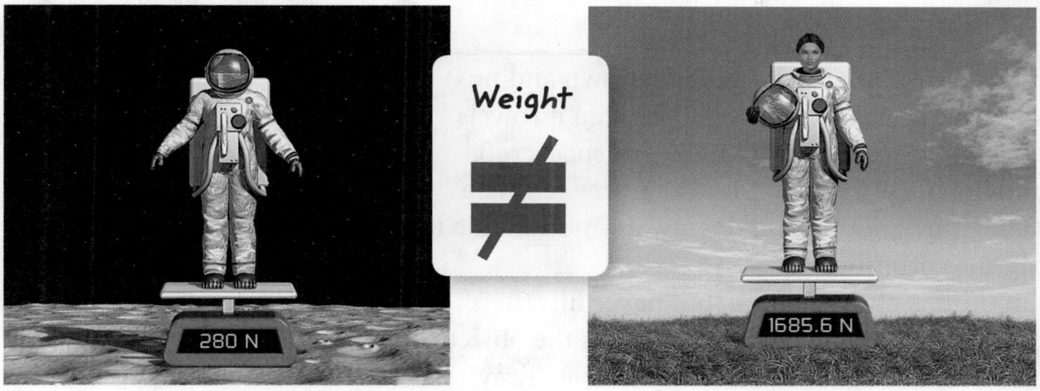
280 N
Weight
1685.6 N

The moon does not pull as hard on an astronaut, so the force of her weight on the scale is less. The astronaut weighs less on the moon than on Earth.

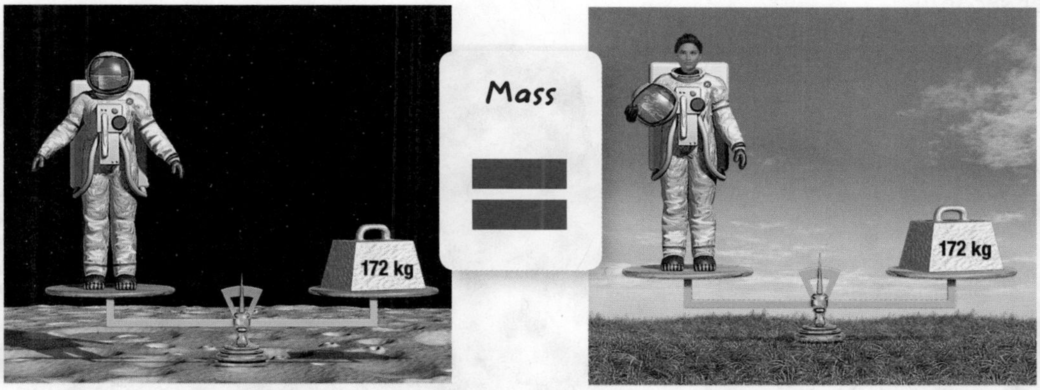
172 kg
Mass
172 kg

The astronaut has the same mass on the moon and Earth.

9 List This table lists the weights of a 80 kg person on different planets. List these planets in decreasing order of mass.

Planet	Weight of 80 kg
Venus	710 N
Earth	784 N
Mars	297 N
Jupiter	1983 N

10 Justify The weight of 80 kg of mass on Mercury is 296 N, almost identical to the weight of the same mass on Mars. But Mercury has much less mass than Mars! Explain how this can be. (What else could affect gravitational force?)

DOWN

How does gravity keep objects in orbit?

Something is in **free fall** when gravity is pulling it down and no other forces are acting on it. An object is in **orbit** when it travels around another object in space. When a satellite or spacecraft orbits Earth, it is moving forward. But it is also in free fall. The combination of the forward motion and downward motion due to gravity combine to cause orbiting.

A spacecraft in orbit is always falling, but never hits the ground! This happens because of forward motion. As the object falls, it moves forward far enough that the planet curves away under it, so it has exactly that much farther to fall. It never actually gets closer to Earth. In order to move forward far enough to counteract the fall, objects in orbit must travel very fast—as much as 8 kilometers per second!

Active Reading

11 Identify When is an object in free fall?

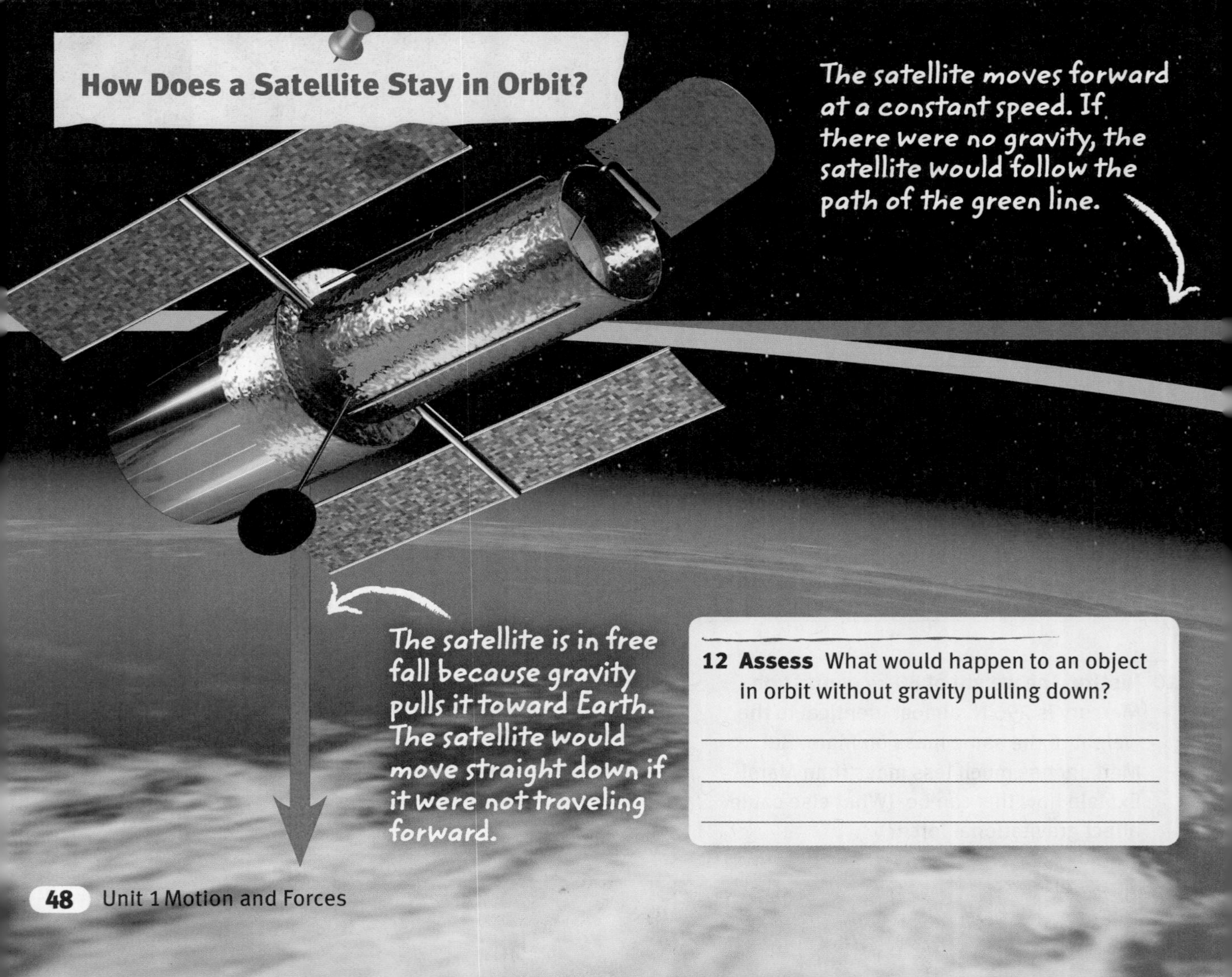
How Does a Satellite Stay in Orbit?
The satellite moves forward at a constant speed. If there were no gravity, the satellite would follow the path of the green line.
The satellite is in free fall because gravity pulls it toward Earth. The satellite would move straight down if it were not traveling forward.

12 Assess What would happen to an object in orbit without gravity pulling down?

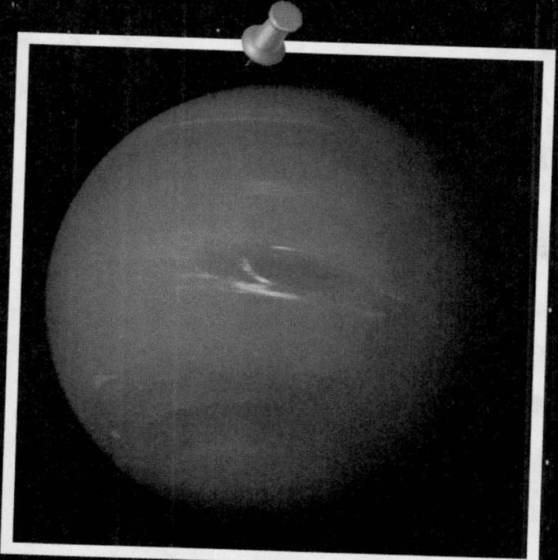

The discovery of the planet Neptune (above) was predicted by observing the effect that its gravity had on the motions of the planet Uranus.

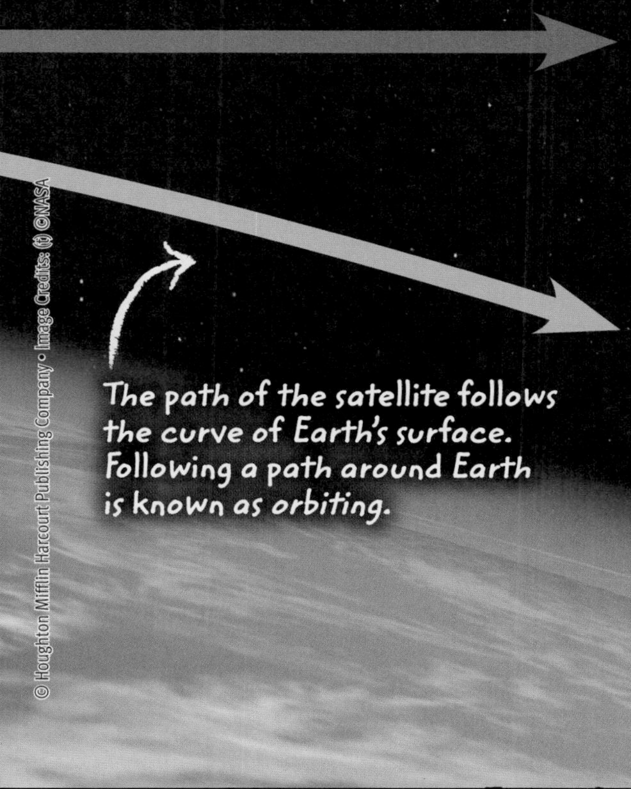

The path of the satellite follows the curve of Earth's surface. Following a path around Earth is known as orbiting.

Gravity Can Make Objects Move in Circles

Besides spacecraft and satellites, many other objects in the universe are in orbit. The moon orbits Earth. Planets orbit the sun. Many stars orbit large masses in the center of galaxies. These objects travel along circular or elliptical paths. As an object moves along a curve, it changes direction constantly. The change in motion is due to an unbalanced force. The direction of the force must change constantly to produce curved motion. The force must be directed inward, toward the center of the curve or circle.

Gravity provides the force that keeps objects in orbit. This force pulls one object into a path that curves around another object. Gravitational force is directed inward. For example, this inward force pulls the moon toward Earth and constantly changes the moon's motion.

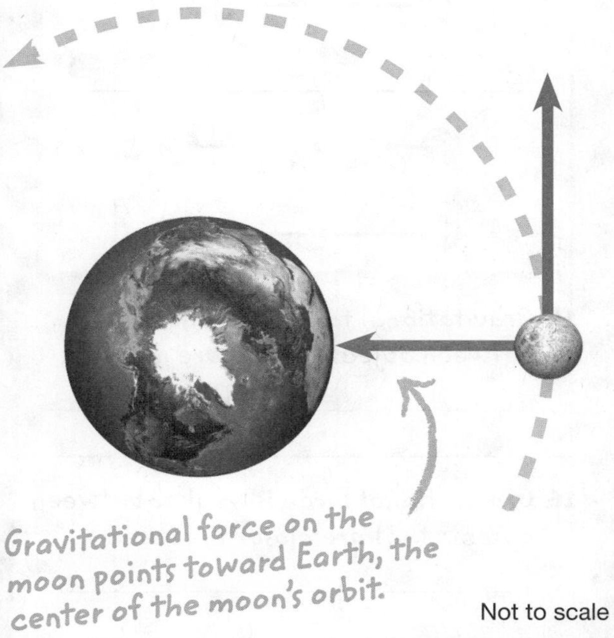
Gravitational force on the moon points toward Earth, the center of the moon's orbit.
Not to scale

13 Model Imagine tying a string to a ball and twirling it around you. How is this similar to the moon orbiting Earth? In this example, what is providing the constantly changing, inward force?

Visual Summary

To complete this summary, read the statements in the boxes below. Circle any that are true. Cross out any that are false, and correct the statement so that it is true. You can use this page to review the main concepts of the lesson.

Gravity and Motion

Gravity is an attractive force that exists between all objects with mass.

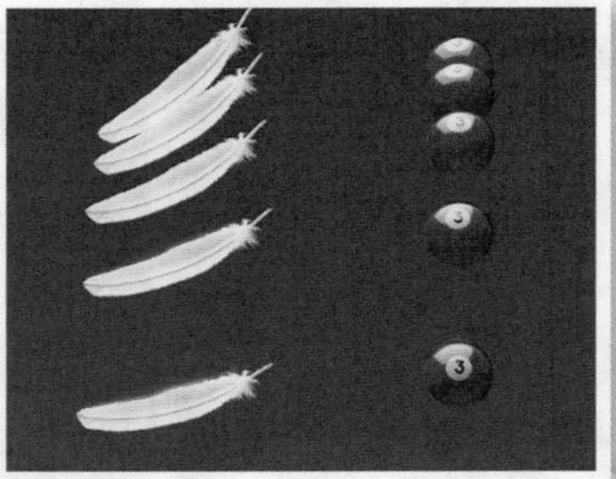

14 The acceleration due to gravity is the same for all falling objects when there is no air resistance.

Gravity depends on mass and distance.

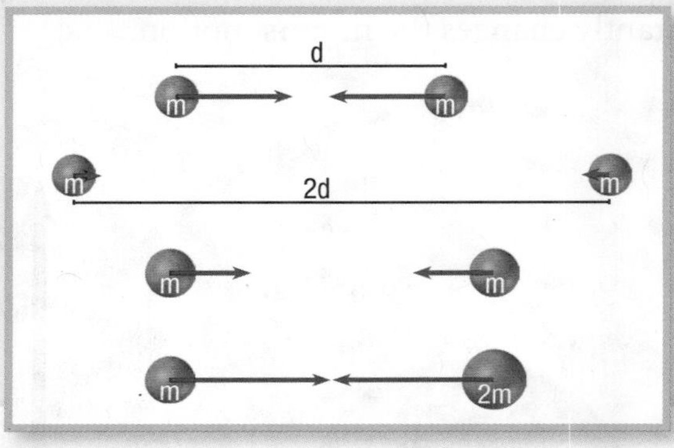

d
m
m
m
m
2d
m
m
m
2m

15 Gravitational force is stronger between objects with more mass.

16 Gravitational force is weaker between objects that are closer together.

Gravity keeps objects in orbit.

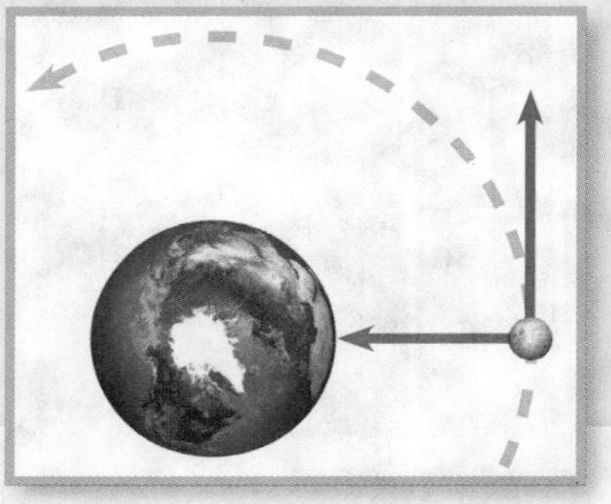

17 The moon does not fall to Earth because of friction.

Answers: 14 True; 15 True; 16 False, gravity is stronger when objects are closer; 17 False, the force keeping the moon orbiting the Earth is gravity.

18 Justify If Earth were replaced by an object with the same mass but much smaller in size, would the moon continue to orbit the new object, fall into it, or fly off into space? Why?

Lesson Review

Vocabulary

Fill in the blanks with the term that best completes the following sentences.

1 _______________ is a force that attracts all matter to each other.

2 When the only force affecting an object is gravity, that object is in _______________

3 An object traveling around another object in space is in _______________

Key Concepts

4 Relate The gravitational attraction between two objects will _______________ if one object acquires more mass.

5 Relate The gravitational attraction between two objects will _______________ if the objects move farther apart.

6 Explain Why are large astronomical bodies such as planets and stars round?

7 Identify What two motions combine to produce an orbit?

8 Distinguish Explain the difference between mass and weight.

Critical Thinking

9 Infer The weight of an object on a planet depends not only on its mass, but also on its distance from the planet's center. This table lists the weight of 80 kg on each planet in the solar system. Uranus has more than 14 times as much mass as Earth, yet the gravitational force is less. Explain how this could be.

Planet	Weight of 80 kg
Mercury	296 N
Venus	710 N
Earth	784 N
Mars	297 N
Jupiter	1983 N
Saturn	838 N
Uranus	708 N
Neptune	859 N

10 Apply Why don't satellites in orbit fall to the ground? Why don't they fly off into space?

My Notes

People in Science

Steve Okamoto

ROLLER COASTER DESIGNER

A day in the life of a roller coaster designer is filled with twists and turns—just ask designer Steve Okamoto. As a kid, he became interested in roller coasters after a trip to Disneyland. To become a product designer, Steve studied subjects like math and science. He later earned a degree in product design that involved studying mechanical engineering and studio art.

Before he starts designing roller coasters, Steve has to think about all of the parts of a roller coaster and how it will fit in the amusement park. It's like putting together a huge puzzle. Different parts of the puzzle include the safety equipment needed, what the roller coaster will be made out of, and how the track will fit in next to other rides. He also has to think about what visitors to the park will want to see and experience in a roller coaster ride.

As he is designing a roller coaster, Steve's math and science background comes in handy. For example, in order to make sure that a roller coaster's cars make it up each hill, he has to calculate the speed and acceleration of the cars on each part of the track. To create the curves, loops, and dips of the roller coaster track, he uses his knowledge of physics and geometry.

MAMBA

Acceleration from the downhill run provides the speed for the next climb.

JOB BOARD

Machinists

What You'll Do: Use machine tools, such as lathes, milling machines, and machining centers, to produce new metal parts.

Where You Might Work: Machine shops and manufacturing plants in industries including the automotive and aerospace industries.

Education: In high school, you should take math courses, especially trigonometry, and, if available, courses in blueprint reading, metalworking, and drafting. After high school, most people acquire their skills in an apprenticeship program. This gives a person a mix of classroom and on-the-job training.

Bicycle Mechanic

What You'll Do: Repair and maintain different kinds of bikes, from children's bikes to expensive road bikes.

Where You Might Work: Independent bicycle shops or large chain stores that carry bicycles; certain sporting events like Olympic and national trials.

Education: Some high schools and trade schools have shop classes that teach bicycle repair. Most bicycle mechanics get on-the-job training. To work as a mechanic at national and international cycling events, you will have to earn a bicycle mechanic's license.

PEOPLE IN SCIENCE NEWS

Mike Hensler

The Surf Chair

As a Daytona Beach lifeguard, Mike Hensler realized that the beach was almost impossible for someone in a wheelchair. Although he had never invented a machine before, Hensler decided to build a wheelchair that could be driven across sand without getting stuck. He began spending many evenings in his driveway with a pile of lawn-chair parts, designing the chair by trial and error.

The result looks very different from a conventional wheelchair. With huge rubber wheels and a thick frame of white PVC pipe, the Surf Chair not only moves easily over sandy terrain but also is weather resistant and easy to clean. The newest models of the Surf Chair come with optional attachments, such as a variety of umbrellas, detachable armrests and footrests, and even places to attach fishing rods.

Lesson 5

Fluids and Pressure

The water in the river is a fluid. The air used to inflate the raft is also a fluid.

ESSENTIAL QUESTION

What happens when fluids exert pressure?

By the end of this lesson, you should be able to explain why fluids exert pressure and how the resulting pressure causes motion and the buoyant force.

Lesson Labs

Quick Labs
- Finding the Buoyant Force
- Pressure Differences

Field Lab
- Pressure in Fluids

Engage Your Brain

1 Describe Fill in the blank with the word that you think correctly completes the following sentences.

A cork will ____________________ on top of water.

A rock will ____________________ in water.

An object that sinks in water is more ____________________ than water.

2 Describe Write your own caption to this photo. Include a description of the liquid's properties.

Active Reading

3 Apply Many scientific words, such as *pressure*, also have everyday meanings. Use context clues to write your own definition for each meaning of the word *pressure*.

Example sentence
Damien felt a lot of pressure because he knew the team was relying on him to hit a home run.

pressure:

Example sentence
When Jodie applied pressure to the clay, it started to flatten.

pressure:

Vocabulary Terms

- **fluid**
- **pressure**
- **pascal**
- **atmospheric pressure**
- **buoyant force**
- **Archimedes' principle**

4 Identify As you read, create a reference card for each vocabulary term. On one side of the card, write the term and its meaning. On the other side, draw an image that illustrates or makes a connection to the term. These cards can be used as bookmarks in the text so that you can refer to them while studying.

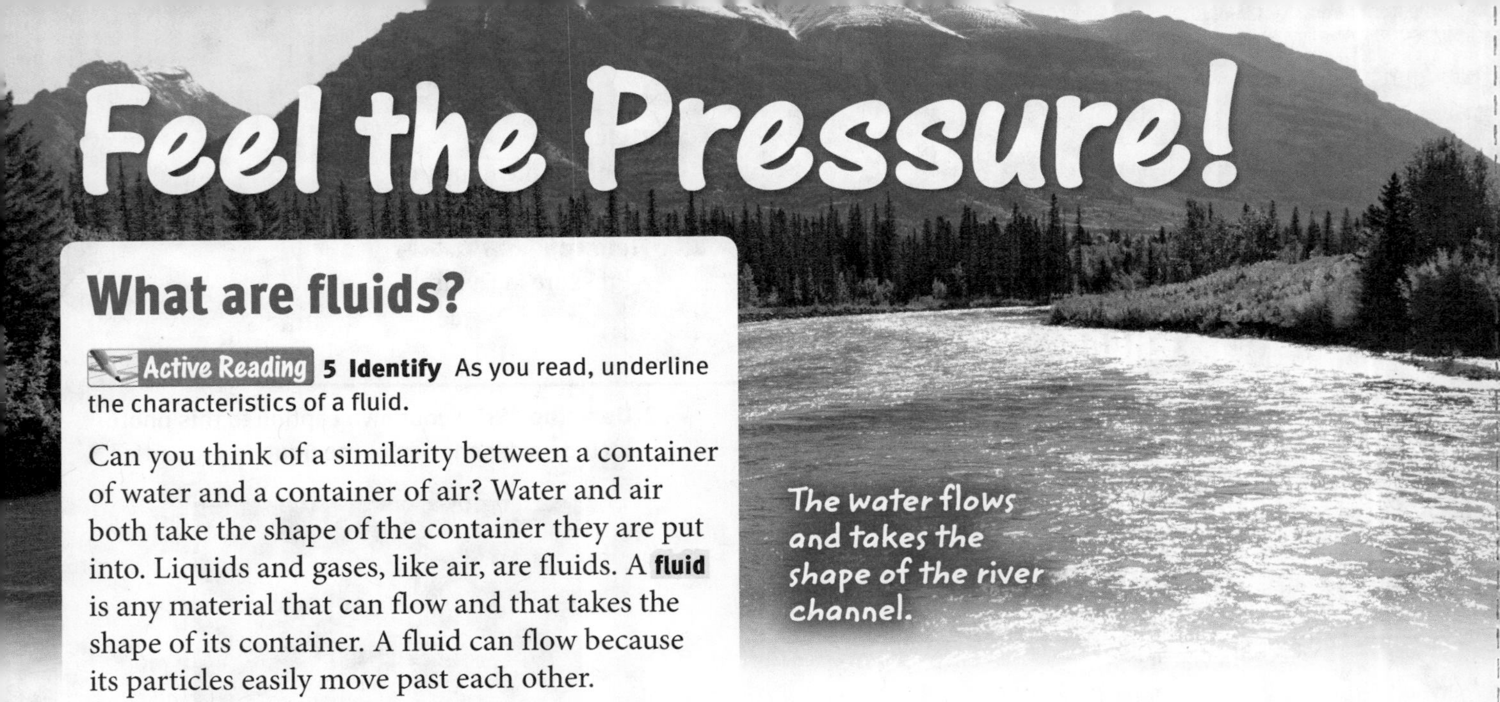

Feel the Pressure!

What are fluids?

Active Reading **5 Identify** As you read, underline the characteristics of a fluid.

Can you think of a similarity between a container of water and a container of air? Water and air both take the shape of the container they are put into. Liquids and gases, like air, are fluids. A **fluid** is any material that can flow and that takes the shape of its container. A fluid can flow because its particles easily move past each other.

The water flows and takes the shape of the river channel.

Why do fluids exert pressure?

All fluids exert pressure. So, what is pressure? **Pressure** is the measure of how much force is acting on a given area. Any force exerted over an area, such as your body weight pushing down on the ground, creates pressure. When you pump up a bicycle tire, you push air into the tire. And like all matter, air is made of tiny particles that are constantly moving. Inside the tire, the air particles bump against one another and against the walls of the tire. The bumping of particles creates a force on the tire. The particles move in all directions and act on every part of the tire.

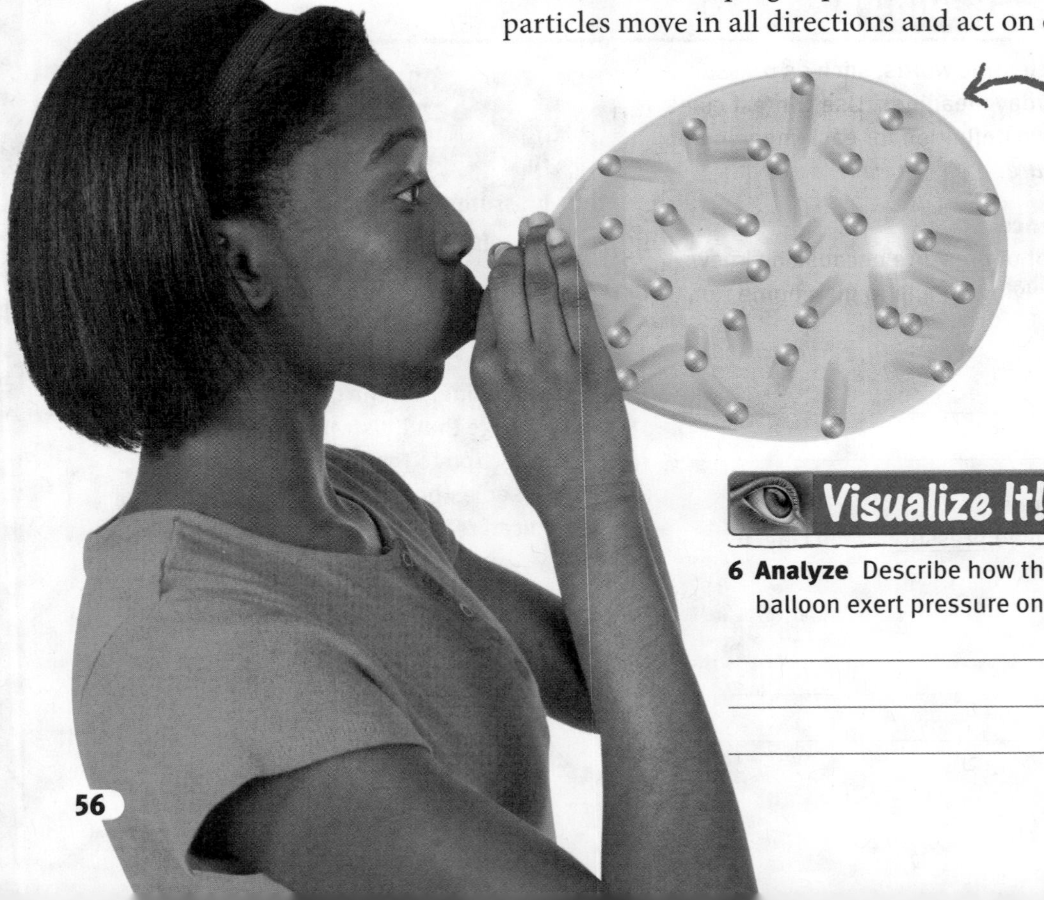

The air in the balloon exerts pressure on the balloon. As more air is added to the balloon, more pressure is exerted.

Visualize It!

6 Analyze Describe how the gas particles inside the balloon exert pressure on the balloon.

___

___

___

How is pressure calculated?

Pressure can be calculated by using the following equation:

$$pressure = \frac{force}{area}$$

The SI unit for pressure is the **pascal**. One pascal (1 Pa) is the force of one newton exerted over an area of one square meter (1 N/m^2). This equation can be used to find the pressure exerted by fluids as well as other materials.

As you can see from the equation, a greater force results in greater pressure. Pressure also depends on the area over which the force is exerted. A greater area results in less pressure.

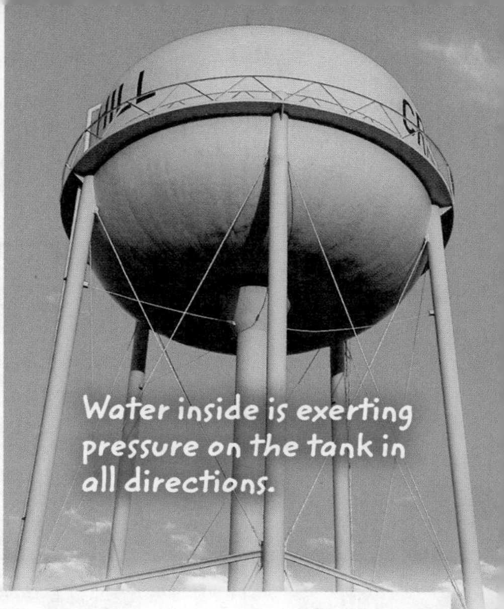
Water inside is exerting pressure on the tank in all directions.

Do the Math

Sample Problem

Calculate the pressure that water exerts on the bottom of a fish tank. The water presses down on the bottom with a force of 2,000 N, and the area of the bottom of the tank is 0.4 m^2.

Identify

A What do you know? area = 0.4 m^2, force = 2,000 N

B What do you want to find? pressure

Plan

C Write the formula: $pressure = \frac{force}{area}$

D Substitute the given values into the formula: $pressure = \frac{2{,}000\ N}{0.4\ m^2}$

Solve

E Divide: $\frac{2{,}000\ N}{0.4\ m^2} = 5{,}000\ N/m^2$

F Check that your units agree: A pascal is a N/m^2, so the units are correct.

Answer: 5,000 Pa

You Try It

7 Calculate Calculate the pressure that the air outside exerts on a window pane that is 1.5 m^2. The force with which the air pushes on the window is 150,000 N.

Identify

A What do you know?

B What do you want to find?

Plan

C Write the formula:

D Substitute the given values into the formula:

Solve

E Divide:

F Check that your units agree:

Answer:

Under Pressure

What are two familiar fluids that exert pressure?

All matter exerts pressure when it exerts force over an area. The atmosphere and water are two familiar fluids that exert pressure.

Active Reading **8 Identify** As you read, underline the similarities between air pressure and water pressure.

As altitude decreases, pressure increases.

The Atmosphere

The atmosphere is the layer of nitrogen, oxygen, and other gases that surrounds Earth. Gravity pulls these gases toward Earth's center, which results in the atmosphere having weight. The pressure caused by the weight of the atmosphere is called **atmospheric pressure**. Atmospheric pressure is exerted on everything on Earth, including you. Atmospheric pressure is usually expressed in kilopascals (kPa). A kilopascal is equal to 1,000 pascals.

As water depth increases, pressure increases.

Water

Gravity pulls water toward Earth's center just as it pulls the atmosphere. The weight of water causes pressure on objects under its surface. In addition to the weight of water above it, anything under water, such as a scuba diver, also has the weight of the air above the water pushing down on it. As a result, the total pressure under water is the sum of the pressures of the atmosphere and the water above.

Think Outside the Book — Inquiry

9 Predict In a small group, research the connection between Earth's gravity and the pressure of fluids. Write a short essay predicting how fluids may behave differently on the moon or on other planets.

Visualize It!

10 Identify Match each pressure with where it is found. Write the pressure 40 kPa, 100 kPa, or 130 kPa in the appropriate box.

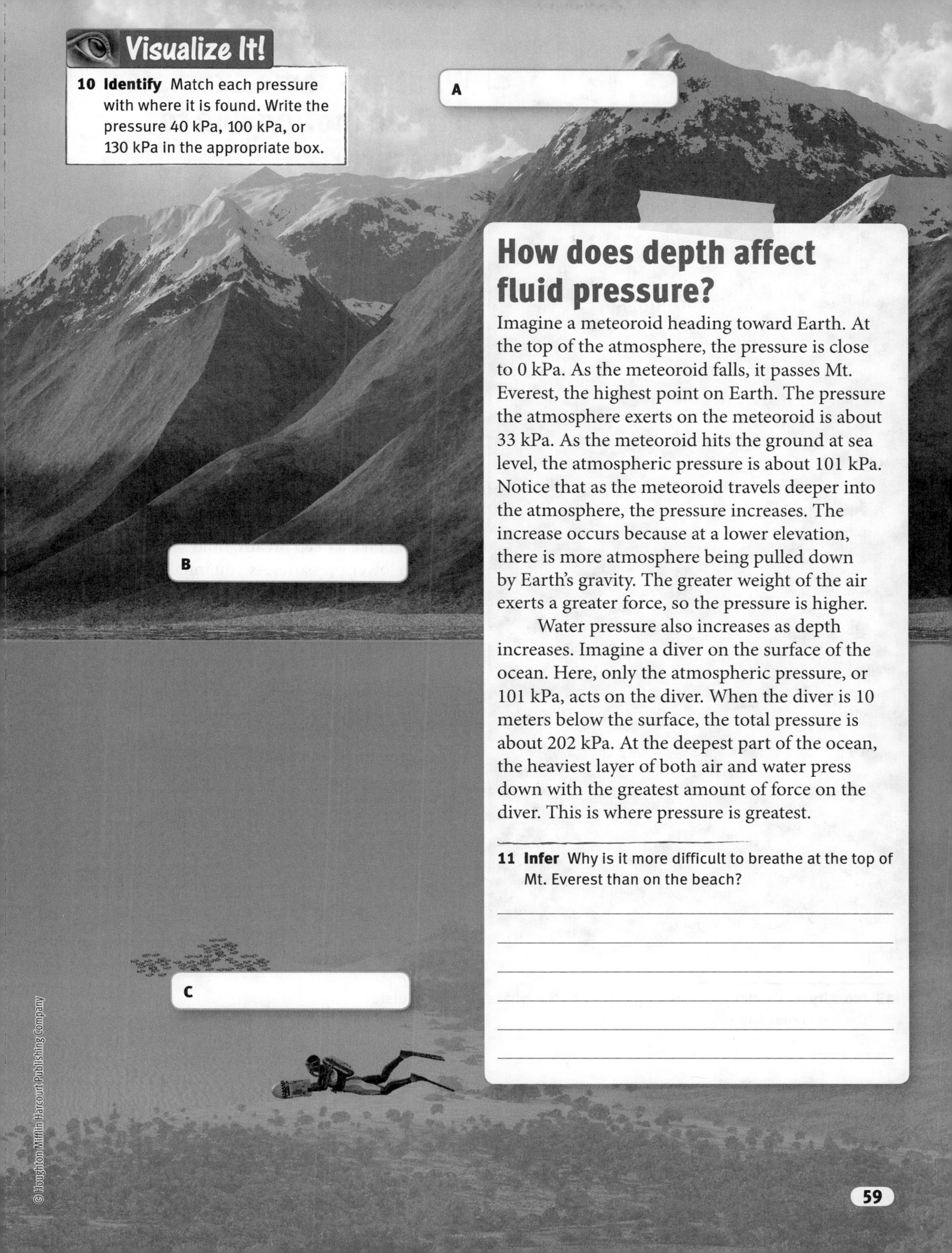

A
B
C

How does depth affect fluid pressure?

Imagine a meteoroid heading toward Earth. At the top of the atmosphere, the pressure is close to 0 kPa. As the meteoroid falls, it passes Mt. Everest, the highest point on Earth. The pressure the atmosphere exerts on the meteoroid is about 33 kPa. As the meteoroid hits the ground at sea level, the atmospheric pressure is about 101 kPa. Notice that as the meteoroid travels deeper into the atmosphere, the pressure increases. The increase occurs because at a lower elevation, there is more atmosphere being pulled down by Earth's gravity. The greater weight of the air exerts a greater force, so the pressure is higher.

Water pressure also increases as depth increases. Imagine a diver on the surface of the ocean. Here, only the atmospheric pressure, or 101 kPa, acts on the diver. When the diver is 10 meters below the surface, the total pressure is about 202 kPa. At the deepest part of the ocean, the heaviest layer of both air and water press down with the greatest amount of force on the diver. This is where pressure is greatest.

11 Infer Why is it more difficult to breathe at the top of Mt. Everest than on the beach?

Thar She Blows!

This whale exhales air explosively through its blowhole before taking another breath. The exhaled air forms a stream of air and water vapor.

What are some examples of fluid motion due to pressure?

When you drink through a straw, you remove some of the air in the straw. Because there is less air inside the straw, the pressure in the straw is reduced. However, the atmospheric pressure on the surface of the liquid outside of the straw remains the same. So, there is a difference between the pressure inside the straw and the pressure outside the straw. The outside pressure forces the liquid up the straw and into your mouth. So, just by drinking through a straw, you can observe an important property of fluids: At any given altitude, fluids flow from areas of higher pressure to areas of lower pressure.

Fluid Motion and Breathing

When you take a deep breath, fluid flows from higher to lower pressure. As you inhale, your lungs expand. This expansion lowers the pressure in your lungs. The pressure in your lungs is now lower than the air pressure outside your lungs. Air flows into your lungs—from higher to lower pressure. When your lungs are filled, the pressure inside your lungs increases. When you exhale, the air in your lungs flows out from a region of higher pressure to a region of lower pressure.

Active Reading **12 Describe** In your own words, describe the movement of air when you inhale.

____

____

____

____

13 Identify Is greater pressure exerted inside the whale's body or outside the blowhole? Explain.

____

____

____

____

Fluid Motion and Weather

At any given altitude in the atmosphere, there are areas of higher pressure and areas of lower pressure. Air moves from areas of higher pressure to areas of lower pressure. The movement of the air is known as wind.

Some of the damaging winds caused by tornadoes are the result of pressure differences. There is a great difference between the very low air pressure inside a tornado and the higher air pressure outside a tornado. This difference causes air to rush into the center of the tornado.

Visualize It!

14 Analyze Write *low pressure* or *high pressure* in each of the blank boxes.

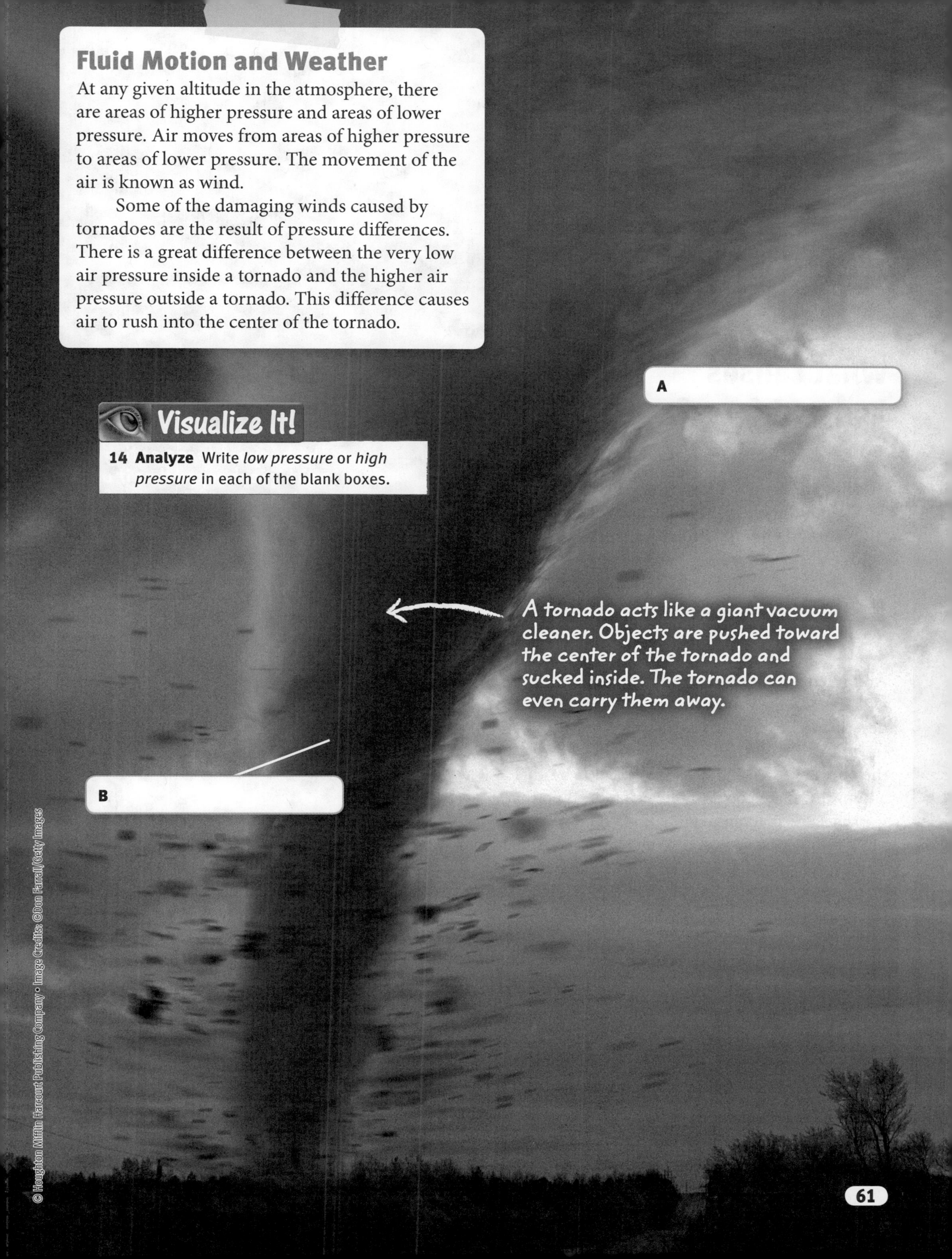
A
A tornado acts like a giant vacuum cleaner. Objects are pushed toward the center of the tornado and sucked inside. The tornado can even carry them away.
B

Sink or Swim?

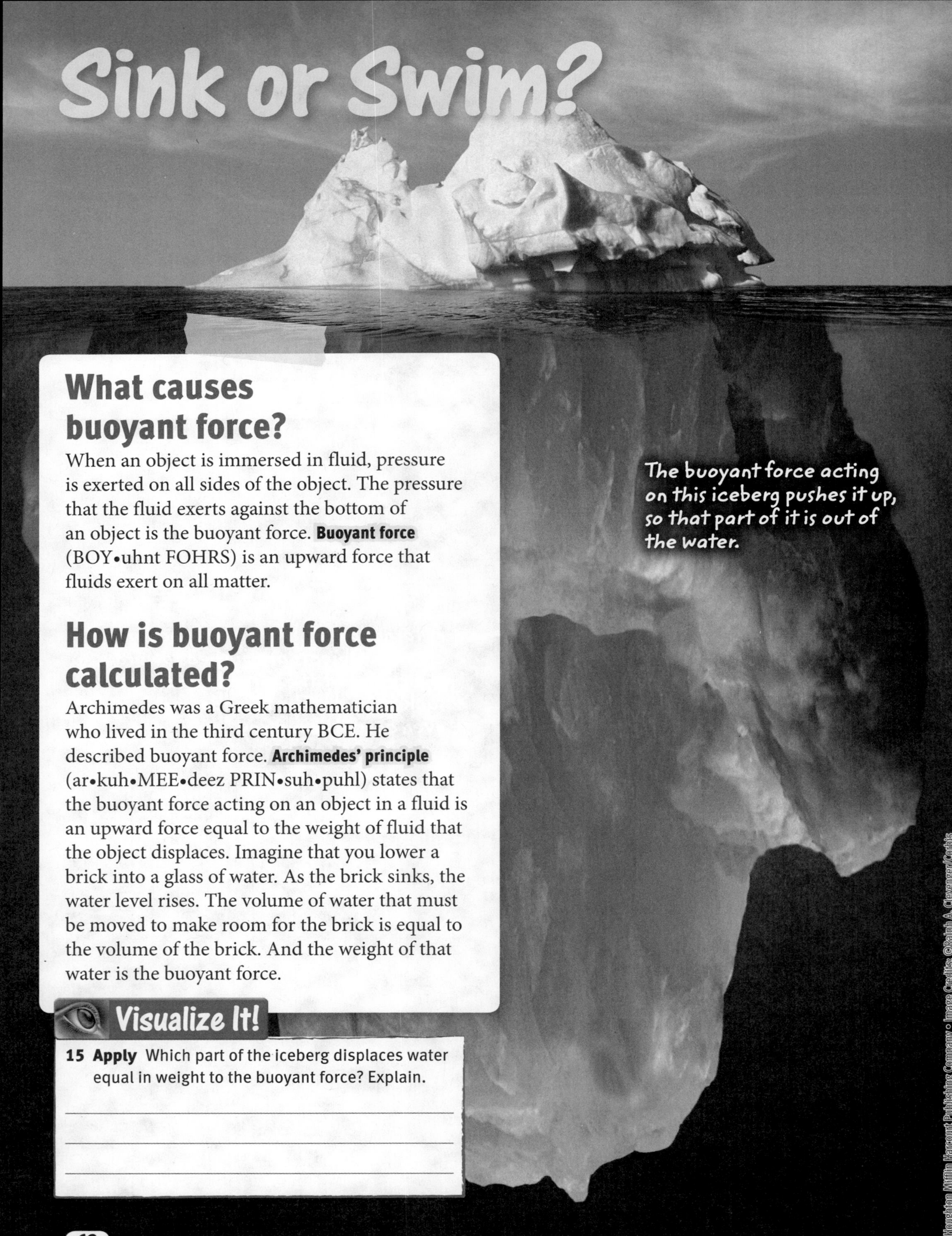

The buoyant force acting on this iceberg pushes it up, so that part of it is out of the water.

What causes buoyant force?

When an object is immersed in fluid, pressure is exerted on all sides of the object. The pressure that the fluid exerts against the bottom of an object is the buoyant force. **Buoyant force** (BOY•uhnt FOHRS) is an upward force that fluids exert on all matter.

How is buoyant force calculated?

Archimedes was a Greek mathematician who lived in the third century BCE. He described buoyant force. **Archimedes' principle** (ar•kuh•MEE•deez PRIN•suh•puhl) states that the buoyant force acting on an object in a fluid is an upward force equal to the weight of fluid that the object displaces. Imagine that you lower a brick into a glass of water. As the brick sinks, the water level rises. The volume of water that must be moved to make room for the brick is equal to the volume of the brick. And the weight of that water is the buoyant force.

Visualize It!

15 Apply Which part of the iceberg displaces water equal in weight to the buoyant force? Explain.

____

____

____

What can happen as a result of weight and buoyant force?

Imagine that you use a straw to push an ice cube under water. Then you release the ice cube. Will it sink or pop back up to the surface? This depends on its weight and the buoyant force.

Active Reading

16 Identify As you read, underline the relationships between weight and buoyant force that cause an object to float, sink, or be buoyed up.

Some Objects Float

An object in a fluid will float if the object's weight is equal to the buoyant force. In this case, the buoyant force pushing the object up is the same as the force pushing the object down. If the object and the fluid have the same density, the object will float suspended under the surface of the fluid. If the object is less dense than the fluid, it will float at the surface, and will be only partly submerged.

Some Objects Sink

An object in a fluid will sink if the object's weight is greater than the buoyant force. The object's weight will be greater than the buoyant force if the object is denser than the fluid.

Some Objects Are Buoyed Up

If the buoyant force on an object is greater than the object's weight, the object is buoyed up. This means that an object moves upward in a fluid until the buoyant force equals the object's weight, causing the object to float. This principle explains why an ice cube pops to the surface when it is pushed to the bottom of a glass of water.

Visualize It!

17 Predict Examine each of the three pictures below and determine whether the object shown floats, sinks, or is buoyed up when submerged in water.

A The duck has a weight of 9 N. The buoyant force is 15 N.

____

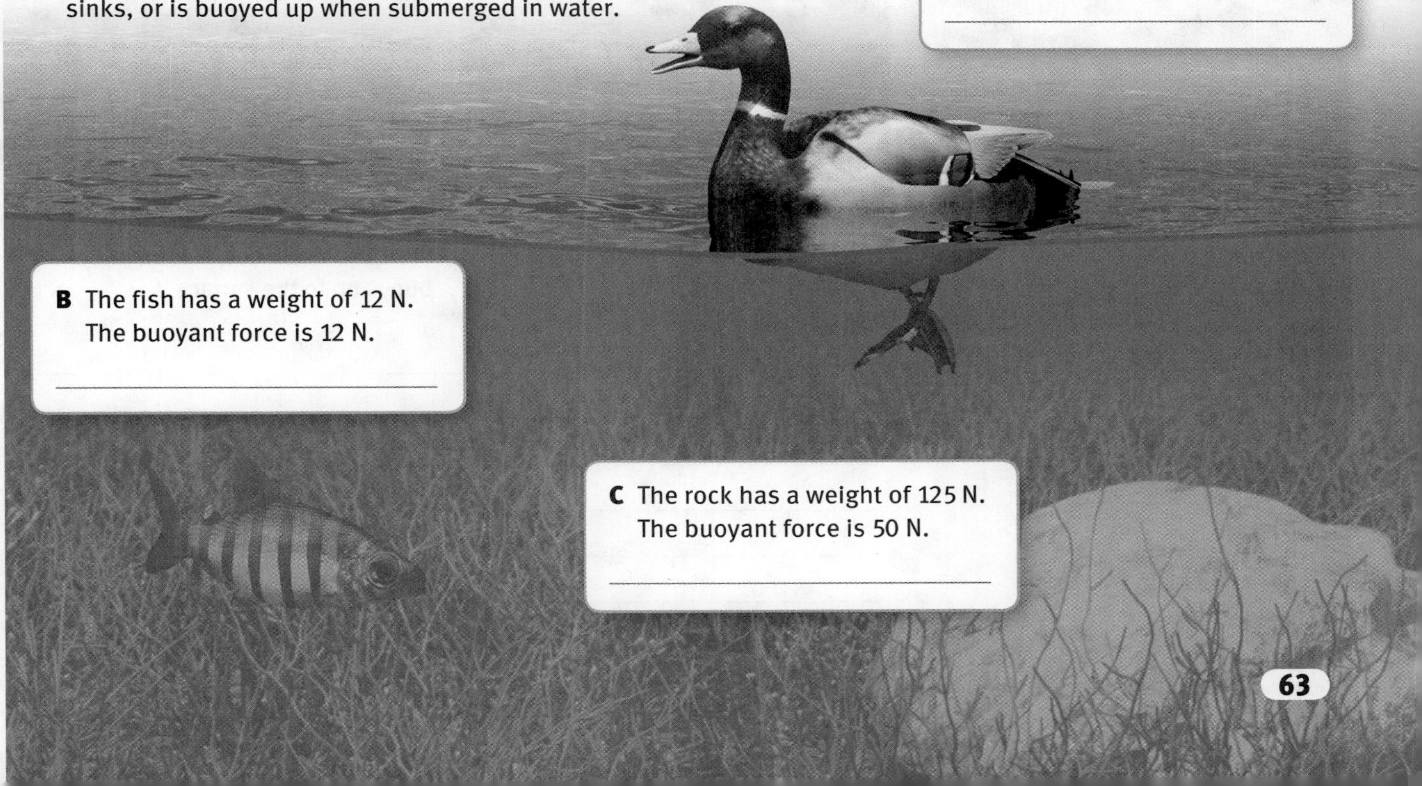

B The fish has a weight of 12 N. The buoyant force is 12 N.

____

C The rock has a weight of 125 N. The buoyant force is 50 N.

____

What affects the density of an object?

The density of an object is related to its ability to sink or float. Sometimes it is possible to change the density of an object to control whether it sinks or floats. Density is related to mass and volume. This relationship can be expressed in a mathematical formula.

$$\text{density} = \frac{\text{mass}}{\text{volume}}$$

Active Reading **18 Describe** If an object's density is decreasing but its mass stays constant, what must be true of the object's volume?

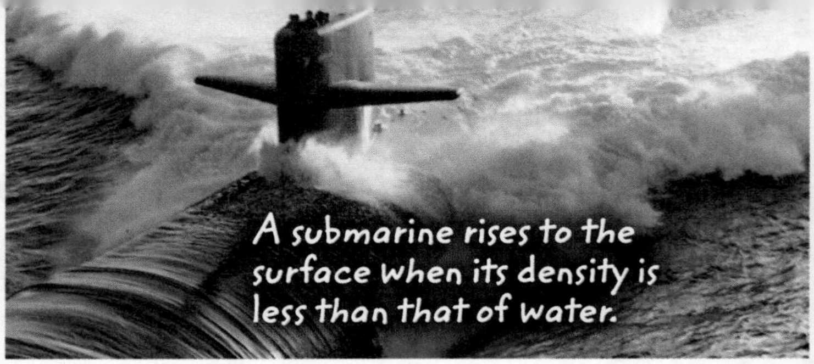

A submarine rises to the surface when its density is less than that of water.

Its Mass

A submarine can travel both on the surface of the ocean and under water. Submarines have large ballast tanks that can be opened to allow seawater to flow in. As water is added, the submarine's mass increases, but its volume stays the same. The submarine's overall density increases so that it sinks below the surface. Adding more water allows the submarine to dive deeper. When the submarine needs to rise, air is added to its tanks and the water is blown out. The submarine's mass decreases as water is expelled, and so the density also decreases. The submarine rises to the surface.

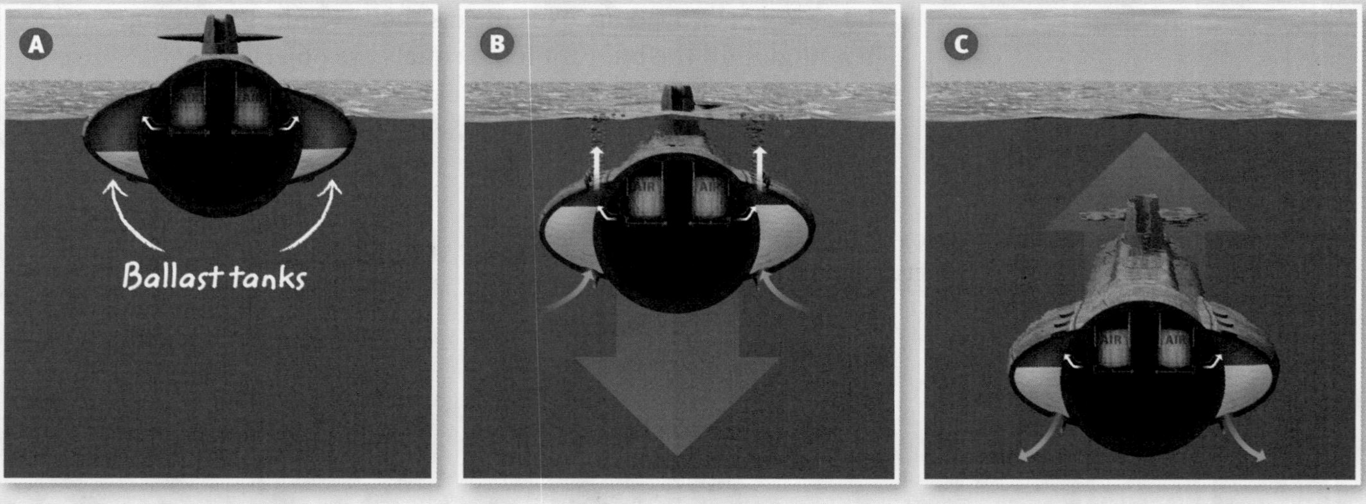

A
Ballast tanks
B
C

A: When a submarine's tanks are mostly filled with air, the submarine floats on the surface.

B: As water fills the tanks from below and air escapes from the top, a submarine sinks.

C: As air is pumped into the tanks to force the water out, a submarine buoys up to the surface.

Visualize It!

19 Analyze Explain how the density of the submarine changes in each image.

Its Volume

Steel is almost eight times denser than water. Yet huge steel ships cruise the oceans with ease. How is this possible? It all depends on the shape of the ship. What if a ship were just a big block of steel? If you put that block into water, the block would sink because it is denser than water. So ships are built with a hollow shape. The amount of steel in the ship is the same as in the block. But the hollow shape increases the overall volume of the ship. An increase in the ship's volume leads to a decrease in its density. Ships float because their overall density is less than the density of water.

Like a submarine, some fish adjust their density to stay at a certain depth in the water. Most bony fish have an organ called a *swim bladder.* This organ is filled with gases. The inflated swim bladder increases the fish's volume, which decreases the fish's overall density. By adjusting the volume of gas in its swim bladder, the fish can move to different depths.

This fish uses its swim bladder to change its volume so that it can float at different depths in water.

20 Predict Each row of the table below shows the density of an object and the density of a fluid. Predict whether each object will sink or float on the surface of the fluid. Write your prediction, *sink* or *float,* in the table.

Object and its density	Fluid and its density	Prediction
cork, 0.24 g/cm^3	water, 1.0 g/cm^3	
penny, 8.96 g/cm^3	mercury, 13.53 g/cm^3	
boiled egg, 1.02 g/cm^3	cooking oil, 0.93 g/cm^3	
ice cube, 0.92 g/cm^3	vinegar, 1.01 g/cm^3	

21 Identify Placing the egg in which fluid would give a different result?

Visual Summary

To complete this summary, fill in the blanks with the correct word. Then use the key below to check your answers. You can use this page to review the main concepts of the lesson.

Fluids and Pressure

Pressure is the amount of force exerted on a given area.

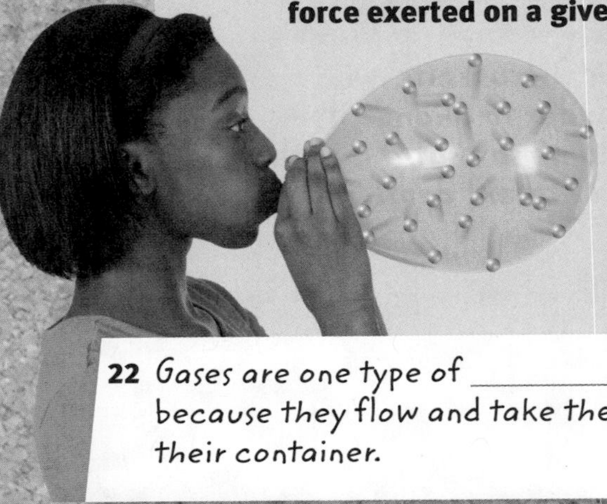

22 Gases are one type of ______________ because they flow and take the shape of their container.

Fluids flow from higher pressure areas to lower pressure areas.

23 The force of ______________ causes atmospheric pressure by pulling down on the air.

Archimedes' principle explains buoyant force.

24 An object that has a weight greater than the buoyant force will ______________

25 The mass of an object divided by its volume is its ______________

Answers: 22 fluid; 23 gravity; 24 sink; 25 density

26 Design Imagine you want to design a toy boat from a block of clay. What would you need to consider to make sure that your boat can float?

Lesson Review

Vocabulary

Draw a line to connect the following terms to their definitions.

1 pascal	**A** the amount of force exerted per unit area of a surface
2 fluid	**B** the SI unit of pressure
3 pressure	**C** a material that can flow and takes the shape of its container

Key Concepts

4 Compare A pebble sinks in water. A twig floats on top of the water. Compare the densities of the water, the pebble and the twig.

5 Describe Explain why atmospheric pressure changes as atmospheric depth changes.

6 Define What does Archimedes' principle state?

7 Calculate An object exerts 140 N of force on a surface that has an area of 2.0 m^2. How much pressure does the object exert?

8 Apply Describe the motion of air particles inside an inflated balloon.

Critical Thinking

Use this photo to answer the following questions.

9 Analyze What two properties show that the drink is a fluid?

10 Apply Explain how drinking through a straw illustrates fluid flowing from high-pressure to low-pressure areas.

11 Evaluate Your friend tells you that all heavy objects sink in water. Do you agree or disagree? Explain your answer in terms of buoyant force.

My Notes

Unit 1 **Big Idea**

Unbalanced forces cause changes in the motion of objects, and these changes can be predicted and described.

Lesson 1

ESSENTIAL QUESTION

How are distance, time, and speed related?

Analyze how distance, time, and speed are related.

Lesson 2

ESSENTIAL QUESTION

How does motion change?

Analyze how acceleration is related to time and velocity.

Lesson 3

ESSENTIAL QUESTION

How do forces affect motion?

Describe different types of forces and explain the effect force has on motion.

Lesson 4

ESSENTIAL QUESTION

How do objects move under the influence of gravity?

Describe the effect that gravity, including Earth's gravity, has on matter.

Lesson 5

ESSENTIAL QUESTION

What happens when fluids exert pressure?

Explain why fluids exert pressure and how the resulting pressure causes motion and the buoyant force.

Connect ESSENTIAL QUESTIONS

Lessons 2 and 3

1 Synthesize How is force related to acceleration and gravity?

____

____

____

____

Think Outside the Book

2 Synthesize Choose one of these activities to help synthesize what you have learned in this unit.

☐ Using what you learned in lessons 1–4, create a brochure to explain why the following statement is false: An object's motion can change only if a force is applied to the object through direct contact.

☐ Using what you learned in lessons 3–5, make a poster presentation describing the forces acting on a falling skydiver with an open parachute.

Unit 1 Review

Name ______________________________

Vocabulary

Fill in each blank with the term that best completes the following sentences.

1 The ______________________ of an object describes the speed and the direction in which it is going.

2 The change in the velocity of an object is defined as its ______________________.

3 An object that is traveling around another body in space is in ______________ around that body.

4 The ______________________ on an object is the combination of all the forces acting on the object.

5 The ______________________ is the upward force that fluids exert on all matter.

Key Concepts

Read each question below, and circle the best answer.

6 An airplane leaves New York to fly to Los Angeles. It travels 3,850 km in 5.5 hours. What is the average speed of the airplane?

A 700 km

B 700 hours

C 700 km/hour

D 700 hours/km

7 The law of universal gravitation says all bodies attract each other. If you drop a cup, it falls to Earth. Why doesn't the gravitational attraction between your hand and the cup keep the cup from falling?

A The law of universal gravitation only applies to planets in space.

B There is a gravitational attraction between you and the cup, but Earth's gravity is stronger, so Earth's gravity pulls the cup down.

C The gravitational attraction between you and the cup is so strong that the force pushes the cup down.

D There is no gravitational attraction between you and the cup, so Earth's gravity pulls the cup down.

8 This distance-time graph shows the speeds of four toy cars.

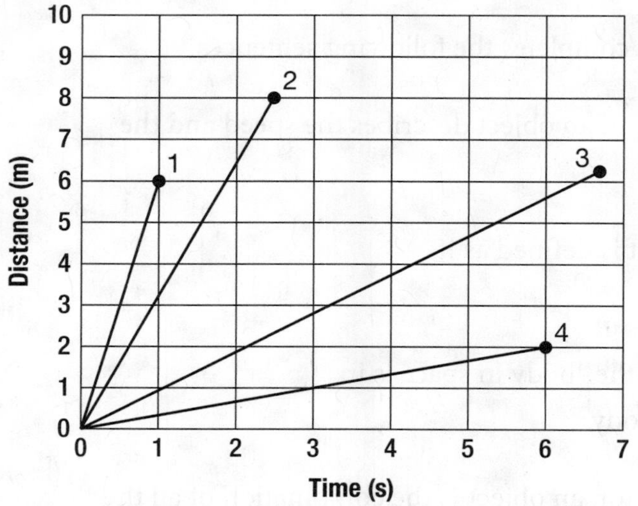
10
9
8
7
6
5
4
3
2
1
0
Distance (m)
0
1
2
3
4
5
6
7
Time (s)
1
2
3
4

Which car is the fastest?

A Car 1

B Car 2

C Car 3

D Car 4

9 The diagram below shows the forces acting on a sneaker. As the force F is applied, the sneaker does not move.

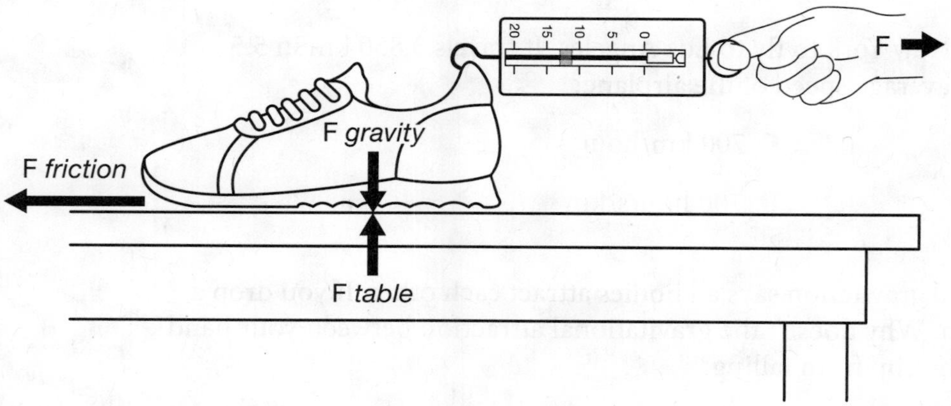
F
F gravity
F friction
F table
0
5
10
15
20

Which statement below correctly describes the forces?

A The net force is acting in an upward direction.

B The net force is acting to the left.

C The net force is moving to the right.

D The net force is zero and all the forces are balanced.

Name ____________________

10 The diagram below shows a satellite in orbit around Earth. It is orbiting in the direction shown and is pulled toward Earth by gravity.

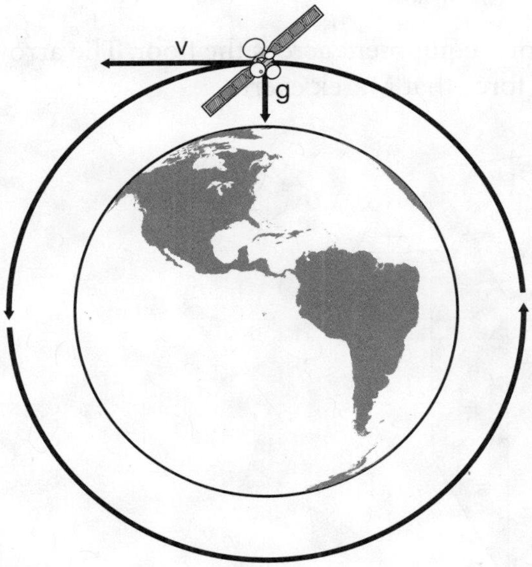
v
g

What would happen if Earth's gravity suddenly disappeared?

A The satellite would continue to orbit Earth.

B The satellite would fall to Earth.

C The satellite would move into space in a straight line.

D The satellite would stop moving.

11 Julia is in a car with her father. The car is undergoing centripetal acceleration. What is happening to the car?

A The car is changing direction at a constant speed.

B The car is changing direction and speeding up.

C The car is stopping suddenly.

D The car is slowing down.

12 Rajiv made a model of a boat. When he places it in water, it sinks. According to Archimedes' principle, why does the boat sink?

A The boat is too small.

B The buoyant force is less than the boat's weight.

C The buoyant force is equal to the boat's weight.

D The buoyant force is greater than the boat's weight.

Critical Thinking

Answer the following questions in the space provided.

13 Marek is trying to push a box of sports equipment across the floor. The arrow on the box is a vector representing the force that Marek exerts.

What are the forces acting upon the box?

14 What does the formula $F = ma$ mean, and which of Newton's three laws does it describe?

Connect ESSENTIAL QUESTIONS

Lessons 1 and 2

Answer the following question in the space provided.

15 What is the difference between the speed of an object, the velocity of an object, and the acceleration of an object?

UNIT 2

Work, Energy, and Machines

Big Idea

Energy is transferred when a force moves an object.

Machines are found everywhere—even in the skate park.

What do you think?

Machines make work and play easier. Skateboards are complex machines made of simple machines. Can you identify two basic parts of this skateboard?

Simple machines make up complex machines.

Unit 2

Work, Energy, and Machines

CITIZEN SCIENCE

A Day at the Races

Both simple and complex machines can make work easier and play more exciting. Creating a small-scale downhill racing machine is a fun way to learn about simple machines.

1 Think about It

A Investigate some ways to create a small-scale downhill racer with everyday objects. Make notes about your research.

B Most downhill racers will have two axles and four wheels. Define *axle* and *wheel* below and explain what function each would serve in a racer.

C Check out the recycling bin in your school, classroom, or home. Can you use any recyclable materials to make a downhill racer? (Safety note: Some materials are toxic or dangerous. Before you touch anything, ask your teacher.)

② Ask a Question

What are some ways that you could make a downhill racer go faster? Do some research and write notes below.

____

____

____

____

____

③ Make a Plan

Draw a sketch of a small-scale downhill racer that you would make. Label it, and note if any of the parts are reused or recyclable.

The downhill racer is traveling over 20 mph! Do you think the driver is frightened or exhilarated?

Take It Home

With an adult, make the small-scale downhill racer you designed. Challenge the adult to design and help you make a different downhill racer. Conduct a race to find out which racer was faster. Think about how the design may affect speed.

Lesson 1

Work, Energy, and Power

This basketball player has to do work in order to make a basket!

ESSENTIAL QUESTION

How is work related to energy?

By the end of this lesson, you should be able to relate work to energy and power.

Lesson Labs

Quick Labs
- Investigating Work
- Calculating Power

STEM Lab
- Using Water to Do Work

Engage Your Brain

1 Identify Circle the correct words in the paragraph below to make true statements.

Max, Jorge, and Wendy are in a race. They push identical rolling carts for the same distance. Max finishes the race first, so he did *more / the same / less* work than Jorge. Wendy finishes the race second, so she has *more / the same / less* power than Max.

2 Illustrate What do you think of when you hear the word *work*? Draw a picture of yourself doing work. Then write a caption describing what you are doing.

Active Reading

3 Apply Many scientific words, such as *work* and *power*, also have everyday meanings. Use context clues to write your own definition for each meaning of the words *work* and *power*.

Example sentence
My mom always waves goodbye before leaving for work.

work:

Example sentence
The team coach has the power to decide when to meet for practice.

power:

Vocabulary Terms

- work
- power
- energy

4 Apply As you learn the definition of each vocabulary term in this lesson, create your own definition or sketch to help you remember the meaning of the term.

Work It Out

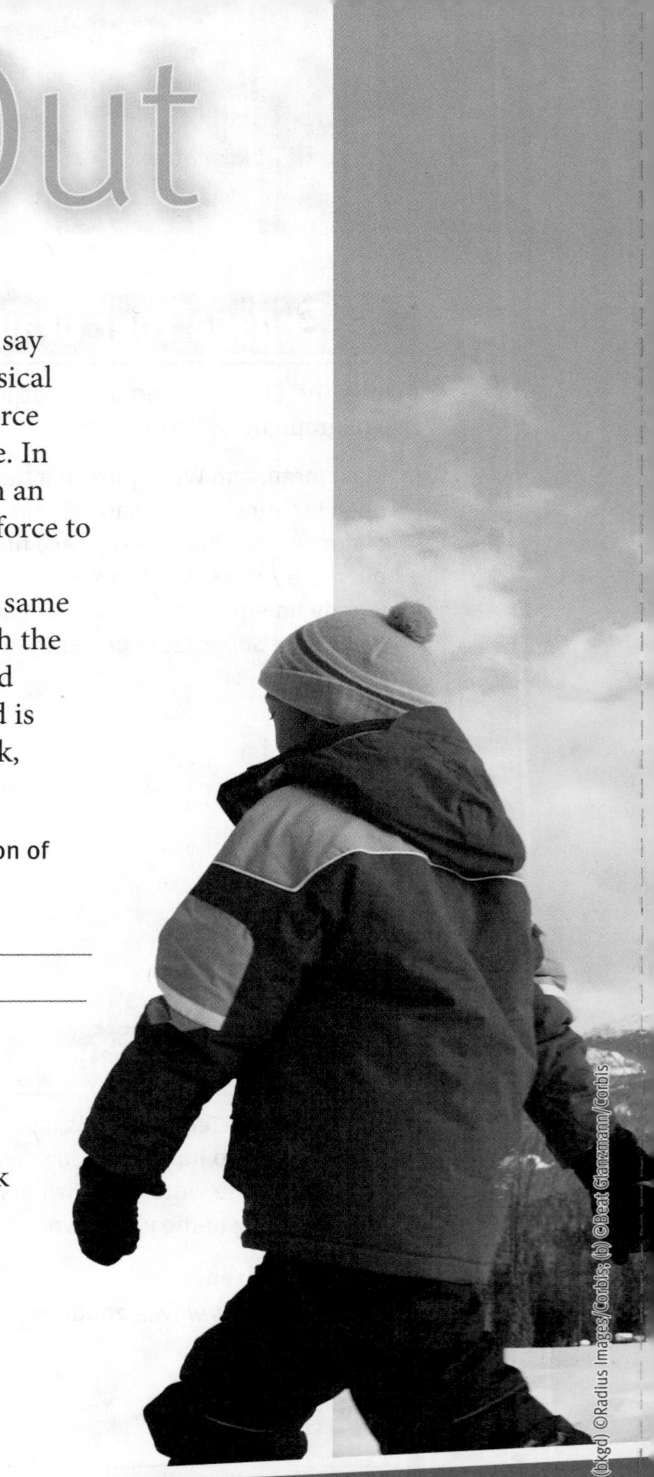

What is work?

What comes to mind when you think of work? Most people say they are working when they do anything that requires a physical or mental effort. But in physical science, **work** is the use of force to move an object some distance in the direction of the force. In scientific terms, you do work only when you exert a force on an object and move it. If you want to do work, you have to use force to move something.

Work is done only by the part of the force that is in the same direction as the motion. Imagine that you pull a sled through the snow. You pull the rope up at an angle while you pull the sled forward. Only the part of your force pulling the sled forward is doing work. The upward part of your force is not doing work, because the sled is not moving upward.

Active Reading **5 Summarize** How does the scientific definition of work differ from the familiar definition?

____

____

How is work calculated?

Work is a measure of how much force is applied to move an object through a certain distance. You can calculate the work a force does if you know the size of the force applied to an object and the distance through which the force acts. The distance involved is the distance the object moved. You can calculate work using the following formula:

$$\text{work} = \text{force} \times \text{distance}$$
$$W = F \times d$$

Force can be expressed in newtons, and distance can be expressed in meters. When you multiply a force in newtons by a distance in meters, the product is a unit called the *newton-meter* (N•m), or the *joule*. The joule (J) is the standard unit used to express work. One joule of work is done when a force of one newton moves an object one meter. To get an idea of how much a joule of work is, lift an apple (which weighs about one newton) from your foot to your waist (about one meter).

Most of the force that the dogs are using is in the direction of motion. So nearly all of the dogs' force does work.

Do the Math

Sample Problem

A boy pulls a sled 22 m. The force that he applies in the direction of motion is 20 N. How much work does he do?

Identify

A. What do you know? force = 20 N, distance = 22 m

B. What do you want to find out? work

Plan

C. Draw and label a sketch:

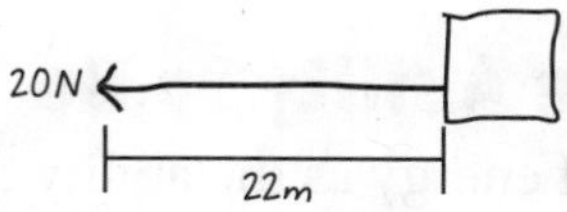

20N
22m

D. Write the formula: $W = F \times d$

E. Substitute into the formula: $W = 20 \text{ N} \times 22 \text{ m}$

Solve

F. Calculate and simplify: $W = 20 \text{ N} \times 22 \text{ m}$

$= 440 \text{ N} \times \text{m}$

$= 440 \text{ J}$

G. Check that your units agree: Unit is J.

Unit of work is J.

Units agree.

Answer: 440 J

You Try It

6 Calculate A team of dogs pulls a sled 15 m using a force of 200 N. How much work did the dogs do?

Identify

A. What do you know?

B. What do you want to find out?

Plan

C. Draw and label a sketch:

D. Write the formula:

E. Substitute into the formula:

Solve

F. Calculate and simplify:

G. Check that your units agree:

Answer:

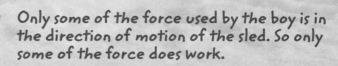

Only some of the force used by the boy is in the direction of motion of the sled. So only some of the force does work.

Energizing

How are work and energy related?

"It's important to conserve energy!" your teacher might say as she turns off the classroom lights when everyone leaves. "I'm all out of energy," you might say when you just ran outside for a long time. What does the word *energy* actually mean? And what does it have to do with work?

Active Reading

7 Identify As you read this page and the next, underline examples of energy provided in the text.

Energy Is the Ability to Do Work

You might think of energy as the ability to cause a change. But now that you know more about work, you can learn more about energy. **Energy** is the ability to do work. This means that energy is the ability to apply force to cause movement in the direction of the force. For example, when a dog pulls a sled, the dog is using energy. When you do work by swinging a tennis racket and hitting a ball, you are using energy. The work done by energy doesn't have to be visible, however. For example, when energy is transferred to an object in the form of heat, the particles in the object move faster even though the object itself does not move. Work and energy are so related that they are both expressed in the same unit, the *joule*. You can think of work as a transfer of energy. In fact, energy is transferred every time work is done.

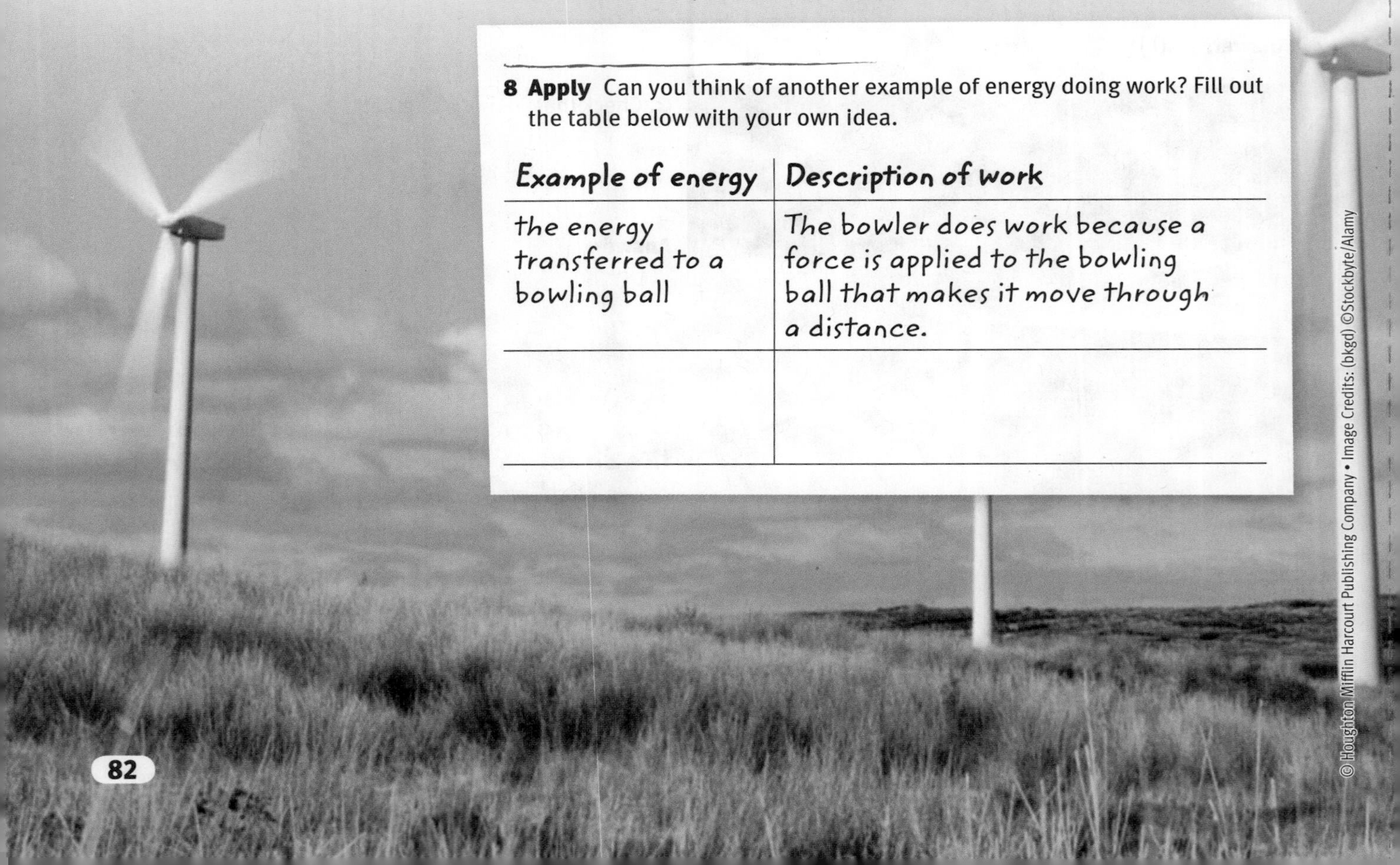

8 Apply Can you think of another example of energy doing work? Fill out the table below with your own idea.

Example of energy	Description of work
the energy transferred to a bowling ball	The bowler does work because a force is applied to the bowling ball that makes it move through a distance.

Work Transfers Energy

When a person does work on an object, he or she can transfer energy to that object. For example, you may know that wind turbines are a way to produce clean and renewable energy. But how is work involved? The wind does work moving the blades so that they spin. The wind has the capacity to do this work because of the energy of its motion. Inside the turbines, more energy transfers occur so that the energy of the blades is transformed into electrical energy that can be used at home.

A carnival game can be an example of work transferring energy. The goal of the game is to hit a target with a ball. You do work on the ball as you throw with your arm. When you change the position and speed of the ball, you transfer energy to the ball. The ball then does work on the target and you win a prize.

Work is done inside wind turbines to transform mechanical energy from the wind into electrical energy.

Visualize It!

9 Synthesize The wind does work on the wind turbines below. Describe how the work is done.

____

____

____

____

Think Outside the Book Inquiry

10 Design Imagine that you work for a wind turbine company. Your company would like to provide tours of the wind farms to students and tourists. Make an advertising brochure that explains what wind turbines do and why people might be interested in learning more about them.

Superpower

A crane's power depends on how quickly it lifts a crate.

What is power?

The word *power* has different common meanings. It is used to mean a source of energy, as in a power plant, or strength, as in a powerful engine. When you talk about a powerful swimmer, for example, you would probably say that the swimmer is very strong or very fast. However, if you use the scientific definition of power, you would instead say that a powerful swimmer is one who does the work of moving herself through the water in a short time.

Power is the rate at which work is done. For example, when two cranes lift the same crate the same height, they do the same amount of work. The one that lifts the crate the fastest is the more powerful crane. Because work is also a measure of energy transfer, you can also think of power as the rate at which energy is converted from one form to another.

This is an incandescent light bulb.

Do the Math — Sample Problem

Here's an example of how to find the power used by an incandescent light bulb. A light bulb uses 600 J of energy in 6 s. What is the power of the light bulb?

To calculate power, divide energy by time.

$$P = \frac{E}{t}$$

$$P = \frac{600\ J}{6\ s}$$

$$P = \frac{100\ J}{s}$$

Unit is J/s. Unit for power is W, which is also J/s. Units agree.

$$P = 100\ W$$

How is power calculated?

Because power is a measure of how much energy is transferred in a given time, power can be calculated from energy and time. Sometimes you know that energy is being transferred, but you cannot directly measure the work being done. For example, you know that a TV uses energy. But there is no way to measure all of the work that every part of the TV does. To calculate the TV's power, divide the amount of energy used by the time it is used.

$$\text{power} = \frac{\text{energy}}{\text{time}}$$

$$P = \frac{E}{t}$$

Remember that energy is expressed in joules. So power is often expressed in joules per second. One joule of energy transferred in one second is equal to one *watt* (W). The watt is the unit of measurement for power. You have probably heard the term *watt* used in connection with light bulbs. A 60-watt light bulb requires 60 joules of energy every second to shine at its rated brightness.

Active Reading

11 Apply What two things would you need to know to calculate the power of a microwave oven?

You Try It

12 Calculate A compact fluorescent light bulb, called a CFL, is advertised as being just as bright as an incandescent 100 W light bulb but using less energy. The CFL uses only 156 J of energy in 6 s. What is the power of this CFL bulb?

13 Analyze Why might someone buy a more expensive CFL instead of an incandescent light bulb?

A compact fluorescent light bulb uses less energy each second than an equally bright incandescent light bulb.

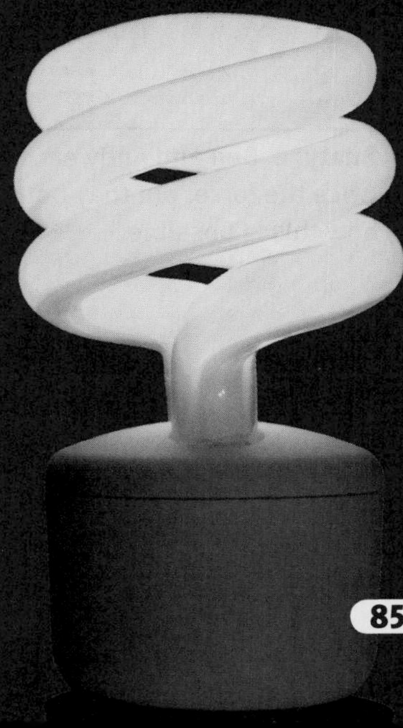

Visual Summary

To complete this summary, fill in the blanks with the correct word or phrase. Then, use the key below to check your answers. You can use this page to review the main concepts of the lesson.

Work, Energy, and Power

Work is the use of force to move an object a distance.

14 *Work is force multiplied by* ________________

15 *Work is done only by the part of the force that acts in the* ________________ *as the motion of an object.*

Energy is the ability to do work.

16 ________________ *transfers energy.*

Power is the rate at which energy is transferred.

17 *Power is* ________________ *divided by time.*

18 *Power is typically expressed in* ________________

Answers: 14 distance; 15 same direction; 16 Work; 17 energy or work; 18 watts

19 Analyze Ben and Andy each pushed an empty grocery cart. Ben used twice the force, but they both did the same amount of work. Explain how this is possible.

Lesson Review

Vocabulary

Fill in the blanks with the term that best completes the following sentences.

1 The joule is the standard unit of measurement for both ______________ and ______________

2 The watt is the standard unit of measurement for ______________

Key Concepts

3 Apply If you push very hard on an object but it doesn't move, have you done any work? Why or why not?

____

____

____

4 Describe What two factors do you need to know to calculate how much work was done in any situation?

____

____

5 Relate Explain the relationship between power, energy, and time.

____

____

____

____

6 Calculate If an electric hair dryer uses 2,400 J of energy in 2 s, what is its power? Use the space below to solve this problem.

Critical Thinking

Use the photo below to answer the following questions.

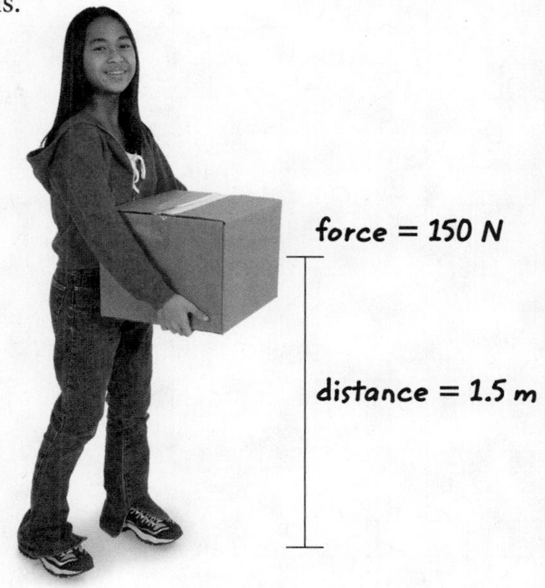
force = 150 N
distance = 1.5 m

7 Apply Is this girl doing any work while she stands still and holds the box? Why or why not?

____

____

8 Calculate When the girl lifted the box from the floor, did she do any work? If so, how much work did she do?

9 Synthesize Think of an activity that involves work. Write about how the work is transferring energy and where the transferred energy goes.

____

____

____

____

____

My Notes

Lesson 2

Kinetic and Potential Energy

ESSENTIAL QUESTION

What are kinetic and potential energy?

By the end of this lesson, you should be able to calculate kinetic and potential energy and know how these two types of energy are related.

Climbing a hill requires a lot of energy but it makes the ride back down fun.

Lesson Labs

Quick Labs
- Investigate Potential Energy
- Identify Potential and Kinetic Energy

Exploration Lab
- Mechanical Energy

Engage Your Brain

1 Predict Check T or F to show whether you think each statement is true or false.

T	F	
☐	☐	Objects that are sitting still have kinetic energy.
☐	☐	The kinetic energy of an object depends on how much space the object takes up.
☐	☐	The gravitational potential energy of an object depends on its height above a surface.

2 Analyze If the baseball and the plastic ball were moving at the same speed, which ball would hit a bat harder? Why?

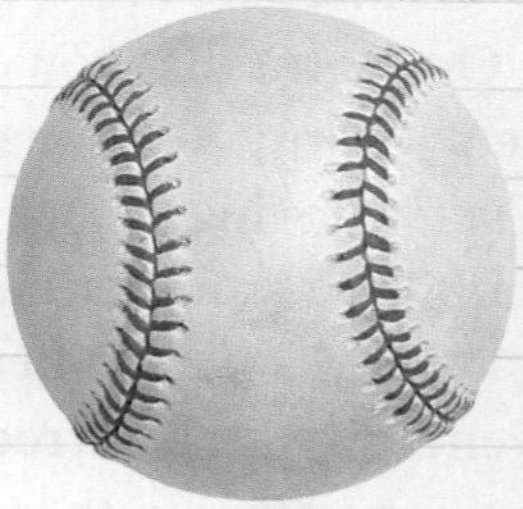

____

____

____

____

____

Active Reading

3 Synthesize Many English words have their roots in other languages. Use the Greek word below to make an educated guess about the meaning of the term *kinetic energy*.

Greek word	Meaning
kinetos	moving

Example sentence:
The harder the football is thrown, the more kinetic energy it has.

kinetic energy:

____

____

____

Vocabulary Terms

- **kinetic energy**
- **potential energy**
- **mechanical energy**

4 Identify As you read, create a reference card for each vocabulary term. On one side of the card, write the term and its meaning. On the other side, draw an image that illustrates or makes a connection to the term. These cards can be used as bookmarks in the text so that you can refer to them while studying.

On the Move

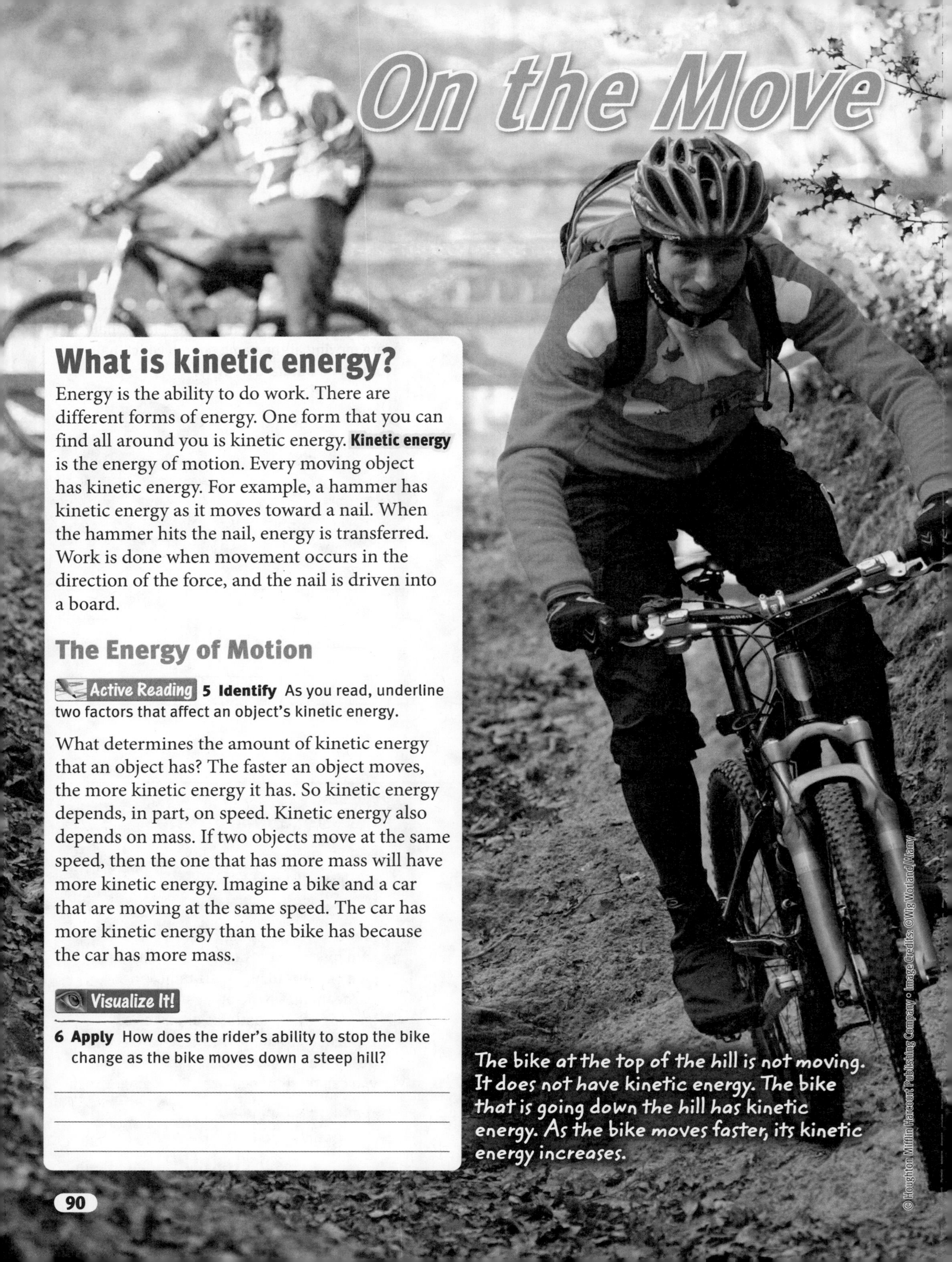

What is kinetic energy?

Energy is the ability to do work. There are different forms of energy. One form that you can find all around you is kinetic energy. **Kinetic energy** is the energy of motion. Every moving object has kinetic energy. For example, a hammer has kinetic energy as it moves toward a nail. When the hammer hits the nail, energy is transferred. Work is done when movement occurs in the direction of the force, and the nail is driven into a board.

The Energy of Motion

Active Reading **5 Identify** As you read, underline two factors that affect an object's kinetic energy.

What determines the amount of kinetic energy that an object has? The faster an object moves, the more kinetic energy it has. So kinetic energy depends, in part, on speed. Kinetic energy also depends on mass. If two objects move at the same speed, then the one that has more mass will have more kinetic energy. Imagine a bike and a car that are moving at the same speed. The car has more kinetic energy than the bike has because the car has more mass.

Visualize It!

6 Apply How does the rider's ability to stop the bike change as the bike moves down a steep hill?

____

____

____

The bike at the top of the hill is not moving. It does not have kinetic energy. The bike that is going down the hill has kinetic energy. As the bike moves faster, its kinetic energy increases.

How is the kinetic energy of an object calculated?

An object's kinetic energy is related to its mass and speed. The speed of an object is the distance that it travels in a unit of time. The following equation shows how kinetic energy is calculated.

$$\text{kinetic energy} = \frac{1}{2}mv^2$$

The letter m is the object's mass, and the letter v is the object's speed. When the mass is expressed in kilograms and the speed in meters per second, kinetic energy is expressed in *joules* (J).

Do the Math

Sample Problem

The foal has a mass of 100 kg and is moving at 8 m/s along the beach. What is the kinetic energy (KE) of the foal?

Identify

A. What do you know? The mass, m, is 100 kg.

The speed, v, is 8 m/s.

B. What do you want to find? kinetic energy

Plan

C. Write the formula: $KE = \frac{1}{2}mv^2$

D. Substitute into the formula: $KE = \frac{1}{2}(100\ kg)(8\ m/s)^2$

Solve

E. Multiply: $KE = \frac{1}{2}(100\ kg)(64\ m^2/s^2) = 3{,}200\ kg \bullet m^2/s^2 = 3{,}200\ J$

Answer: 3,200 J

You Try It

7 Calculate Complete the table at the right to calculate the kinetic energy of the horses.

Horse	m	v	v^2	KE
foal	100 kg	10 m/s		
mare	800 kg	10 m/s		
mare	800 kg	15 m/s		

It Could Change

What is potential energy?

Some energy is stored energy, or potential energy. **Potential energy** is the energy an object has because of its position, condition, or chemical composition. Like kinetic energy, potential energy is the ability to do work. For example, an object has *elastic potential energy* when it has been stretched or compressed. Elastic potential energy is stored in a stretched spring or rubber band. An object has *gravitational potential energy* due to its position above the ground. An object held above the ground has the potential to fall. The higher the object is above the ground, the greater its gravitational potential energy. Potential energy that depends on an object's position is referred to as *mechanical potential energy.* But there are other types of potential energy that do not depend on an object's position. For example, a substance stores *chemical potential energy* as a result of its chemical bonds. Some of that energy can be released during chemical reactions.

Think Outside the Book Inquiry

8 Classify With a partner, create a poster that shows examples of potential energy from everyday life. Label each example as gravitational, elastic, or chemical potential energy.

Visualize It!

9 Identify Fill in the type of potential energy that is illustrated in each image.

Fruit can provide energy to your body.

A ______________________

The boulder is high above the ground.

B ______________________

The archer pulls back on the string and stretches it.

C ______________________

How is the gravitational potential energy of an object calculated?

The following equation describes an object's gravitational potential energy.

$$\text{gravitational potential energy} = mgh$$

The letter m represents the object's mass expressed in kilograms. The letter g represents the acceleration due to Earth's gravity, which is 9.8 m/s^2. The letter h is the object's height from the ground in meters. The height is a measure of how far the object can fall. Like kinetic energy, potential energy is expressed in units of joules.

Do the Math

Sample Problem

The cat has a mass of 4 kg and is 1.5 m above the ground. What is the gravitational potential energy of the cat?

Identify

A. What do you know? mass = 4 kg, height = 1.5 m, acceleration due to gravity = 9.8 m/s^2

B. What do you want to find? gravitational potential energy

Plan

C. Write the formula: $GPE = mgh$

D. Substitute the given values into the formula:

$GPE = (4\ kg)(9.8\ m/s^2)(1.5\ m)$

Solve

E. Multiply: $PE = (4\ kg)(9.8\ m/s^2)(1.5\ m) = 58.8\ kg \cdot m^2/s^2 = 58.8\ J$

Answer: 58.8 J

You Try It

10 Calculate Three books are on different shelves. Calculate the gravitational potential energy of each book based on its mass and its height above the floor.

Object	m	h	PE
picture book	0.2 kg	2 m	
picture book	0.2 kg	3 m	
textbook	1.5 kg	4 m	

It All Adds Up!

How is the mechanical energy of an object calculated?

Active Reading

11 Identify As you read, underline the two components of mechanical energy.

A moving object can have both kinetic and potential energy. **Mechanical energy** is the energy possessed by an object due to its motion and position. For example, a thrown baseball has kinetic energy. It also has potential energy because it is above the ground. The sum of the ball's kinetic energy and mechanical potential energy is its mechanical energy. You can use the following equation to find mechanical energy.

$$\text{mechanical energy} = KE + PE$$

If the object's only potential energy is gravitational potential energy, you can use the following equation to find mechanical energy.

$$ME = \frac{1}{2}mv^2 + mgh$$

Visualize It!

12 Compare Circle the position of the ball when its gravitational potential energy is greatest.

The mechanical energy of the ball is the sum of its kinetic energy and potential energy.

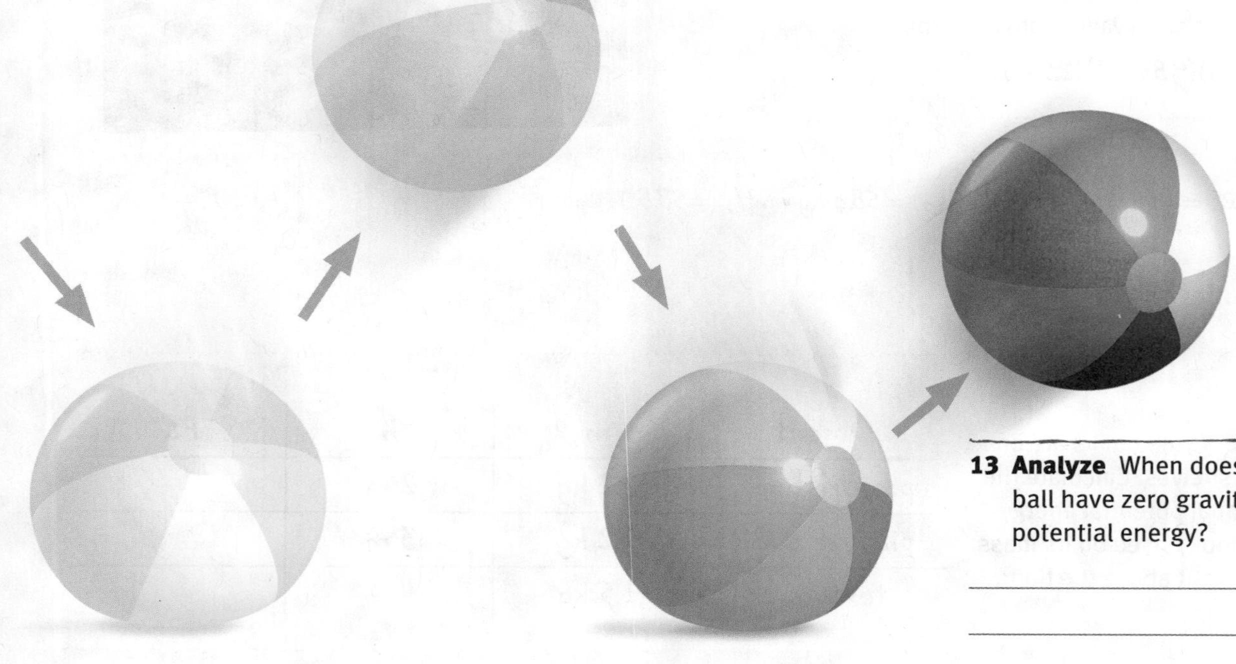

13 Analyze When does the ball have zero gravitational potential energy?

____

____

Do the Math You Try It

14 Calculate When the basketball is at its maximum height of 3 meters, it is not moving. The table below lists the KE and GPE for the basketball at heights of 3 m, 2 m, 1 m, and 0 m. Write the missing values for KE and GPE in the table. Then find the mechanical energy for each height.

Height	KE	GPE	ME
3.0 m		18 J	
2.0 m	6 J	12 J	
1.0 m	12 J	6 J	
0 m	18 J		

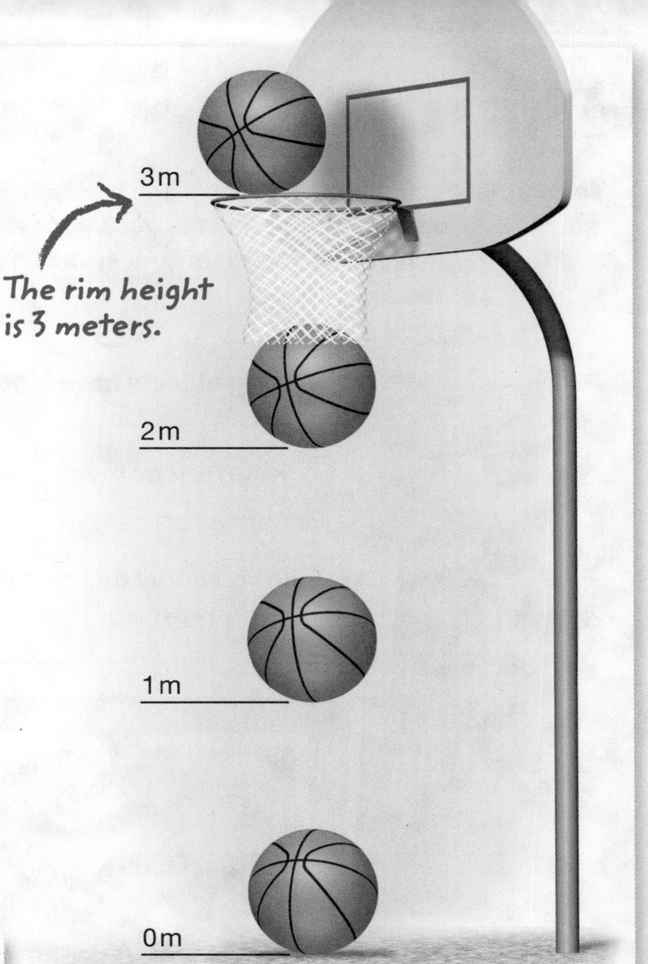

3m
The rim height is 3 meters.
2m
1m
0m

15 Graph Use the data above to plot and label two lines representing the kinetic energy and the gravitational potential energy of the basketball.

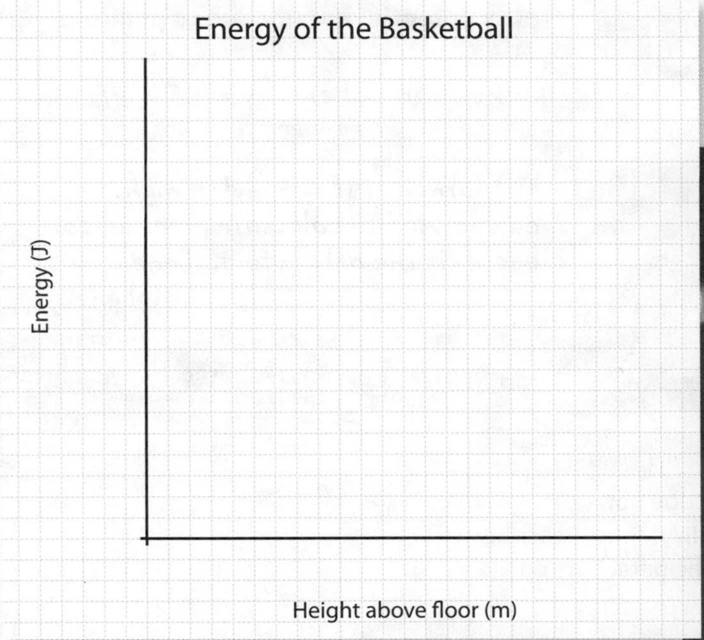

Energy of the Basketball
Energy (J)
Height above floor (m)

16 Analyze What is the relationship between the kinetic energy and the gravitational potential energy of the basketball?

____

____

____

Visual Summary

To complete this summary, fill in the blanks with the correct word. Then, use the key below to check your answers. You can use this page to review the main concepts of the lesson.

Kinetic and Potential Energy

All moving objects have kinetic energy.

$$\text{kinetic energy} = \frac{1}{2}mv^2$$

17 Kinetic energy depends on an object's mass and ________________

Potential energy is stored energy.

$$\text{gravitational potential energy} = mgh$$

18 Potential energy can be gravitational, ________________, or elastic.

Mechanical energy is kinetic energy plus potential energy due to position.

$$\text{mechanical energy} = KE + PE$$

19 The formula $ME = \frac{1}{2}mv^2 + mgh$ can be used to calculate mechanical energy if the only potential energy is ________________ potential energy.

Answers: 17 speed; 18 chemical; 19 gravitational

20 Synthesize A skydiver jumps out of a plane. Describe how gravitational potential energy changes as the skydiver falls. Describe how the skydiver's kinetic energy changes when the parachute opens.

Lesson Review

Vocabulary

In your own words, define the following terms.

1 kinetic energy

2 potential energy

3 mechanical energy

Key Concepts

4 **Relate** Describe the relationship between a moving object's mass and its kinetic energy.

5 **Identify** What are two factors that determine an object's gravitational potential energy?

6 **Analyze** A passenger plane is flying above the ground. Describe the two components of its mechanical energy.

Critical Thinking

7 **Evaluate** Can an object's mechanical energy be equal to its gravitational potential energy? Explain.

Use this graph to answer the following questions.

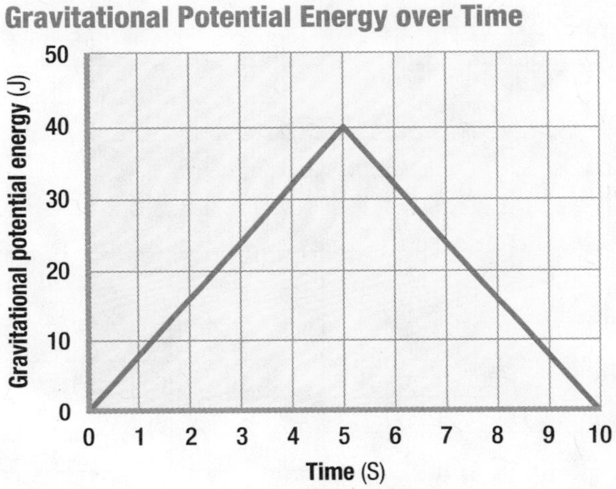
Gravitational Potential Energy over Time
Gravitational potential energy (J)
50
40
30
20
10
0
0 1 2 3 4 5 6 7 8 9 10
Time (S)

8 **Apply** The graph shows the gravitational potential energy of a radio-controlled toy helicopter. Describe the motion of the toy.

9 **Calculate** At 2.5 seconds, the helicopter has a kinetic energy of 20 J. What is its mechanical energy at that time?

My Notes

S.T.E.M. **Engineering & Technology**

Engineering Design Process

Skills
Identify a need
Conduct research
✓ Brainstorm solutions
✓ Select a solution
✓ Design a prototype
✓ Build a prototype
✓ Test and evaluate
✓ Redesign to improve
✓ Communicate results

Objectives
• Build a simple machine.
• Evaluate the design using mechanical advantage.

Testing a Simple Machine

Simple machines are devices that change the way work is done. Some simple machines allow us to lift objects using less force over a longer distance. Others help us to move something faster or farther when we exert a greater force over a shorter distance. Still other machines allow us to change the direction of force. The six types of simple machines are shown below.

Six simple machines

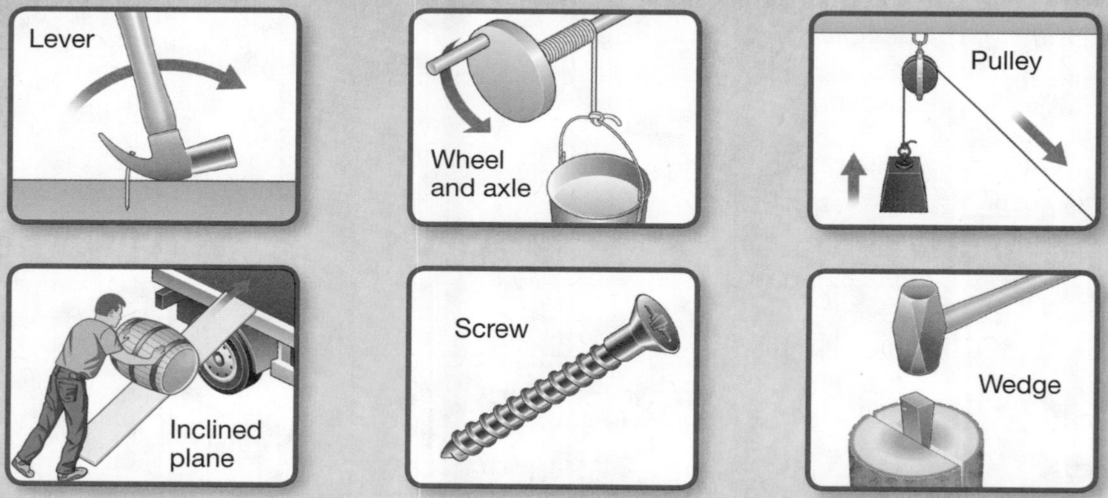
Lever
Wheel and axle
Pulley
Inclined plane
Screw
Wedge

1 Brainstorm What simple machines are found in your home?

Stationary pulley
Output force
Moveable pulley
Input force

Calculating Mechanical Advantage

The *mechanical advantage* of a machine is the ratio of the output force to the input force. The *input force* is the force applied to the machine. It is how hard you have to push or pull, and can be measured with a spring scale. The *output force* is the force the machine exerts on the object being moved. For example, for a machine that lifts an object, the output force is equal to the weight of the object lifted. When we know the value of those two forces, we can calculate the mechanical advantage of the machine using the equation below. Notice that because it is a ratio, mechanical advantage does not have any units.

$$\text{mechanical advantage} = \frac{\text{output force}}{\text{input force}}$$

Do the Math You Try It

2 Apply What is the mechanical advantage of a pulley system that can lift a bicycle weighing 150 N when the student exerts a force of 80 N?

You Try It!

Now it's your turn to build a simple machine and calculate its mechanical advantage.

You Try It!

Now it's your turn to build a simple machine that can lift an object and to calculate the machine's mechanical advantage.

You Will Need

- ✔ blocks or stands
- ✔ board, wooden
- ✔ dowel, wooden
- ✔ duct tape or masking tape
- ✔ mass, 200 g to 1,000 g
- ✔ meterstick or ruler
- ✔ pulley
- ✔ spring scale, calibrated in newtons
- ✔ string
- ✔ wheel and axle

1 Brainstorm Solutions

Brainstorm ideas for a simple machine to lift a mass against gravity.

A Which simple machine or machines could accomplish this task?

B How could you measure the force of gravity on the mass?

C How could you measure the input force?

2 Select a Solution

Which of your ideas seems to offer the best promise for success?

3 Design a Prototype

In the space below, draw a prototype of your simple machine. Be sure to include and label all the parts you will need and show how they will be connected. Show where on the machine you will measure the input force.

4 Build a Prototype

Now build your lifting device. Were there any parts you had to revise as you were building the prototype?

5 Test and Evaluate

What is the output force (the weight in newtons that was lifted)? What is the input force needed to raise the mass? Calculate the mechanical advantage of your machine.

Output force:

Input force:

Mechanical advantage =

6 Redesign to Improve

A How could you redesign your machine to increase its mechanical advantage?

B Make a change and take measurements to see if the mechanical advantage has increased. How many revisions did you have to make to see an increase in mechanical advantage?

7 Communicate Results

What is the largest mechanical advantage that you measured? As the mechanical advantage increased, did you notice any change in function of the machine? Why do you think that was the case?

Lesson 3

Machines

ESSENTIAL QUESTION

How do simple machines work?

By the end of this lesson, you should be able to describe different types of simple machines and to calculate the mechanical advantages and efficiencies of various simple machines.

Machines come in all shapes and sizes. This huge Ferris wheel contains a type of simple machine known as a wheel and axle.

Lesson Labs

Quick Labs
- Mechanical Efficiency
- Investigate Pulleys

S.T.E.M. Lab
- Compound Machines

Engage Your Brain

1 Identify Unscramble the letters below to find the names of some simple machines. Write your words on the blank lines.

VEERL ____________________

EGDWE ____________________

YPLLUE ____________________

HELWE DAN EXAL ____________________

2 Compare How is using the stairs similar to and different from using a ramp to get into a building?

Active Reading

3 Apply Use context clues to write your own definition for the phrases *input force* and *output force*.

Example sentence
An input force was applied to the pedal to make it move.

input force:

Example sentence
The output force of the pedal made the gear of the bike turn.

output force:

Vocabulary Terms

- **machine**
- **mechanical advantage**
- **mechanical efficiency**
- **lever**
- **fulcrum**
- **wheel and axle**
- **pulley**
- **inclined plane**

4 Identify As you read, create a reference card for each vocabulary term. On one side of the card, write the term and its meaning. On the other side, draw an image that illustrates or makes a connection to the term. These cards can be used as bookmarks in the text so that you can refer to them while studying.

Simply Easier

What do simple machines do?

Active Reading

5 Identify As you read, underline the types of simple machines.

What do you think of as a machine—maybe a car or a computer? A **machine** is any device that helps people do work by changing the way work is done. The machines that make up other machines are called *simple machines.* The six types of simple machines are *levers, wheels and axles, pulleys, inclined planes, wedges,* and *screws.*

Change the Way Work Is Done

The wheelbarrow and rake shown below contain simple machines. They change the way you do work. Work is the use of force to move an object some distance. The force you apply to a machine through a distance is called the *input force.* The work that you do on a machine is called *work input.* You do work on a wheelbarrow when you lift the handles. You pull up on the handles to make them move. The wheelbarrow does work on the leaves. The work done by the machine on an object is called *work output.* The *output force* is the force a machine exerts on an object. The wheelbarrow exerts an output force on the leaves to lift them up.

Visualize It!

6 Identify The person raking leaves applies an input force to the handle of the rake. The output force is applied to the leaves. Label the input force and the output force on the rake.

Machines, such as a wheelbarrow and rake, make yard work easier.
Output force
Input force
A ______________________
B ______________________

Change the Size of a Force and the Distance

Machines make tasks easier without decreasing the amount of work done. Work is equal to force times distance. If you apply less force with a machine, you apply that force through a longer distance. So the amount of work done remains the same. A ramp is an example of a machine that can change the magnitude, or size, of the force needed to move an object. You apply less force when you push a box up a ramp than when you lift the box. However, you apply the force through a longer distance. The amount of work you do is the same as when you lift the box to the same height, if friction is ignored. Other machines increase the amount of force needed, but you apply the force over a shorter distance.

Input force

The work done on the box is equal to the input force needed to lift the box times the height to which the box is lifted.

Input force

Less force is applied through a longer distance when the box is pushed up a ramp. But the work done on the box is the same.

7 Summarize Complete the table below by filling in the word *larger, smaller,* or *same* to compare lifting the box with pushing it up the ramp.

	Lifting box	Using ramp
Force applied	larger	smaller
Distance through which force is applied		
Work done		

Change the Direction of a Force

Some machines change the way you do work by changing the direction of a force. For example, you apply a downward force when you pull on the rope to raise a flag. The rope runs over a pulley at the top of the flagpole. The rope exerts an upward force on the flag, and the flag goes up. The direction of the force you applied has changed. But the magnitude of force and distance through which you apply the force are the same.

The pulley on the flagpole changed only the direction of the force. However, other machines can change the direction of a force, the magnitude of the force, and the distance through which the force is applied.

Input force

Pulling down on the rope pulls up the flag.

Input and Output

What is mechanical advantage?

Active Reading

8 Identify As you read, underline what happens when the mechanical advantage of a machine is equal to one.

Machines change force by different amounts. A machine's **mechanical advantage** is the number of times the machine multiplies the input force. It is a way of comparing the input force with the output force. Ignoring friction, you can calculate mechanical advantage, MA, of any machine by dividing the output force by the input force.

$$\text{mechanical advantage} = \frac{\text{output force}}{\text{input force}}$$

The bottle opener, pulley, and hammer shown below have different mechanical advantages. A machine that has a mechanical advantage greater than one multiplies the input force, producing greater output force. A machine that has a mechanical advantage equal to one changes only the direction of the force. A machine that has a mechanical advantage less than one requires greater input force, but the output force is applied through a longer distance.

Do the Math

Sample Problem

The bottle opener changes the input force of 1 N to an output force of 2 N. Calculate the mechanical advantage of the bottle opener.

Output Force
Input Force

$$MA = \frac{\text{output force}}{\text{input force}}$$
$= 2\ N / 1\ N$
$= 2$

You Try It

9 Calculate The pulley changes the direction of a 5 N input force. The output force is equal to the input force. Calculate the mechanical advantage.

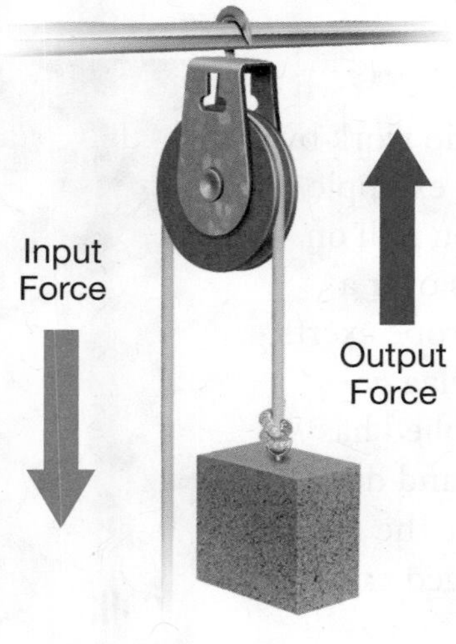

Input Force
Output Force

MA = ______

= ______

= ______

You Try It

10 Calculate The input force applied on the hammer is 6 N. The output force applied to the nail is 2 N. Calculate the mechanical advantage.

Output Force
Input Force

MA = ______

= ______

= ______

What is mechanical efficiency?

Ideally, the work a machine does on an object is the same as the work that you put into it. But even when the mechanical advantage is greater than one, the work input is greater than the work output because some work is done to overcome friction. **Mechanical efficiency** is a comparison of a machine's work output with the work input. Mechanical efficiency, ME, is equal to the work output divided by the work input, expressed as a percentage.

$$\text{mechanical efficiency} = \frac{\text{work output}}{\text{work input}} \times 100\%$$

Do the Math

Sample Problem

Suppose 5,000 J of work is put into a go-cart engine. The work output of the engine is 1,250 J. What is the mechanical efficiency of the engine?

$$ME = \frac{\text{work output}}{\text{work input}} \times 100\%$$

$$= \frac{1{,}250\ \text{J}}{5{,}000\ \text{J}} \times 100\%$$

$$= 25\%$$

What Happens to Input Work

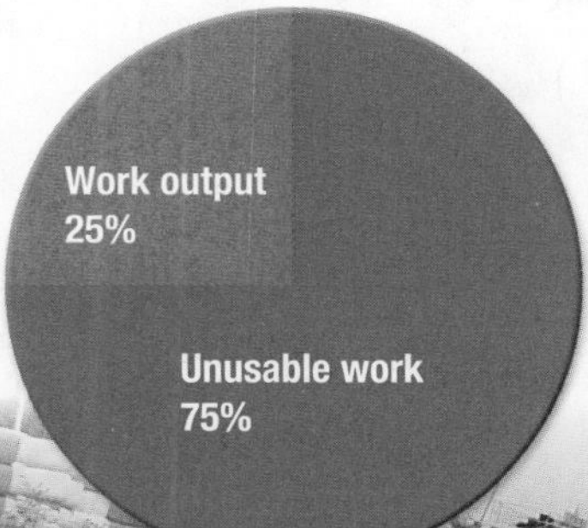

Work output 25%
Unusable work 75%

Only 25% of work that goes into the engine is used to move the go-cart.

You Try It!

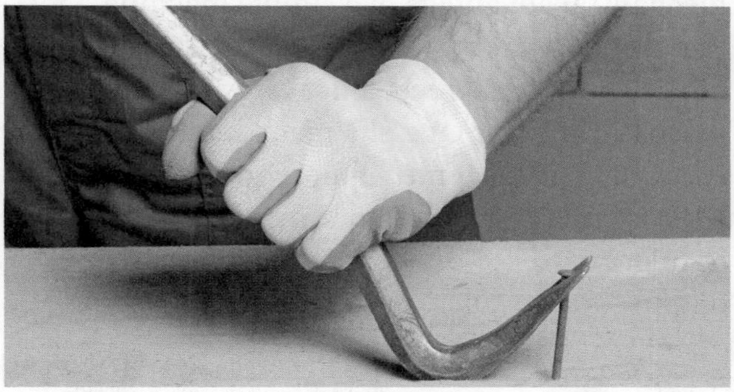

11 Calculate A person does 500 J of work on a crowbar. The crowbar does 475 J of work on a nail. What is the mechanical efficiency of the crowbar?

12 Graph Draw and label a pie graph that shows the percentages of work output and unusable work.

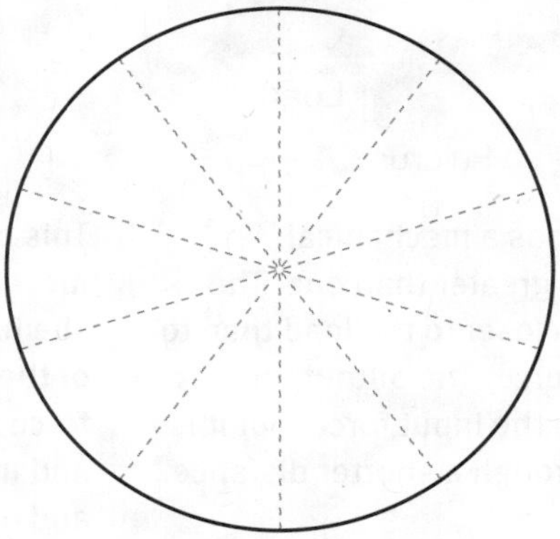

Gaining Leverage

What are the classes of levers?

What do hammers, seesaws, and baseball bats have in common? They are all levers. A **lever** is a simple machine that has a bar that pivots at a fixed point. This fixed point is called a **fulcrum**. Levers are used to apply a force to move an object. The force of the object is called the load.

Ideal mechanical advantage is the mechanical advantage of a simple machine that does not take friction into account. In other words, ideal mechanical advantage is the mechanical advantage of a machine that is 100% efficient. The ideal mechanical advantage of a lever is equal to the distance from input force to fulcrum (d_{input}) divided by the distance from output force to fulcrum (d_{output}).

$$\text{ideal mechanical advantage} = \frac{d_{input}}{d_{output}}$$

First-Class Levers

There are three classes of levers that differ based on the positions of the fulcrum, the load, and the input force. A seesaw is an example of a *first-class lever*. In a first-class lever, the fulcrum is between the input force and the load. First-class levers always change the direction of the input force. They may also increase the force or the distance through which the force is applied. The ideal mechanical advantage of first-class levers can be greater than one, equal to one, or less than one, depending on the location of the fulcrum.

Active Reading **13 Describe** Where is the fulcrum located in a first-class lever?

____

____

____

Visualize It!

14 Illustrate In box C, draw and label a first-class lever that has an ideal mechanical advantage less than one.

A

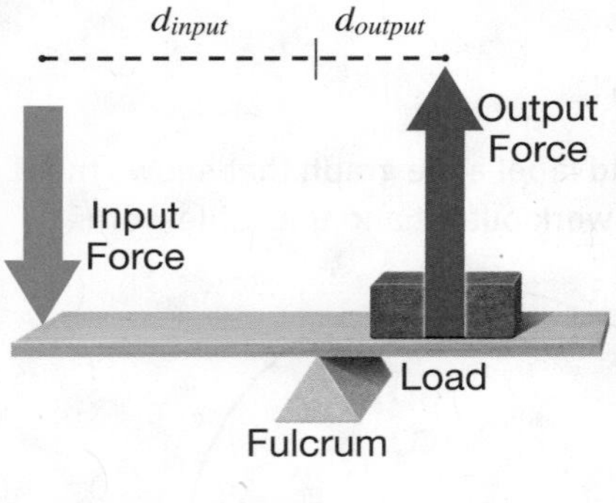

d_{input}
d_{output}
Output Force
Input Force
Load
Fulcrum

This lever has a mechanical advantage greater than one. The fulcrum is closer to the load than to the input force. The output force is larger than the input force, but it is applied through a shorter distance.

B

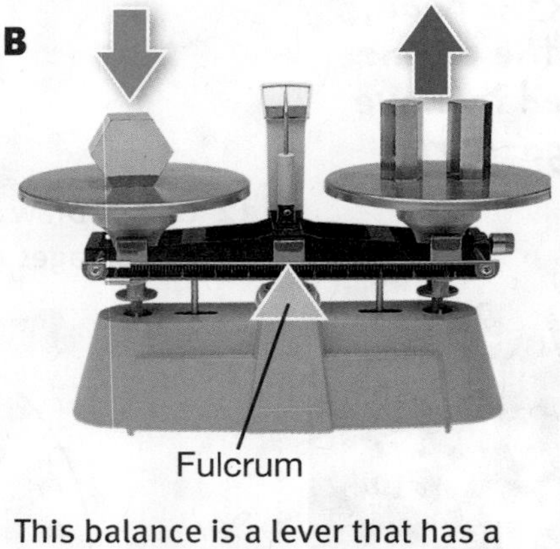

Fulcrum

This balance is a lever that has a mechanical advantage equal to one. The fulcrum is exactly in the middle of the lever. The direction of the force is changed, but the distance and magnitude of the input force and output force are the same.

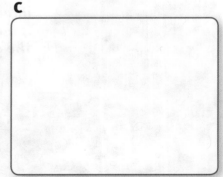

C

This lever has a mechanical advantage of less than one. The fulcrum is closer to the input force than to the load. The output force is less than the input force, but it is applied through a longer distance.

Second-Class Levers

In a *second-class lever,* the load is between the fulcrum and the input force. Second-class levers do not change the direction of the input force. They allow you to apply less force than the load. But you must exert the input force through a greater distance. The ideal mechanical advantage for a second-class lever is always greater than one. Wheelbarrows, bottle-cap openers, and staplers are second-class levers. A stapler pivots at one end when you push on the other end. The output force of the stapler drives the staple into the paper. The output force is applied between where you push and where the stapler pivots.

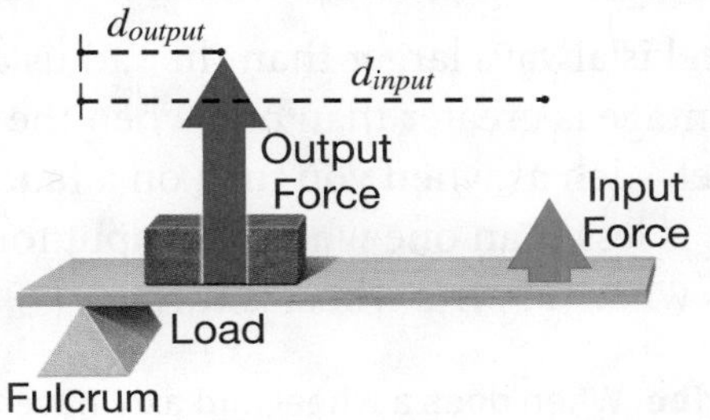

d_{output}
d_{input}
Output Force
Input Force
Load
Fulcrum

The load is between the fulcrum and input force in a stapler.

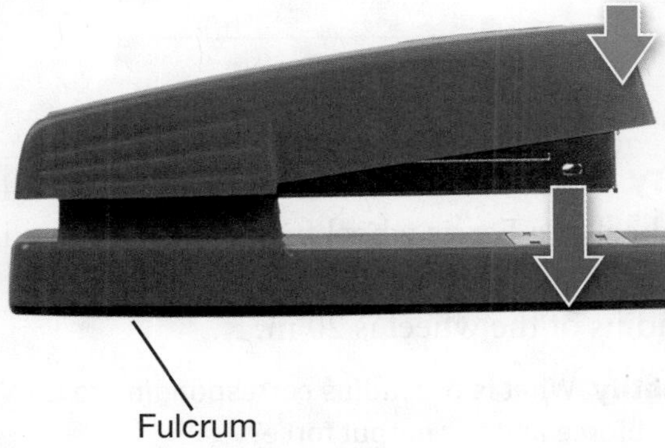

Fulcrum

Third-Class Levers

In a *third-class lever,* the input force is between the fulcrum and the load. Like second-class levers, third-class levers do not change the direction of the input force. The mechanical advantage for a third-class lever is always less than one. The output force is less than the input force. But the output force is applied through a longer distance. Hammers and baseball bats are examples of third-class levers. When you swing a baseball bat, the fulcrum is at the base of the handle. The output force is at the end of the bat where it hits the ball. A bat applies a force to the ball in the same direction as you swing the bat. Your hands move a much shorter distance than the end of the bat moves when you swing.

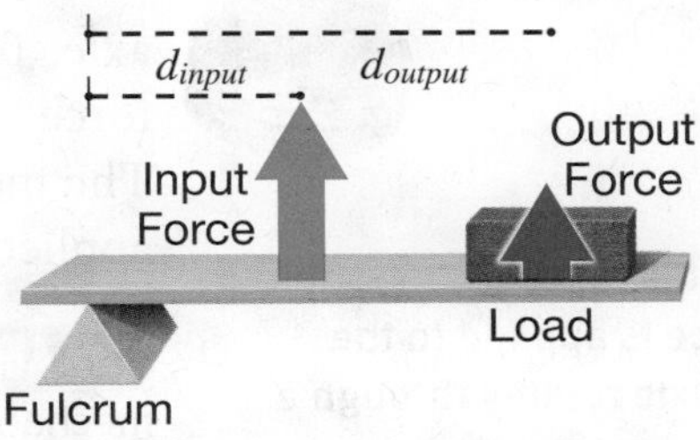

d_{input}
d_{output}
Input Force
Output Force
Load
Fulcrum

The input force is between the fulcrum and the load in a baseball bat.

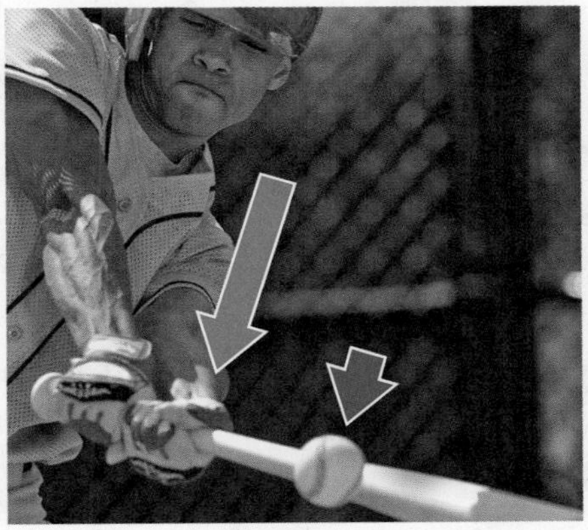

Do the Math You Try It!

15 Calculate The input force of a third-class lever is 5 cm away from the fulcrum. The output force is 20 cm away from the fulcrum. What is the ideal mechanical advantage of the lever?

16 Model Draw and label a diagram of the lever described in question 15. Make sure to show the correct relative distances of the input and output forces from the fulcrum.

Turn, Turn, Turn

What is a wheel and axle?

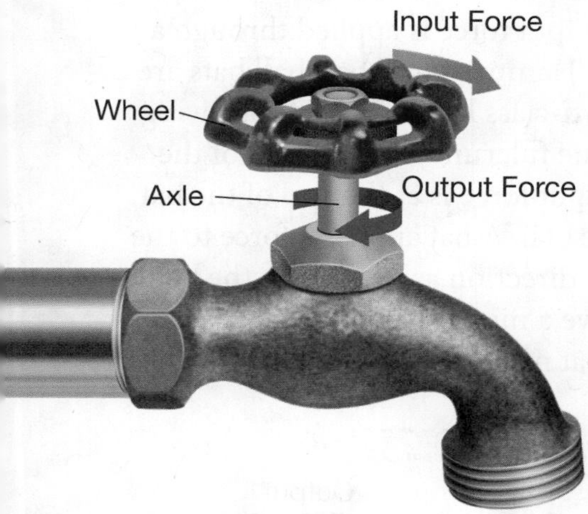

Input Force
Wheel
Axle
Output Force

The axle of this faucet turns when an input force is applied to the wheel. The axle rotates through a shorter distance than the wheel does. So the output force is larger than the input force.

A **wheel and axle** is a simple machine that is made of a wheel connected to a smaller cylindrical object, the axle. Doorknobs, tires, and screwdrivers are machines that contain wheels and axles.

The ideal mechanical advantage of a wheel and axle equals the radius corresponding to the input force divided by the radius corresponding to the output force.

$$\text{ideal mechanical advantage} = \frac{\text{radius}_{input}}{\text{radius}_{output}}$$

The radius of the wheel is always larger than the radius of the axle. The mechanical advantage is greater than one when the input force is applied to the wheel, such as when you turn on a faucet. The mechanical advantage is less than one when the input force is applied to the axle, such as when a Ferris wheel is turned.

Active Reading **17 Describe** When does a wheel and axle have a mechanical advantage greater than one?

____

____

Do the Math

Sample Problem

The faucet has a wheel radius of 5 cm and an axle radius of 1 cm. What is its ideal mechanical advantage?

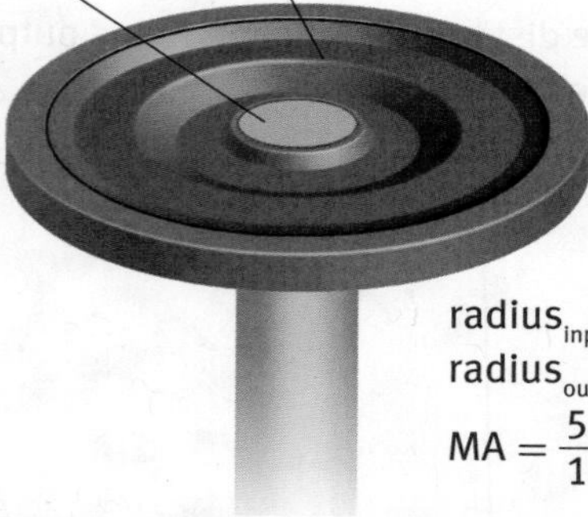

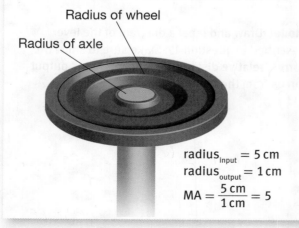

Radius of wheel
Radius of axle

$\text{radius}_{input} = 5\text{ cm}$

$\text{radius}_{output} = 1\text{ cm}$

$\text{MA} = \frac{5\text{ cm}}{1\text{ cm}} = 5$

You Try It!

The wheel of a Ferris wheel turns when a force is applied to the axle. The radius of its axle is 1 m. The radius of the wheel is 20 m.

18 Identify What is the radius corresponding to the input force and the output force?

radius_{input}: ______________

radius_{output}: ______________

19 Calculate What is the ideal mechanical advantage of the Ferris wheel?

What are the types of pulleys?

When you open window blinds by pulling on a cord, you're using a pulley. A **pulley** is a simple machine that has a grooved wheel that holds a rope or a cable. A load is attached to one end of the rope, and an input force is applied to the other end. There are three different types of pulleys.

Fixed Pulleys

The pulley at the top of a flagpole is a *fixed pulley.* A fixed pulley is attached to something that does not move. It allows you to pull down on the rope to lift the load up. The wheel of the pulley turns and changes the direction of the force. Fixed pulleys do not change the size of the force. The size of the output force is the same as the size of the input force. Therefore, a fixed pulley has an ideal mechanical advantage of one.

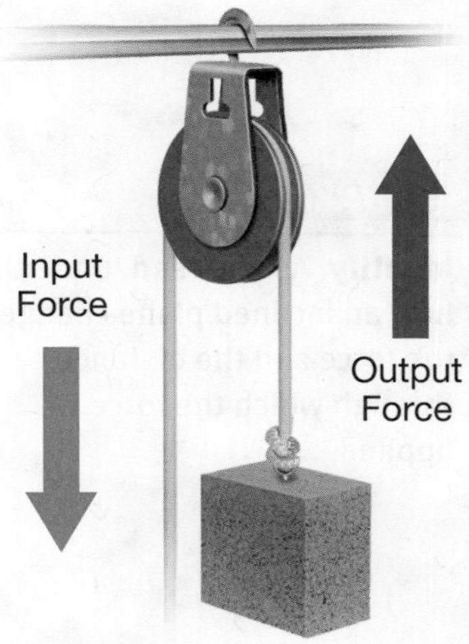

Input Force
Output Force

Movable Pulleys

Unlike a fixed pulley, the wheel of a *movable pulley* is attached to the object being moved. One end of the rope is fixed. You can pull on the other end of the rope to make the wheel and load move along the rope. A movable pulley moves up with the load as the load is lifted. A movable pulley does not change the direction of a force, but does increase the force. The ideal mechanical advantage of all movable pulleys is two. They also increase the distance through which the input force must be applied. The rope must be pulled twice the distance that the load is moved.

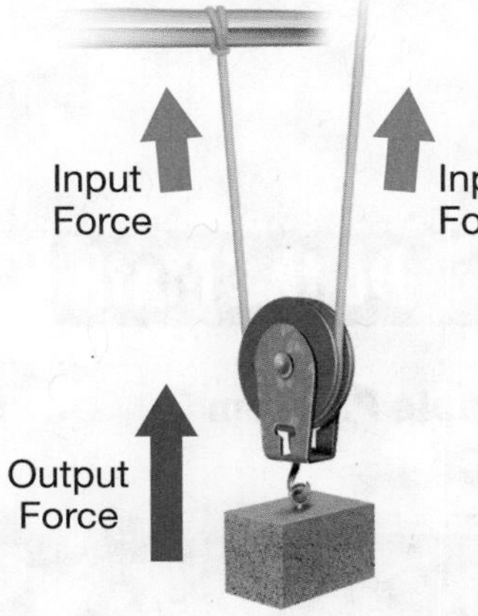

Input Force
Input Force
Output Force

Block and Tackle Pulleys

A *block and tackle pulley* is a pulley system made by combining a fixed pulley and a movable pulley. Cranes at construction sites use block and tackle pulleys to lift heavy objects. Block and tackle pulleys change the direction of the force and increase the force. The ideal mechanical advantage of a block and tackle pulley depends on the number of rope segments. The ideal mechanical advantage of a block and tackle with four rope segments is four. It multiplies your input force by four. But you have to pull the rope four times as far.

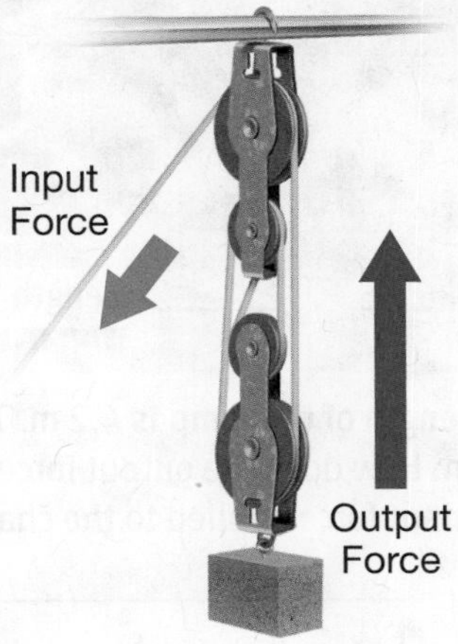

Input Force
Output Force

20 Identify Which type(s) of pulley could you use to increase your output force?

So Inclined

What are inclined planes?

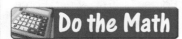

Active Reading

21 Identify As you read, underline how an inclined plane changes the force and the distance through which the force is applied.

Why is pushing furniture up a ramp easier than lifting the furniture? When you push something up a ramp, you are using a machine called an *inclined plane.* An **inclined plane** is a simple machine that is a straight, slanted surface. A smaller input force is needed to move an object using an inclined plane than is needed to lift the object. However, the force must be applied through a longer distance. So, the amount of work done on the object is the same. The ideal mechanical advantage of an inclined plane can be calculated by dividing the length of the incline by the height that the load is lifted.

$$\text{ideal mechanical advantage} = \frac{\text{length}}{\text{height}}$$

Do the Math

Sample Problem

Length
Height

The length of the ramp is 4.2 m. The height of the ramp is 1.2 m. How does the output force on the chair compare to the input force applied to the chair?

$$\text{ideal mechanical advantage} = \frac{\text{length}}{\text{height}} = \frac{4.2\ m}{1.2\ m} = 3.5$$

The output force on the chair is 3.5 times the input force.

You Try It!

22 Illustrate Use the grid below to draw and label a diagram of an inclined plane that has a length of 6 meters and an ideal mechanical advantage of 3. Use the squares to approximate the length. (Hint: In the space below, use the mechanical advantage to calculate the height.)

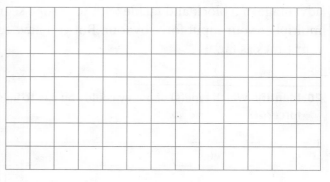

What are wedges?

Sculptors use chisels to break rock and wood. Chisels, ax heads, and knife blades are wedges. A *wedge* is a pair of inclined planes that move. They have one thick end and one thin end. Wedges are used to cut and split objects. For example, a sculptor applies an input force to the thick end of a chisel. The thin end of the chisel exerts an outward force that splits open the object. The output force of the wedge is greater than the input force, but the output force is applied through a shorter distance. The longer and thinner the wedge is, the greater its ideal mechanical advantage. So a longer chisel has a greater mechanical advantage than a shorter chisel that is the same width at the thick end.

Input Force
Width
Output Force
Output Force
Length

Wedges have two sloped sides and help split objects.

What are screws?

Screws are often used to hold wood together. A *screw* is an inclined plane that is wrapped in a spiral around a cylinder. Think of wrapping a long triangular piece of paper around a pencil, as shown below. The ridges formed by the paper are like the threads of a screw. When a screw is turned, a small force is applied through the distance along the inclined plane of the screw. The screw applies a large force through the short distance it is pushed.

Imagine unwinding the inclined plane of a screw. You would see that the plane is very long and has a gentle slope. The longer an inclined plane is compared with its height, the greater its ideal mechanical advantage. Similarly, the longer the spiral on a screw is and the closer together the threads are, the greater the screw's mechanical advantage.

The threads of a screw are made by wrapping an inclined plane around a cylinder.

Think Outside the Book Inquiry

23 Apply Make a list of simple machines you use every day. In a small group, try to classify all the machines identified by the group members.

Visual Summary

To complete this summary, check the box that indicates true or false. Then, use the key below to check your answers. You can use this page to review the main concepts of the lesson.

Machines

Mechanical efficiency is a way to compare a machine's work output with work input.

	T	F	
24	☐	☐	Mechanical advantage is calculated by dividing the output force by the input force and multiplying by 100.
25	☐	☐	Friction causes the real mechanical advantage of a ramp to be less than the ideal mechanical advantage.

The six types of simple machines:

- **levers**
- **wheel and axles**
- **pulleys**
- **inclined planes**
- **wedges**
- **screws**

	T	F	
26	☐	☐	The location of the fulcrum differs for first-class levers, second-class levers, and third-class levers.
27	☐	☐	Types of pulleys include fixed pulleys, movable pulleys, and wheel and axles.
28	☐	☐	Using ramps, wedges, and screws reduces the amount of work that is done.

Answers: 24 False; 25 True; 26 True; 27 False; 28 False

29 Apply A third-class lever has an ideal mechanical advantage of less than one. Explain why it is useful for some tasks, and identify two examples of third-class levers.

Lesson Review

Vocabulary

Draw a line to connect the following terms to their definitions.

1 machine	**A** a simple machine that has a grooved wheel that holds a rope
2 lever	**B** a simple machine consisting of two circular objects of different sizes
3 wheel and axle	**C** a simple machine that is a straight, slanted surface
4 pulley	**D** a device that helps people do work by changing the way work is done
5 inclined plane	**E** a simple machine that has a bar that pivots at a fixed point

Key Concepts

6 Explain In what two ways can machines change the way work is done?

____

____

____

____

7 Identify What equation would you use to calculate the ideal mechanical advantage of a wheel and axle if the input force is applied to the axle?

____

____

____

____

8 Solve A stone block is pushed up a ramp that is 120 m long and 20 m high. What is the ideal mechanical advantage of the ramp?

____

____

Critical Thinking

9 Apply A person does 50 J of work to lift a crate using a pulley. The pulley's work output is 42 J. What is the pulley's mechanical efficiency?

____

____

Use this drawing to answer the following questions.

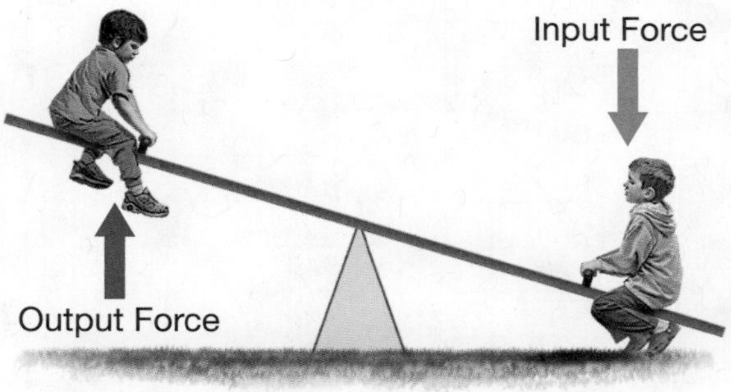
Input Force
Output Force

10 Classify What type of lever is the seesaw? Explain.

____

____

____

11 Calculate The input force is 245 N, and the output force is 245 N. Calculate the ideal mechanical advantage of the seesaw.

____

____

12 Predict The boy applying the input force moves so that he is 1.5 m from the fulcrum. The seesaw applies an output force to the other boy, who is 2 m from the fulcrum. What is the new ideal mechanical advantage?

____

____

____

____

My Notes

Unit 2 Big Idea

Energy is transferred when a force moves an object.

Lesson 1

ESSENTIAL QUESTION

How is work related to energy?

Relate work to energy and power.

Lesson 2

ESSENTIAL QUESTION

What are kinetic and potential energy?

Calculate kinetic and potential energy and know how these two types of energy are related.

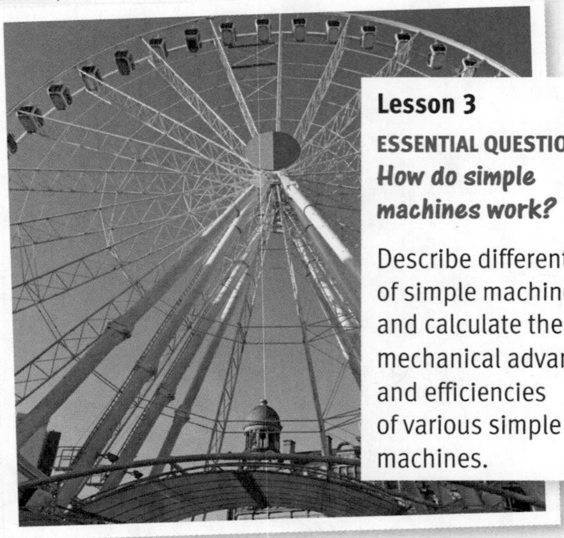

Lesson 3

ESSENTIAL QUESTION

How do simple machines work?

Describe different types of simple machines, and calculate the mechanical advantages and efficiencies of various simple machines.

Connect ESSENTIAL QUESTIONS

Lessons 1 and 2

1 Synthesize What happens when you lift a basket of laundry and move it to the washing machine? Explain in terms of work, potential energy, kinetic energy, and power.

____

____

____

____

____

____

Think Outside the Book

2 Synthesize Choose one of these activities to help synthesize what you have learned in this unit.

☐ Using what you learned in lessons 1 and 2, create a poster presentation to explain what happens when you wind up a music box and release the key. Illustrate the events in terms of energy.

☐ Using what you learned in lessons 1 and 3, in an informative brochure, describe a machine that you have used recently. Explain how the machine helped you do work.

Unit 2 Review

Name ______________________________

Vocabulary

Fill in each blank with the term that best completes the following sentences.

1 ______________________ is the use of force to move an object in the direction of the force.

2 The stored energy that an object has due to its position, condition, or chemical composition is called ______________________ .

3 A(n) ______________________ is a device that helps people do work by changing the way work is done.

4 A machine's ______________________ is the ratio of the machine's output force to its input force.

5 A(n) ______________________ is a simple machine that consists of a solid bar that pivots at a fixed point.

Key Concepts

Read each question below, and circle the best answer.

6 Which of the following is an example of the conversion of kinetic energy into gravitational potential energy?

A a person parachuting out of an airplane

B a car racing around an oval track

C a person skiing down a hill

D a person walking up a hill

7 Which is an example of a wedge?

A knife

B hammer

C ramp

D screw

8 A ramp is an example of which type of simple machine?

A a lever

B a wheel and axle

C an inclined plane

D a block and tackle pulley

9 The diagram below shows a swinging pendulum. During every swing, the pendulum's speed and position change. Three positions during the swing are identified as Position 1, Position 2, and Position 3.

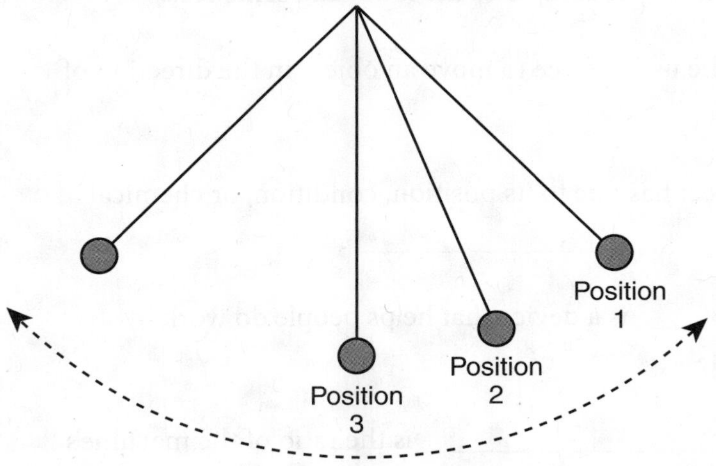
Position 1
Position 2
Position 3

Ignoring the effects of friction or air resistance, at which point would the pendulum have the greatest amount of mechanical energy?

A Position 1

B Position 2

C Position 3

D Mechanical energy does not change.

10 Below is a diagram of a weight on a spring. When the weight is pulled down and then released, the spring compresses and expands. Each position indicates a different point in time.

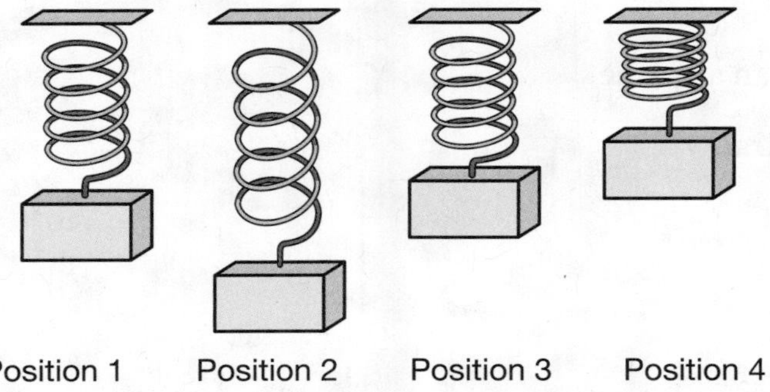
Position 1
Position 2
Position 3
Position 4

Which of the following statements is true?

A In all four positions, mechanical energy is 0 J.

B The elastic potential energy of the spring at Position 2 is converted to kinetic energy.

C The chemical potential energy of the spring is greatest at Position 4.

D In all four positions, the gravitational potential energy of the spring is the same.

Name ____________________________

11 A bottle opener is an example of a second-class lever.

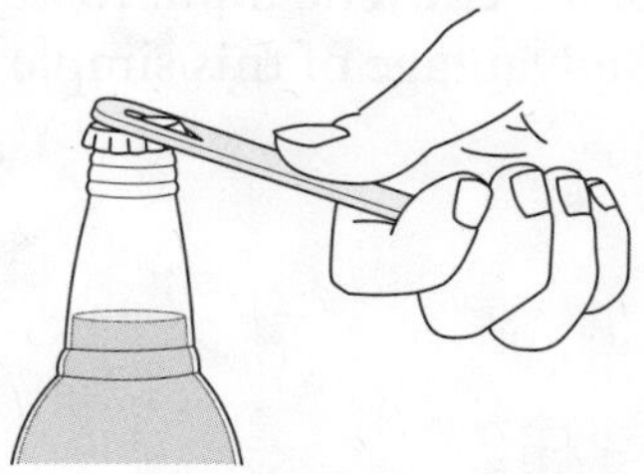

Which of the following statements is true about second-class levers?

A The input force is between the output force and the fulcrum.

B The fulcrum is between the input force and the output force.

C The output force is between the input force and the fulcrum.

D The input force and output force move in opposite directions.

12 All moving objects have kinetic energy. The four vehicles in the diagram below are all moving at the same speed along a road.

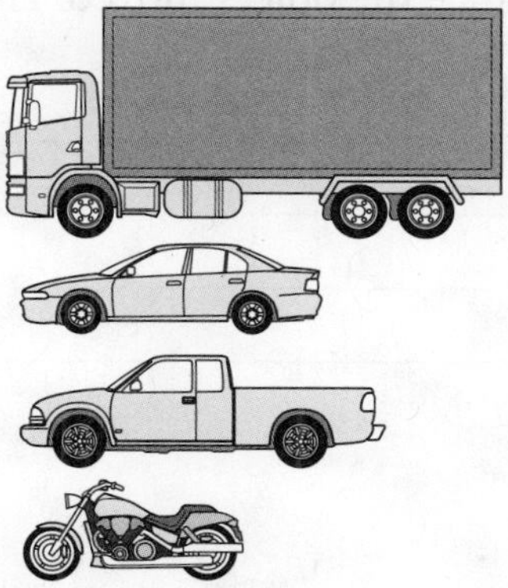

Which of the following statements is correct?

A The motorcycle has the most kinetic energy because it is the vehicle with the least mass.

B All the vehicles have the same kinetic energy because they are moving at the same speed.

C The delivery truck has the greatest kinetic energy because its mass is greater than that of the other vehicles.

D The delivery truck has the greatest kinetic energy because it has the most tires in contact with the pavement.

13 A faucet is an example of a simple machine, a wheel and axle. The faucet wheel has a radius of 5 cm. The axle has a radius of 0.5 cm. The input force is applied to the faucet wheel. What is the mechanical advantage of this simple machine?

A 0.1

B 1

C 5

D 10

Critical Thinking

Answer the following questions in the space provided.

14 What is mechanical efficiency, and how is it calculated?

15 Work is defined as the use of force to move an object in the direction of that force and is equal to the force times the distance the object moved. How do energy and power relate to work?

Connect ESSENTIAL QUESTIONS

Lessons 2 and 3

Answer the following question in the space provided.

16 Explain how an inclined plane makes loading a piano into a truck easier. Refer to the changing potential energy and kinetic energy of the piano as it (a) sits on the ground, (b) is being moved into the truck, and (c) sits in the truck.

UNIT 3

Electricity and Magnetism

Lightning is the discharge of static electricity that builds up in clouds during a storm.

Big Idea

An electric current can produce a magnetic field, and a magnetic field can produce an electric current.

What do you think?

Static electricity can make your hair stand on end. What other effects of static electricity can you think of?

This Van de Graaff generator makes a safe but hair-raising demonstration.

Unit 3

Electricity and Magnetism

CITIZEN SCIENCE

Be Lightning Safe

Lightning can be an impressive display, but it is also very dangerous. Lightning strikes carry a great deal of energy that can split apart trees, damage property, and start fires. People can be injured or killed if they are struck by lightning.

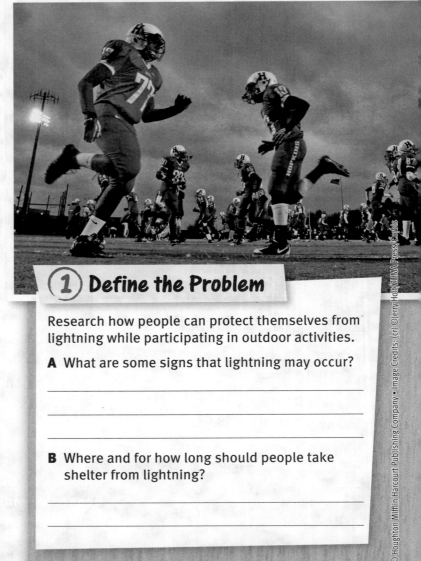

77
10

1 Define the Problem

Research how people can protect themselves from lightning while participating in outdoor activities.

A What are some signs that lightning may occur?

____

____

____

B Where and for how long should people take shelter from lightning?

____

____

RAIDERS
58
RAIDERS
12
12
Game Canceled due to severe weather

To be safe from lightning, people should wait out a storm by going inside a school building that is completely enclosed.

2 Ask Some Questions

A Where is your school's lightning-safety plan posted?

B Are students and teachers aware of your school's plan for lightning safety?

C What is your school's current policy for canceling outdoor events when there is a risk of lightning?

D Is your school's current plan for lightning safety adequate?

3 Make a Plan

A What are two ways in which your school's lightning-safety plan could be improved?

B Describe two steps that you could take to promote your improved lightning-safety plan at your school.

Take It Home

With an adult, make a lightning-safety plan for your family. And, discuss the weather conditions that would cause you to put your plan into action.

Lesson 1

Electric Charge and Static Electricity

This electrically charged metal dome is part of a device called a Van de Graaff generator. Touching the dome has made this student electrically charged.

ESSENTIAL QUESTION

What makes something electrically charged?

By the end of this lesson, you should be able to describe electric charges in objects and distinguish between electrical conductors and insulators.

Lesson Labs

Quick Labs

- Making a Static Detector
- Investigate Conductors and Insulators

Engage Your Brain

1 Predict Check T or F to show whether you think each statement is true or false.

T	F	
☐	☐	Electrons have a negative charge.
☐	☐	Objects with like charges attract each other.
☐	☐	Copper is an electrical conductor.
☐	☐	Objects must be touching to exert an electric force on each other.

2 Describe Write your own caption describing what is happening to this student's hair.

Active Reading

3 Synthesize Many scientific words, such as *charge*, also have everyday meanings. Use context clues to write your own definition for each meaning of the word *charge*.

Example sentence
The charge for entry to the zoo goes up every year.

charge:

Example sentence
When Andre touched the doorknob, the charge gave him a shock.

charge:

Vocabulary Terms

- **electric charge**
- **static electricity**
- **electrical conductor**
- **electrical insulator**
- **semiconductor**

4 Identify As you read, create a reference card for each vocabulary term. On one side of the card, write the term and its meaning. On the other side, draw an image that illustrates or makes a connection to the term. These cards can be used as bookmarks in the text so that you can refer to them while studying.

Opposites Attract

What is electric charge?

Have you ever touched a doorknob and felt a shock? Have you ever seen clothes cling to each other after they are taken from a dryer? Both of these events are due to a fundamental property of matter called *electric charge.* **Electric charge** is a property that leads to electromagnetic interactions between the particles that make up matter. An object can have a positive (+) charge, a negative (–) charge, or no charge. An object that has no charge is *neutral.*

The diagram below shows charges within an atom. All atoms have a dense center called a *nucleus.* The nucleus contains two types of particles: *protons* and *neutrons.* A proton has a charge of 1+. A neutron has no charge. *Electrons* are a third type of particle and are found outside the nucleus. An electron has a charge of 1–. When an atom has the same number of protons as electrons, the atom has no overall charge. This is because the charges of its protons and electrons add up to zero. However, atoms can lose or gain electrons. When this happens, the atom has an overall positive or negative charge and is called an *ion.* Positively charged ions have more protons than electrons. Negatively charged ions have fewer protons than electrons. The overall charge of an object is the sum of the charges of its atoms.

Pieces of paper cling to a ruler due to the electric charge of the ruler.

5 Apply An atom gains an additional electron. What is the overall charge of the ion that is formed? ______________________

Visualize It!

6 Label Complete the diagram by labeling the nucleus and an electron.

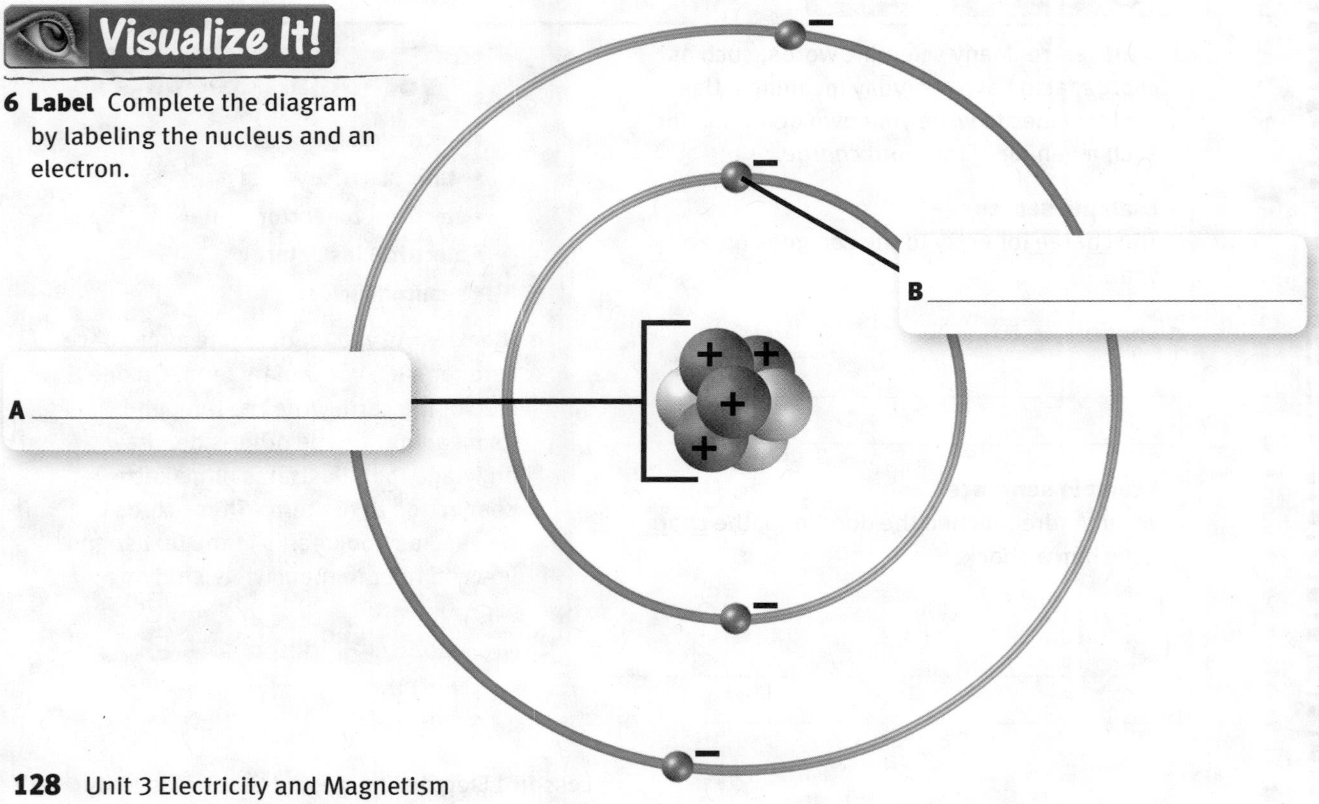
A ______________________
B ______________________

What affects the electric force between two objects?

Any two charged objects exert a force on each other called an *electric force*. Like gravity, electric force acts between objects even when they do not touch. But gravity always pulls objects together. Unlike gravity, the electric force can either pull objects together or push them apart. How strongly the electric force pushes or pulls depends on the charge of each object and how close together the objects are.

Charge

If objects have like charges, they repel each other. The objects exert an electric force that pushes them apart. The balls in the diagram A at the right both have a positive charge. The arrows show the electric force acting on each ball.

Two objects with unlike charges attract each other. So an object with a positive charge and an object with a negative charge are attracted. Each object exerts a force on the other, pulling the objects together.

The amount of charge on each object also affects the strength of the electric force between them. The greater an object's charge is, the greater the electric force is. This is true whether the objects repel or attract each other.

Distance

The distance between two objects affects the size of the electric force, too. The closer together the charged objects are, the greater the electric force is. As charged objects move farther apart, they attract or repel each other less strongly.

Active Reading **7 Identify** What factors affect how strong the electric force is between two charged objects?

____

____

____

____

Visualize It!

8 Analyze Label diagrams B and C with the missing charge signs. Then add a caption below each diagram to describe the forces between the objects.

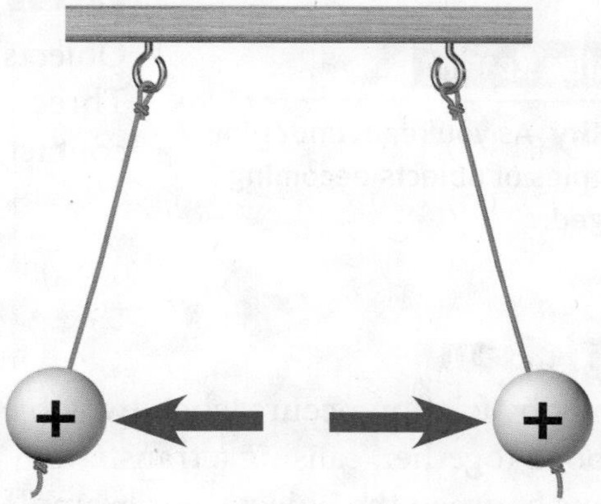

+
+

A *The balls have like positive charges. They push each other apart.*

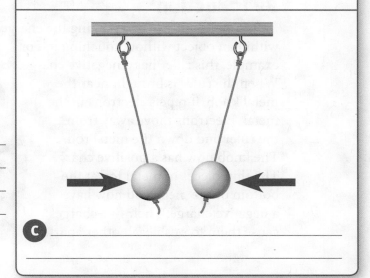

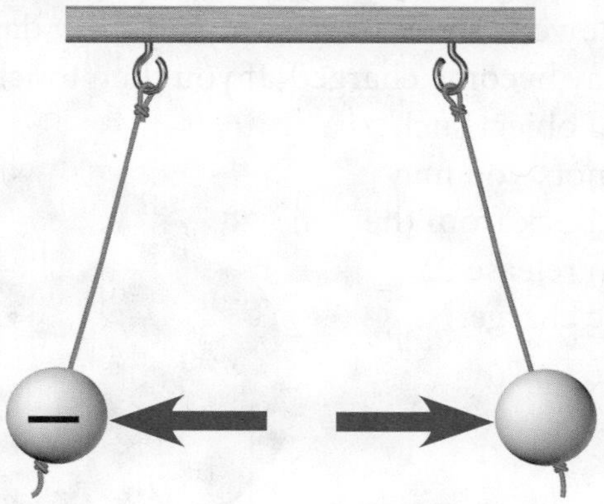

–

B ______________________________

____

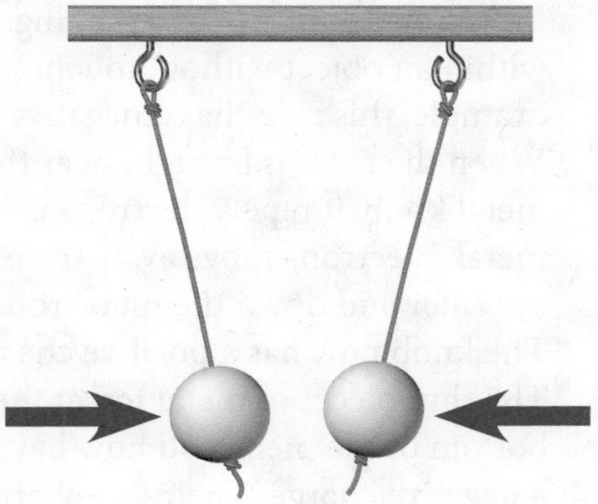

C ______________________________

____

What a *Shock!*

How can an object become charged?

Active Reading

9 Identify As you read, underline examples of objects becoming charged.

Objects become charged when their atoms gain or lose electrons. Three ways that objects can gain or lose electrons are by friction, contact, or induction.

By Friction

Charging by friction occurs when two objects are rubbed together, causing a transfer of electrons between the objects. For example, rubbing a balloon on your hair moves electrons from your hair to the balloon. Your hair becomes positively charged, and the balloon becomes negatively charged. Similarly, when you rub your shoes on a carpet on a dry day, you may become charged. If you then touch a metal object such as a doorknob, you may feel a shock from the sudden release of electric charge.

By Contact

If a charged object and an uncharged object touch each other, the charged object can transfer some of its charge to the area it touches. The sphere at the right is part of a *Van de Graaff generator.* The generator places a charge on its dome. An uncharged object that touches the dome becomes charged by contact. This student's hair is standing on end because the charged hairs repel each other.

By Induction

Induction is a way of rearranging the charges within an object without touching it. For example, this ruler has a negative charge. When the ruler is brought near the metal knob, it repels electrons in the metal. Electrons move away from the ruler and down the metal rod. The knob now has a positive charge. The thin pieces of metal foil at the bottom of the metal rod now have a negative charge. Their like charges cause them to push each other apart.

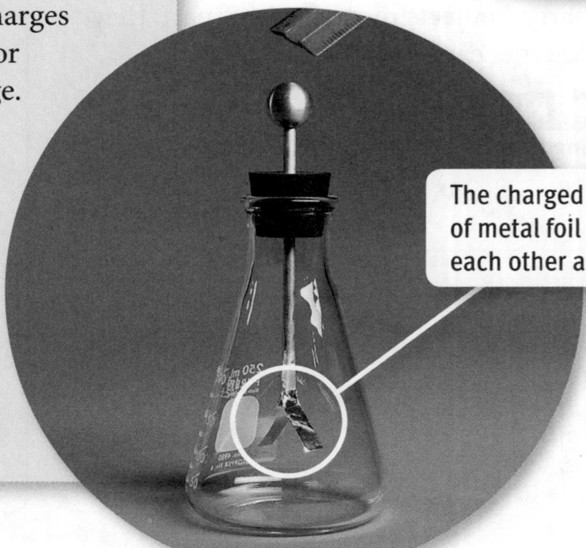

The charged pieces of metal foil push each other apart.

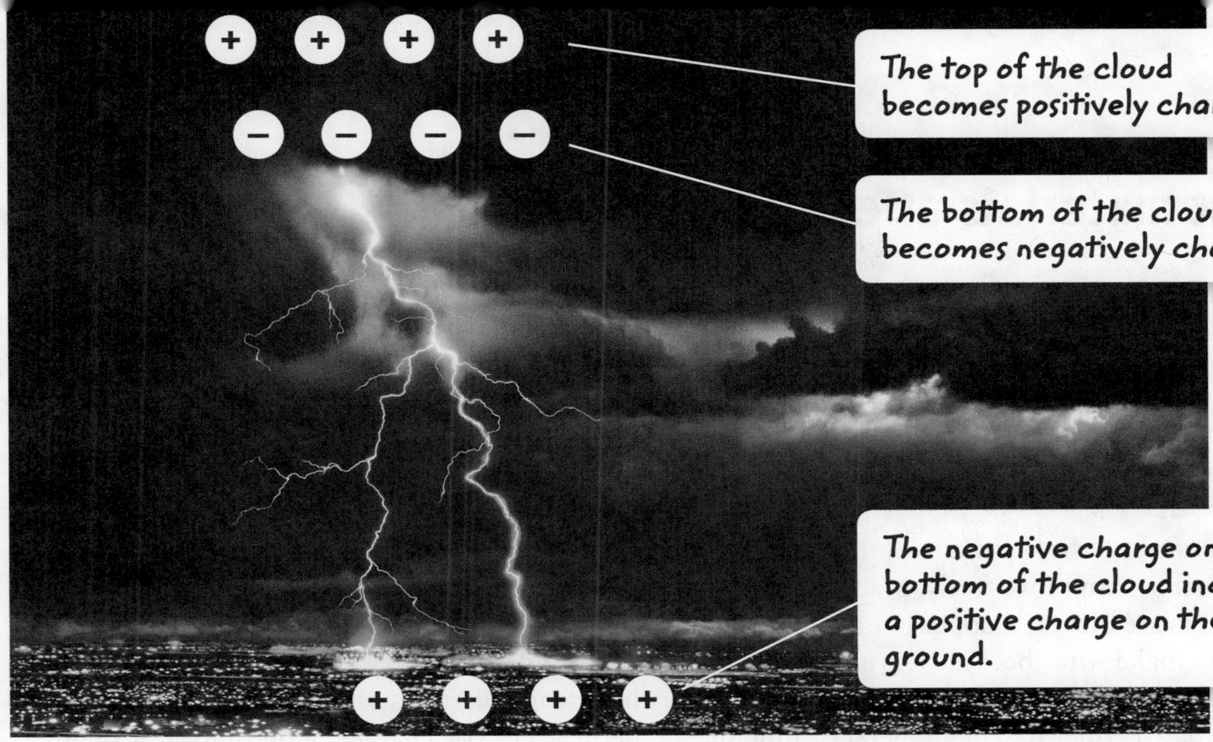
The top of the cloud becomes positively charged.
The bottom of the cloud becomes negatively charged.
The negative charge on the bottom of the cloud induces a positive charge on the ground.

What is static electricity?

After you take your clothes out of the dryer, they sometimes are stuck together. They stick together because of static electricity. **Static electricity** is the buildup of electric charge on an object. When something is static, it is not moving. Static electricity is the extra positive or negative charge that builds up on an object until it eventually moves elsewhere.

The Buildup of Charge on an Object

For an object to have static electricity, charge must build up on the object. For example, static electricity can build up inside storm clouds. The top of the cloud becomes positively charged. The bottom of the cloud becomes negatively charged. The negative charge in the bottom of the cloud can cause the ground to become positively charged by induction.

Charges that build up as static electricity eventually leave the object. This loss of charges is known as *electric discharge.* Electric discharge may happen slowly or quickly. Lightning is an example of rapid electric discharge. Lightning can occur between clouds. It can also occur between the negative part of the cloud and the positively charged ground. When lightning strikes, charged particles move toward places with opposite charge.

Active Reading **10 Analyze** During a lightning storm, what can cause the ground to become positively charged?

____

____

Think Outside the Book Inquiry

11 Apply Think of an everyday example of an object becoming charged. Draw and label a diagram that shows how charges moved. (Hint: You may need to use reference materials to learn more about the process you have chosen.)

Charging Ahead

What materials affect the flow of charge?

Have you ever noticed that electrical cords are often made from both metal and plastic? Different materials are used because electric charges move through some materials more easily than they move through others.

Conductors

An **electrical conductor** is a material through which charges can move freely. Many electrical conductors are metals. Copper is a metal that is used to make wires because it is an excellent electrical conductor. When an electrically charged plastic ruler touches a metal conductor, the charge it transfers to the metal can move freely through the metal.

Insulators

An **electrical insulator** is a material through which charges cannot move easily. The electrons are tightly held in the atoms of the insulator. Plastic, rubber, glass, and dry air are all good electrical insulators. Plastic is often used to coat wires because electric charges cannot move through the plastic easily. This stops the charges from leaving the wire and prevents you from being shocked when you touch the lamp cord.

Visualize It!

12 Identify What is the purpose of the material surrounding the metal inside the lamp cord?

____

____

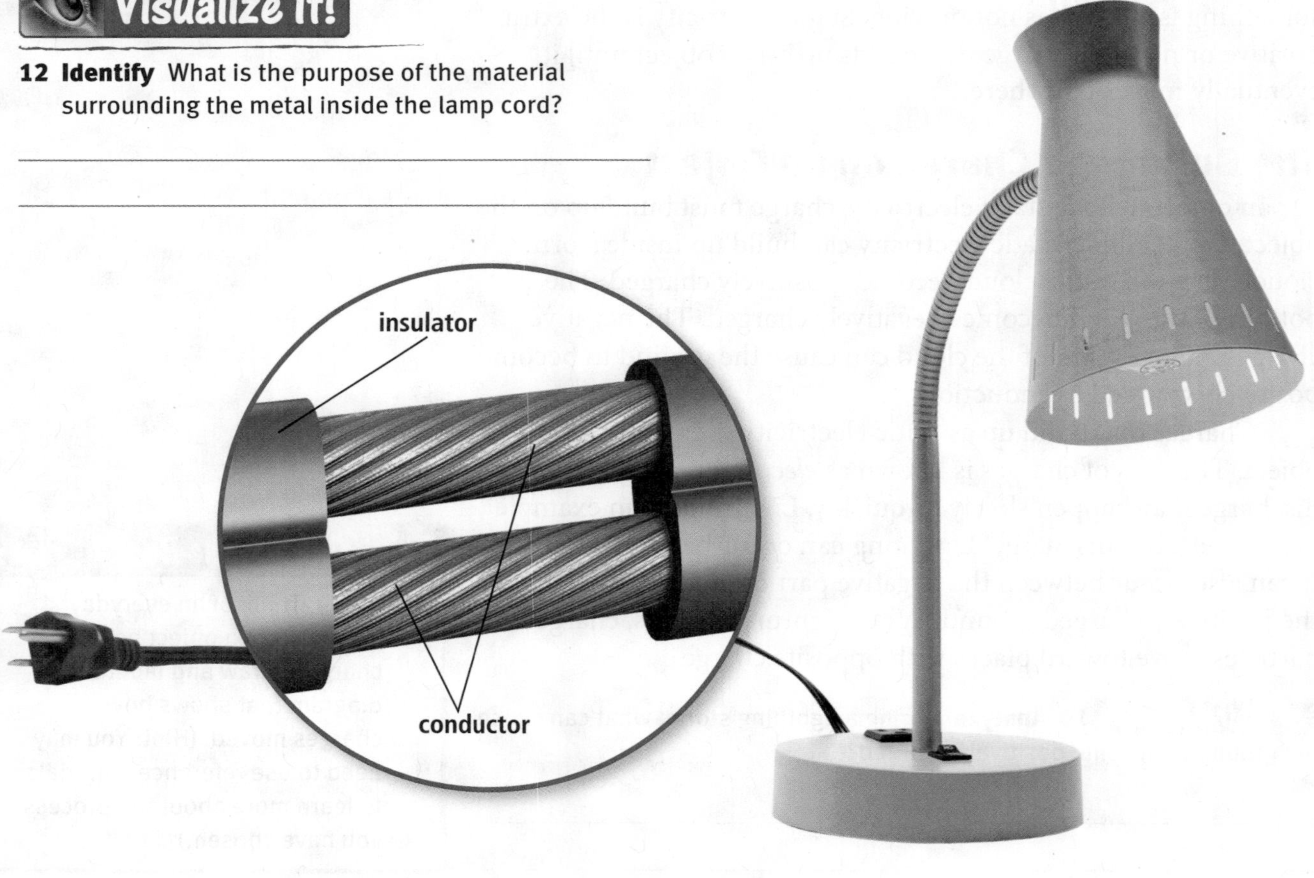
insulator
conductor

Semiconductors are used to make the computer chips found in electronic devices such as cell phones and calculators.
TEXAS INSTRUMENTS Explorer Plus

Semiconductors

Semiconductors are a special class of materials that conduct electric charge better than electrical insulators but not as well as electrical conductors. Their properties allow them to be used to control the flow of charge. Electrical devices use semiconductors to process electrical signals in many different ways. Silicon is the basis of many kinds of semiconductors. It is used to make computer chips found in electronic devices such as the ones shown above.

13 Summarize Fill in the table at the right to summarize what you have learned about conductors, insulators, and semiconductors.

	Example	Effect on the movement of charges
Conductor		
Insulator		
Semiconductor		

How is charge conserved?

All objects contain positive charges from the protons and negative charges from the electrons within their atoms. A neutral object becomes negatively charged when it gains one or more electrons and then has more negative charges than positive charges. Where do these electrons come from? They might come from a second object that loses the electrons and becomes positively charged. So electrons are not really lost. Charging objects involves moving electrons from one object to another. The total amount of charge always stays the same. This principle is called the conservation of charge.

Active Reading **14 Describe** What happens to the charge lost by an object?

Visual Summary

To complete this summary, fill in the blanks with the correct word. Then use the key below to check your answers. You can use this page to review the main concepts of the lesson.

Electric Charge and Static Electricity

Like charges repel each other, while unlike charges attract each other.

15 An object that has a positive charge equal to its negative charge is ______________________

Electrical conductors allow electric charges to move freely, while electrical insulators do not.

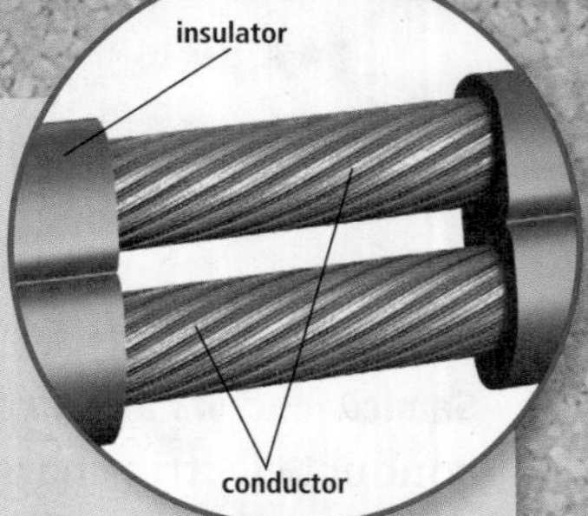
insulator
conductor

17 A ______________________ is a material whose conductivity is between that of an electrical conductor and an electrical insulator.

Objects can become charged by friction, contact, or induction.

16 ______________________ is the buildup of electric charges on an object.

Electric charge is always conserved.

18 The electrons lost by one object are ______________________ by another.

Answers: 15 neutral; 16 Static electricity; 17 semiconductor; 18 gained

19 Predict Suppose an electrically charged ruler transfers some of its charge by contact to a tiny plastic sphere. Will the ruler and the sphere attract or repel afterwards? Why?

Lesson Review

Vocabulary

Draw a line to connect the following terms to their definitions.

1 electric charge	**A** a material that allows electrons to flow easily
2 electrical conductor	**B** a material that does not allow electrons to flow easily
3 electrical insulator	**C** property that leads to electromagnetic interactions

Key Concepts

4 Explain Describe electric discharge.

5 Compare What properties of semiconductors make them useful in electronic devices?

6 Predict Two objects have unlike charges. How would the electric force between the two objects change as they are moved apart?

Critical Thinking

Use this diagram to answer the following questions.

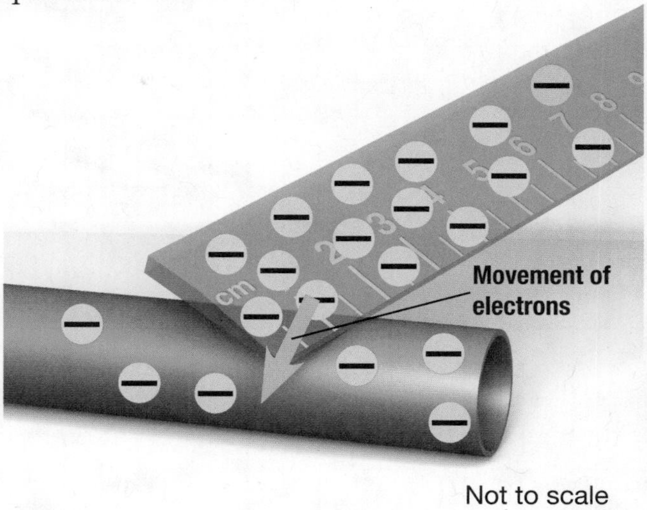
Movement of electrons
cm
Not to scale

7 Analyze Describe how charge is transferred from the ruler to the metal rod.

8 Describe Explain how this transfer observes the conservation of charge.

9 Evaluate A student places two charged objects near each other. The objects repel each other. The student concludes that the objects must both be negative. Do you agree? Explain.

My Notes

Lesson 2

Electric Current

Electric current sent over wires from power plants supplies this city with energy for lights and other uses.

ESSENTIAL QUESTION

What flows through an electric wire?

By the end of this lesson, you should be able to describe how electric charges flow as electric current.

Lesson Labs

Quick Labs
- Investigate Electric Current
- Lemon Battery

S.T.E.M. Lab
- Voltage, Current, and Resistance

Engage Your Brain

1 Identify Unscramble the letters below to find terms related to electric current. Write your words on the blank lines.

SGARCHE ______________________

EGATOVL ______________________

EERPAM ______________________

EIRW ______________________

2 Describe Describe what makes this electric sign light up when it is in use.

OPEN

____

____

____

____

Active Reading

3 Apply Many scientific words such as *resistance* also have everyday meanings. Use context clues to write your own definition for the word *resistance*.

Example sentence
John's request to go to the movies met with resistance from his friends.

resistance:

____

____

____

Example sentence
The composition of a wire determines its electrical resistance.

resistance:

____

____

____

Vocabulary Terms

- electric current
- resistance
- voltage

4 Identify As you read, place a question mark next to any words that you do not understand. When you finish reading the lesson, go back and review the text that you marked. If the information is still confusing, consult a classmate or a teacher.

Current Events

What is an electric current?

When you watch TV, use a computer, or even turn on a light bulb, you depend on moving charges to provide the electrical energy that powers them. *Electrical energy* is the energy of electric charges. In most devices that use electrical energy, the electric charges flow through wires. The rate of flow of electric charges is called **electric current**.

How is electric current measured?

To understand an electric current, think of people entering the seating area for a sporting event through turnstiles. A counter in each turnstile records the number of people who enter. The number of people who pass through a turnstile each minute describes the rate of flow of people into the stadium. Similarly, an electric current describes the rate of flow of charges, such as the slow flow of many electrons through a wire. Electric current is the amount of charge that passes a location in the wire every second. Electric current is expressed in units called *amperes* (AM•pirz), which is often shortened to "amps." The symbol for ampere is A. A wire with a current of 2 A has twice as much charge passing by each second as a wire with a current of 1 A.

Active Reading

5 Identify As you read, underline the units used to express electric current.

Visualize It!

6 Identify How can you express the rate of flow of people into a stadium? How can you express the rate of flow of charges through a wire?

____

____

____

____

Tigers
17

What are two kinds of current?

Two kinds of electric current are *direct current* (DC) and *alternating current* (AC). Both kinds of current carry electrical energy. They differ in the way that the charges move.

Direct Current (DC)

In direct current, charges always flow in the same direction. The electric current generated by batteries is DC. Some everyday devices that use DC from batteries are flashlights, cars, and cameras.

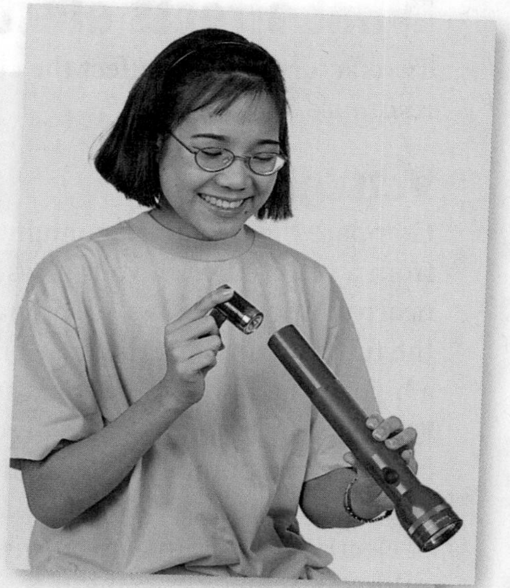

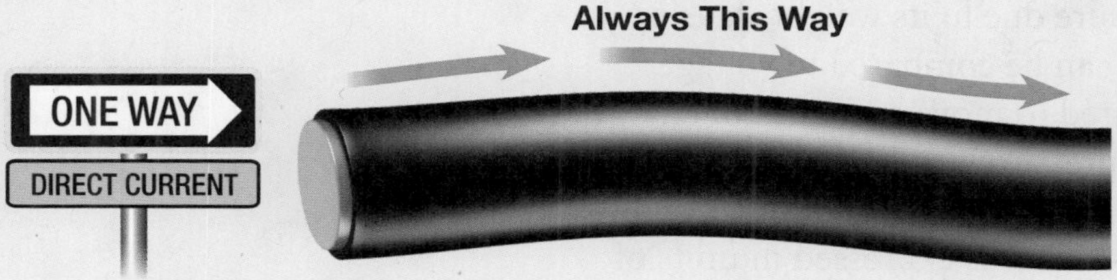
Always This Way
ONE WAY
DIRECT CURRENT

Charges move in one direction in DC.

Alternating Current (AC)

In alternating current, charges repeatedly shift from flowing in one direction to flowing in the reverse direction. The current *alternates* direction. The electric current from outlets in your home is AC. So, most household appliances run on alternating current. In the United States, the alternating current reverses direction and then returns back to the original direction 60 times each second.

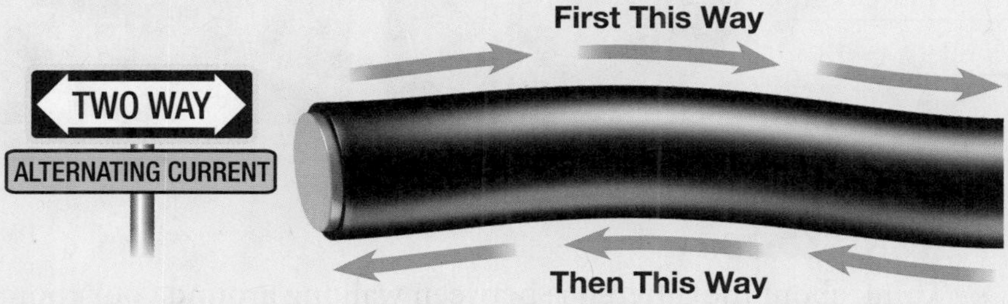
First This Way
TWO WAY
ALTERNATING CURRENT
Then This Way

Charges repeatedly change direction in AC.

Active Reading

7 Explain What alternates in alternating current?

____

____

You've Got *Potential*

What affects electric current?

Two factors that can affect the current in a wire are *voltage* and *resistance*.

Voltage

Compare the two drink containers below. If you pour lemonade from a full container, your glass fills quickly. If the container is nearly empty, the flow of lemonade is weaker. The lemonade in the full container exerts more pressure due to its weight, causing a higher rate of flow. This pressure can be compared to voltage. **Voltage** is the amount of work required to move each unit of charge between two points. Just as higher pressure produces a higher rate of flow of lemonade, higher voltage produces a higher rate of flow of electric charges in a given wire. Voltage is expressed in units of volts (V). Voltage is sometimes called *electric potential* because it is a measure of the electric potential energy per unit charge.

Visualize It!

8 Analyze How does the flow of the lemonade coming out of these containers relate to current and voltage?

____

____

____

____

____

____

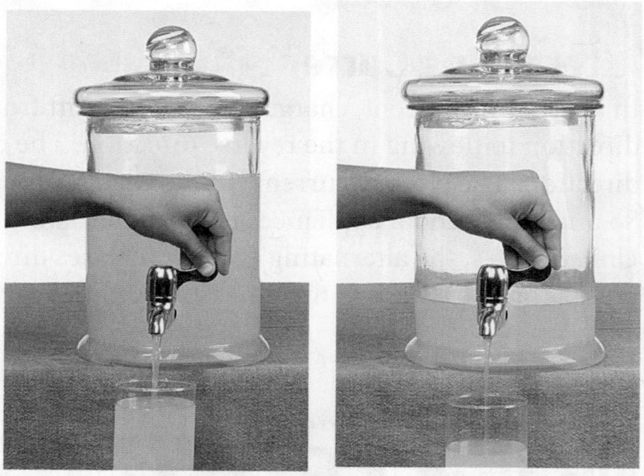

Resistance

Think about the difference between walking around your room and walking around in waist-deep water. The water resists your movement more than the air, so you have to work harder to walk through water. If you walked in waist-deep mud, you would have to work even harder. Similarly, some materials do not allow electric charges to move freely. The opposition to the flow of electric charge is called **resistance**. Resistance is expressed in ohms (Ω, the Greek letter *omega*). Higher resistance at the same voltage results in lower current.

Think Outside the Book **Inquiry**

9 Apply In a small group, create a skit that illustrates the idea of electrical resistance. Be sure to compare high resistance and low resistance.

What affects electrical resistance?

A material's composition affects its resistance. Some metals, such as silver and copper, have low resistance and are very good electrical conductors. Other metals, such as iron and nickel, have a higher resistance. Electrical insulators such as plastic have such a high resistance that electric charges cannot flow in them at all. Other factors that affect the resistance of a wire are thickness, length, and temperature.

- A thin wire has higher resistance than a thicker wire.
- A long wire has higher resistance than a shorter wire.
- A hot wire has higher resistance than a cooler wire.

Conductors with low resistance, such as copper, are used to make wires. But conductors with high resistance are also useful. For example, an alloy of nickel and chromium is used in heating coils. Its high resistance causes the wire to heat up when it carries electric current.

Like lemonade in a drinking straw, electric charges move more easily through a short, wide pathway than through a long, narrow one.

Visualize It!

10 Predict For each pair of images, place a check mark in the box that shows the material that has higher electrical resistance.

Composition Wires made from different materials have different uses in electronic devices.	Pure copper 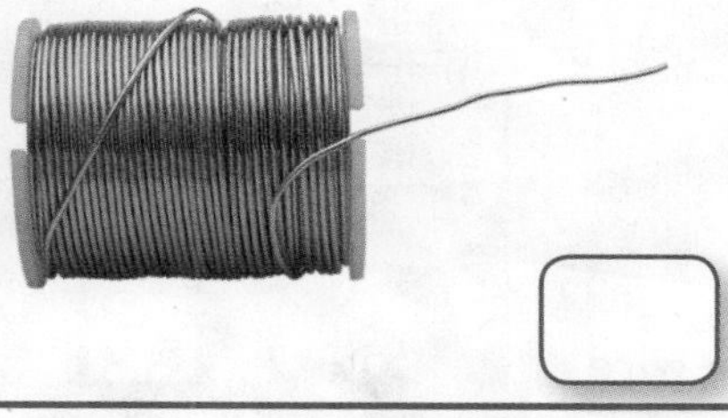	Nickel and chromium alloy 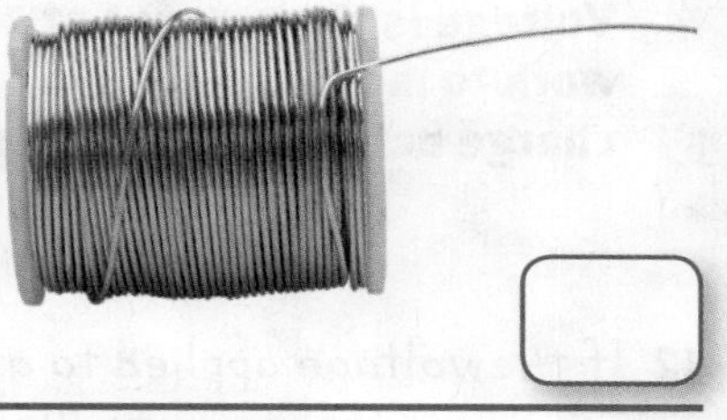
Thickness A three-way light bulb contains a thin filament and a thick filament. Charges move through one filament or the other or both to produce different brightness levels.	Thin filament 	Thick filament 
Temperature The electrical resistance of this heating element changes as its temperature increases.		

Visual Summary

To complete this summary, fill in the blanks with the correct word or phrase. Then use the key below to check your answers. You can use this page to review the main concepts of the lesson.

Electric current is the rate of flow of electric charges.

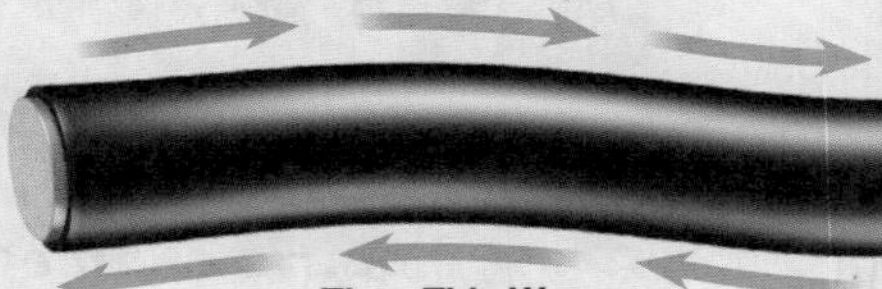

First This Way
Then This Way

11 In ______________________ current, the flow of charge changes direction and then reverses back to the original direction.

The opposition to the flow of electric charges is called resistance.

13 Four factors that determine the resistance of a wire are

____

____

____

____

Electric Current

Voltage is the amount of work to move an electric charge between two points.

12 If the voltage applied to a given wire increases, its current will

____

Answers: 11 alternating; 12 increase
13 composition, temperature, length, and thickness

14 Apply What might happen if a wire in an electronic device is replaced with a thinner, longer wire? Explain.

Lesson Review

Vocabulary

Draw a line to connect the following terms to their definitions.

1 electric current	**A** the opposition to the flow of electric charges
2 voltage	**B** the rate of flow of electric charges
3 resistance	**C** the amount of work required to move each unit of electric charge between two points

Key Concepts

4 Compare How does direct current differ from alternating current?

5 Summarize Describe how resistance affects electric current.

6 Apply What happens to the electric current in a wire as voltage is increased?

7 Apply List two everyday devices that use DC and two everyday devices that use AC.

Critical Thinking

Use the diagram to answer the following questions.

Electrical Resistance of Various Materials

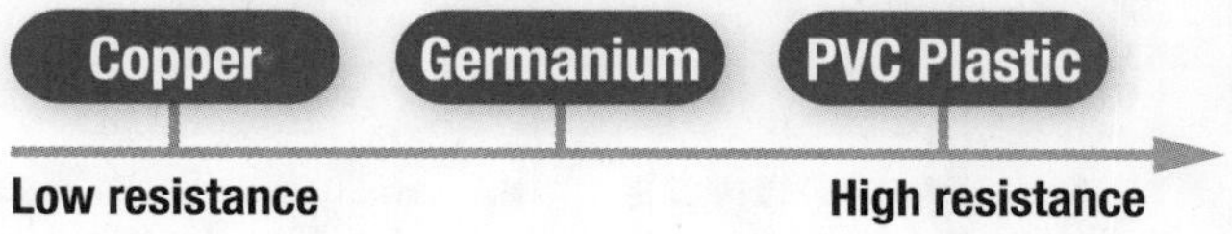
Copper
Germanium
PVC Plastic
Low resistance
High resistance

8 Analyze Which material is likely to slow the flow of electric charges the most? Explain.

9 Infer A certain voltage is applied to a copper wire and to a germanium wire of the same thickness and length. How will the current in the two wires compare?

10 Compare How do the currents produced by a 1.5 V flashlight battery and a 12 V car battery compare if the resistance is the same?

11 Infer What does it mean to say that the electric current from a wall socket is "120 V AC?"

My Notes

Lesson 3

Electric Circuits

Microscopic electric circuits inside these computer chips carry electric charges that can power computers, video games, and home appliances.

ESSENTIAL QUESTION

How do electric circuits work?

By the end of this lesson, you should be able to describe basic electric circuits and how to use electricity safely.

Lesson Labs

Quick Labs
- Compare Parallel and Series Circuits
- Compare Materials for Use in Fuses

Exploration
- Model the Electric Circuits in a Room

Engage Your Brain

1 Predict Check T or F to show whether you think each statement is true or false.

T	F	
☐	☐	A circuit must form a closed loop to have an electric current.
☐	☐	Electricity is dangerous only when it is labeled as high voltage.
☐	☐	Every electric circuit must have an energy source.

2 Describe Write a caption explaining how these light bulbs are connected.

Active Reading

3 Apply Many scientific words, such as *current*, also have everyday meanings. Use context clues to write your own definition for each meaning of the word *current*.

Example sentence
The magazine covered current events.

current:

Example sentence
The circuit had an electric current in it.

current:

Vocabulary Terms

- **electric circuit**
- **series circuit**
- **parallel circuit**

4 Apply As you learn the definition of each vocabulary term in this lesson, create your own definition or sketch to help you remember the meaning of the term.

A Complete Circuit

What are the parts of an electric circuit?

Think about a running track. It forms a loop. The spot where you start running around the track is the same as the spot where you end. This kind of closed loop is called a circuit. Like a track, an electric circuit also forms a loop. An **electric circuit** is a complete, closed path through which electric charges can flow. All electric circuits contain three basic parts: an energy source, an electrical conductor, and a load.

Energy Source

The energy source converts some type of energy, such as chemical energy, into electrical energy. One common household energy source is a battery. A battery changes chemical energy stored inside the battery into electrical energy. A solar cell is an energy source that changes light energy into electrical energy.

Inside a power plant, a form of energy such as chemical or nuclear energy is changed into mechanical energy. Electric generators in the power plant change the mechanical energy into electrical energy. Power transmission lines deliver this energy to wall outlets in homes, schools, and other buildings.

Active Reading

5 Identify As you read this page and the next, underline examples of energy sources, electrical conductors, and electrical loads used in an electric circuit.

Solar cell
12345678
D Battery
9V Battery
AAA
AA
Battery

Power plant

Think Outside the Book **Inquiry**

6 Research Learn how your local power plant uses turbines and generators to produce electrical energy. Then write a short article about how the power plant generates the mechanical energy for the turbines.

Electrical Conductor

Materials in which electric charges can move easily are called *electrical conductors.* Most metals are good conductors of electric current. Electric wires are often made of copper. Copper is a metal that is a good conductor and is inexpensive compared to many other metals. Conducting wires connect all the parts of an electric circuit.

To protect people from harmful electrical shocks, copper wire is often covered with an insulator. An *electrical insulator* is a material, such as glass, plastic, or rubber, through which electric charges cannot move easily.

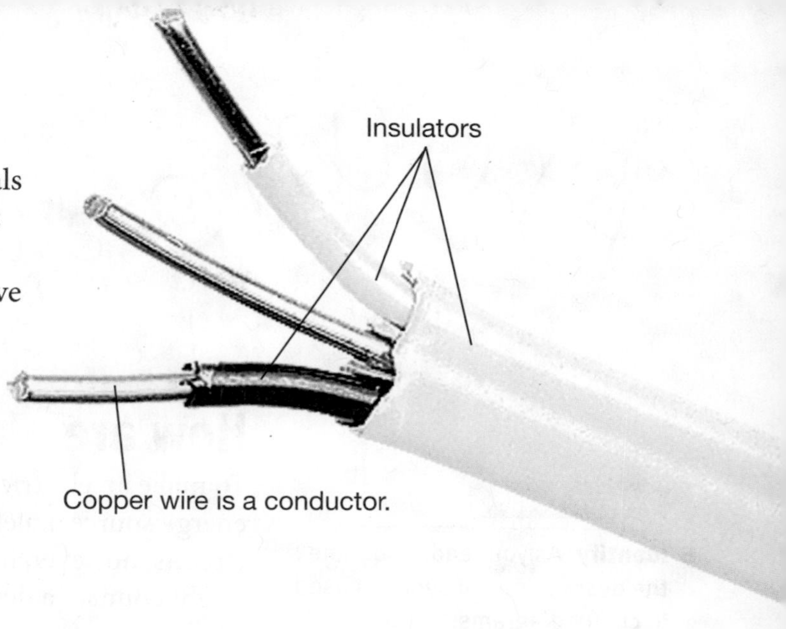
Insulators
Copper wire is a conductor.

Load

A complete circuit also includes a *load,* a device that uses electrical energy to operate. The conductor connects the energy source to the load. Examples of loads include light bulbs, radios, computers, and electric motors. The load converts electrical energy into other forms of energy. A light bulb, for example, converts electrical energy into light and energy as heat. A doorbell produces sound waves, energy that is transmitted through the air to your ear. A cell phone converts electrical energy into electromagnetic waves that carry information.

Visualize It!

7 Identify List the devices in the photograph that could be a load in an electric circuit.

Around and Around

How are electric circuits modeled?

Active Reading

8 Identify As you read, underline the descriptions of symbols used in circuit diagrams.

To make an electric circuit, you need only three basic parts: an energy source, an electrical conductor, and a load. Most electric circuits, however, have more than one load. A circuit in your home might connect a desk lamp, clock radio, computer, and TV set. The circuit may even include devices in more than one room. Circuits can be complex. A single computer chip can have many millions of parts. One tool that can be used to model electric circuits is a circuit diagram.

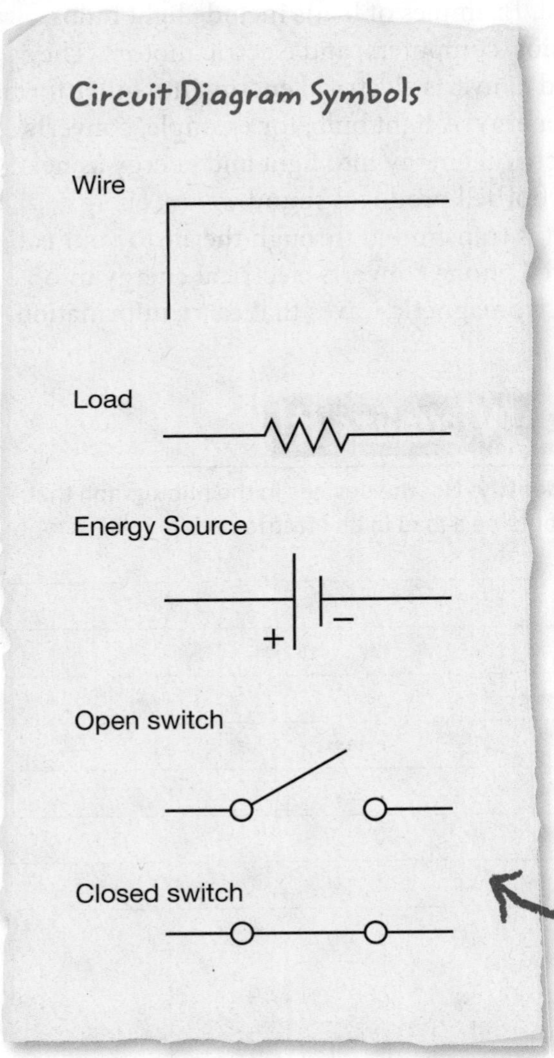

Circuit Diagram Symbols
Wire
Load
Energy Source
+
−
Open switch
Closed switch

With Circuit Diagrams

A circuit diagram helps engineers and electricians design and install electric circuits so that they function correctly and safely. Sometimes, special software is used to create complex circuit designs on computers. A diagram for an electric circuit shows all the parts in the complete circuit and the relationships among the different parts. The chart at the left shows how each part of a circuit can be represented in a circuit diagram. The energy source can be represented by two parallel lines of different length. A wire or other conductor is shown as a line. A load is represented by a zigzag line segment. A small circle shows where two wires are connected. A straight line between two circles shows an on-off switch. When the line of the switch symbol is slanted up, the switch is open. When the line for the switch symbol connects two dots, the switch is closed.

Symbols are put together to show the arrangement of parts in a circuit. A circuit diagram is like a road map for the moving charges.

How does current stop and start?

Electric charges move continuously in the closed loop of an electric circuit. What do you do if you want the charges to stop flowing? You open the switch! A switch is a device that turns electrical devices on and off. A switch is usually made of a piece of conducting material that can move. When the switch is open, the circuit is open. That means it does not form a closed loop, so charges cannot flow. When you turn a light switch on, the switch closes the circuit. Charges flow through the light bulb. If you turn a light switch off, the switch opens the circuit, and the charges stop flowing.

Active Reading

9 Explain Why does an open light switch turn off the light?

____

____

____

____

____

Visualize It!

10 Identify Label the parts in this circuit diagram. Then draw a switch to match the circuit shown in the photograph.

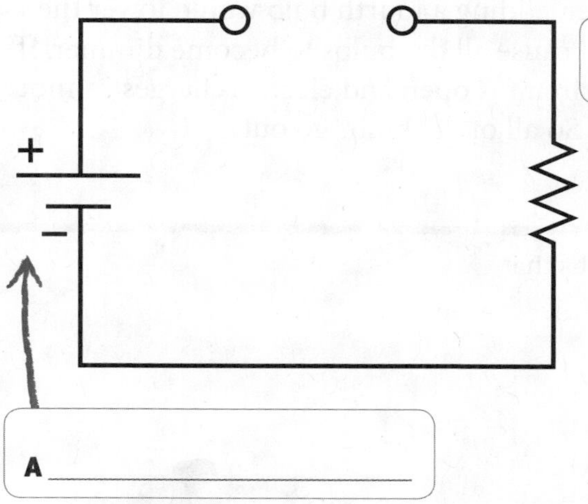

+
−
B
A

6V
Battery

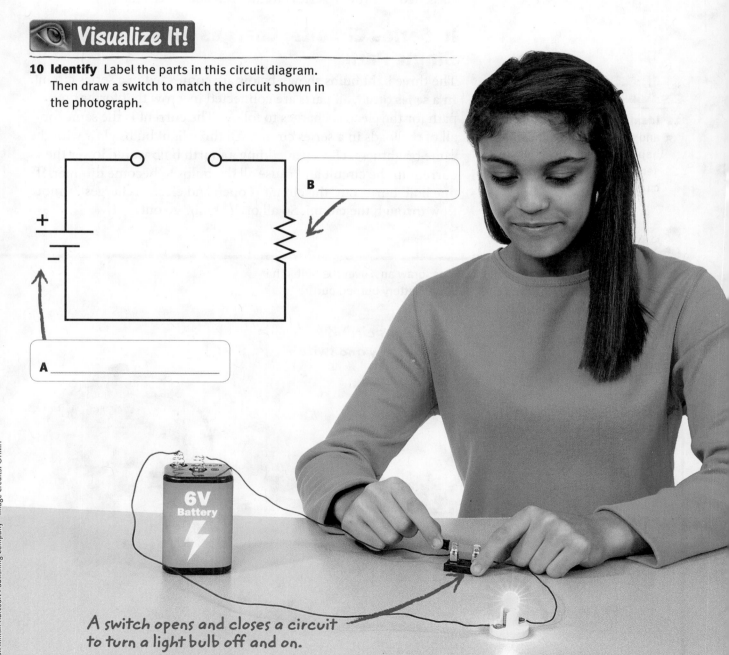

A switch opens and closes a circuit to turn a light bulb off and on.

All Together?

How do series circuits and parallel circuits differ?

Most electric circuits have more than one load. Simple electric circuits that contain one energy source and more than one load are classified as either a series circuit or a parallel circuit.

In Series Circuits, Charges Follow a Single Path

Active Reading

11 Identify As you read this page and the next, underline what happens if you add a bulb to a series circuit and to a parallel circuit.

The three light bulbs shown below are connected in a series circuit. In a **series circuit**, all parts are connected in a row that forms one path for the electric charges to follow. The current is the same for all of the loads in a series circuit. All three light bulbs glow with the same brightness. However, adding a fourth bulb would lower the current in the circuit and cause all the bulbs to become dimmer. If one bulb burns out, the circuit is open and electric charges cannot flow through the circuit. So all of the bulbs go out.

Visualize It!

12 Apply In these two circuit illustrations, draw an *X* over the bulbs that would not glow if the bulb closest to the battery burned out.

Series circuit
with battery and switch

The bulbs are connected to one another in a single loop.

BATTERY

In Parallel Circuits, Charges Follow Multiple Paths

Think about what would happen if all of the lights in your home were connected in series. If you needed to turn on a light in your room, all other lights in the house would have to be turned on, too! Instead of being wired in series, circuits in buildings are wired in parallel. In a **parallel circuit**, electric charges have more than one path that they can follow. Loads in a parallel circuit are connected side by side. In the parallel circuit shown below, any bulb can burn out without opening the circuit.

Unlike the loads in a series circuit, the loads in a parallel circuit can have different currents. However, each load in a parallel circuit experiences the same voltage. For example, if three bulbs were hooked up to a 12-volt battery, each would have the full voltage of the battery. Each light bulb would glow at the same brightness no matter how many more bulbs were added to the circuit.

13 Compare In the table below, list the features of series and parallel circuits.

Series circuits	Parallel circuits

Parallel circuit with battery and switch

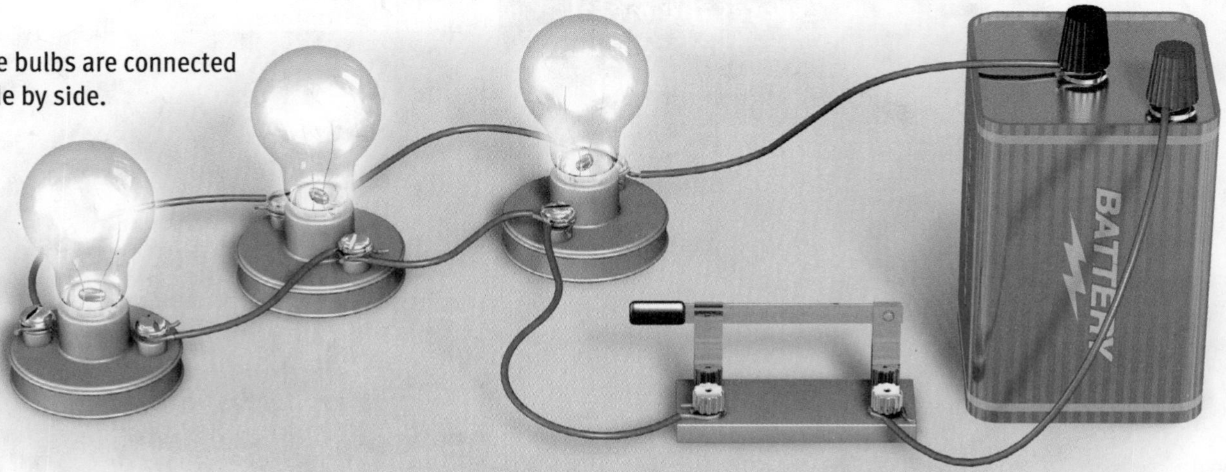
BATTERY

The bulbs are connected side by side.

Safety First!

How can I use electricity safely?

You use many electrical devices every day. It is important to remember that electrical energy can be hazardous if it is not used correctly. Electric circuits in buildings have built-in safeguards to keep people safe. You can stay safe if you are careful to avoid electrical dangers and pay attention to warning signs and labels.

By Avoiding Exposure to Current

Active Reading

14 Identify As you read, underline the reason that electric currents can be harmful to people.

Pure water is a poor conductor of electric current. But water usually has substances such as salt dissolved in it. These substances make water a better conductor. This is especially true of fluids inside your body. The water in your body is a good conductor of electric current. This is why you should avoid exposure to current. Even small currents can cause severe burns, shock, and even death. A current can prevent you from breathing and stop your heart.

Following basic safety precautions will protect you from exposure to electric current. Never use electrical devices around water. Do not use any appliance if its power cord is worn or damaged. Always pay attention to warning signs near places with high-voltage transmission lines. You do not actually have to touch some high-voltage wires to receive a deadly shock. Even coming near high-voltage wires can do serious harm to your body.

A damaged cord exposes the metal wires that conduct electric charges.

Stay away from places where there is high-voltage electrical equipment.

DANGER
High Voltage
Trespassers may
be electrocuted

By Using Electrical Safety Devices

Damage to wires can cause a "short circuit," in which charges do not pass through all the loads. When this happens, current increases and wires can get hot enough to start a fire.

Fuses, circuit breakers, and ground fault circuit interrupters (GFCIs) are safety devices that act like switches. When the current is too high in a fuse, a metal strip that is part of the circuit heats up and melts. Circuit breakers are switches that open when the current reaches a certain level. A GFCI is a type of circuit breaker. GFCIs are often built into outlets that are used near water, such as in a kitchen or bathroom.

Active Reading **15 Identify** Name three safety devices that you might find in electric circuits at home.

____

____

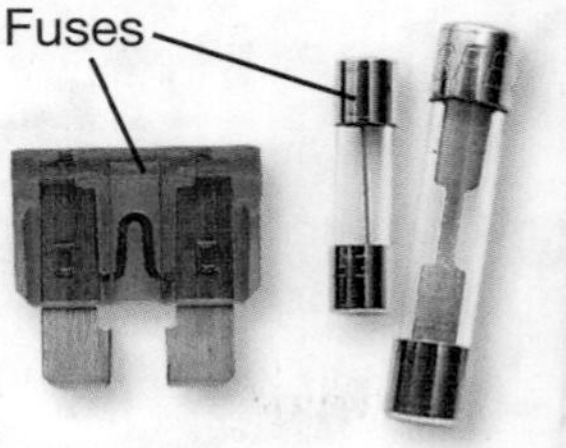
Fuses

When the current is too high in the fuse, the metal strip melts and opens the circuit.

Ground fault circuit interrupter (GFCI)

The lightning rod attached to the top of this building helps to protect it from a lightning strike.

By Taking Precautions during a Lightning Storm

When lightning strikes, electric charges can travel between a cloud and the ground. Lightning often strikes objects that are taller than their surroundings, such as skyscrapers, trees, barns, or even a person in an open field. During a thunderstorm, be sure to stay away from trees and other tall objects. The best place to seek shelter during a thunderstorm is indoors.

Many buildings have lightning rods. These are metal rods at the highest part of the building. The rod is connected to the ground by a thick conducting wire. The rod and wire protect the building by *grounding* it, or providing a path that allows charges to flow into the ground.

16 Infer What would happen if there were no electrical path from the top of the building to the ground?

____

____

____

Visual Summary

To complete this summary, fill in the blanks with the correct word or phrase. Then, use the key below to check your answers. You can use this page to review the main concepts of the lesson.

Electric Circuits

D
Battery
9V
Battery
AAA
Battery
AA
Battery

An electric circuit has three basic parts: an energy source, an electric conductor, and a load.

17 *Batteries are an example of an* ____________________ *in an electric circuit.*

18 *To open and close a circuit, a* ____________________ *can be used.*

Circuits can be connected in series or in parallel.

BATTERY

19 *When one of several bulbs in a series circuit burns out, the other bulbs* ____________________

20 *When one of several bulbs in a parallel circuit burns out, the other bulbs* ____________________

Taking precautions when using electricity and during a lightning storm can keep you safe from electrical dangers.

21 *This outlet contains a GFCI, which acts as a* ____________________ *to protect people from short circuits.*

Answers: 17 energy source; 18 switch; 19 go out; 20 stay lit; 21 circuit breaker

22 Synthesize Compare the function of a switch in an electric circuit to the function of a water faucet. How are they alike and how are they different?

Lesson Review

Vocabulary

Draw a line to connect the following terms to their definitions.

1 series circuit

2 parallel circuit

A a circuit with two or more paths for charges

B a circuit with a single path for charges

Key Concepts

3 Explain Why is an energy source needed in order to have a working electric circuit?

4 Compare Describe the difference between a closed circuit and an open circuit.

5 Apply Why does removing one bulb from a string of lights in a series circuit cause all the lights to go out?

6 Describe How does a lightning rod protect a building from lightning damage?

Critical Thinking

Use this drawing to answer the following questions.

Energy source

7 Identify Circuits can be either series or parallel. What type of circuit is shown above?

8 Infer Imagine that a circuit breaker opened the circuit every time that you operated the light, coffee maker, and microwave at the same time. What could be causing this?

9 Predict What electrical safety device could be used in this kitchen to decrease risk of electric shock? Explain.

My Notes

Lesson 4

Magnets and Magnetism

When cows are grazing, they may eat pieces of metal, such as nails. Farmers can feed the cows a smooth magnet to attract such objects. This prevents the objects from moving farther through the cow's system and causing damage.

ESSENTIAL QUESTION

What is magnetism?

By the end of this lesson, you should be able to describe magnets and magnetic fields and explain their properties.

Lesson Labs

Quick Labs
- Making Magnets
- Studying Magnetism

Engage Your Brain

1 Predict Check Yes or No to show whether you think the object would be attracted to a magnet.

Yes	No	
☐	☐	A paper clip
☐	☐	A plastic water bottle
☐	☐	A piece of notepaper
☐	☐	Another magnet
☐	☐	Aluminum foil
☐	☐	A penny

2 Describe Write your own caption for this photo of a cow magnet.

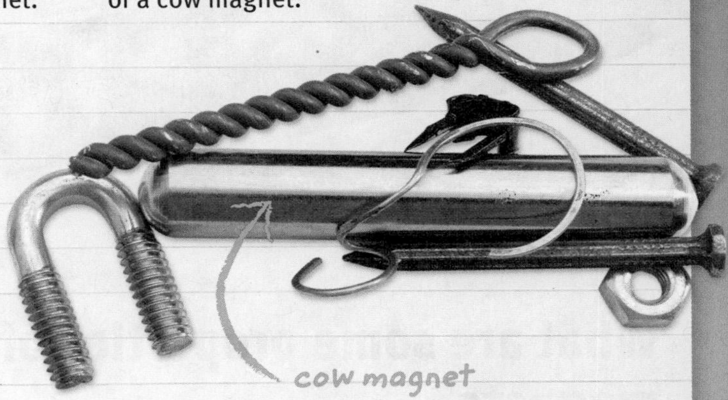
cow magnet

___

Active Reading

3 Apply Many scientific words, such as *field*, also have everyday meanings. Use context clues to write your own definition for each meaning of the word *field*.

Example sentence
The farm animals in the field are eating grass and clover.

field:

___

Example sentence
The magnet attracted all the pins that were within its magnetic field.

field:

___

Vocabulary Terms

- magnet
- magnetic force
- magnetic pole
- magnetic field

4 Identify As you read, place a question mark next to any words you don't understand. When you finish reading the lesson, go back and review the text that you marked. If the information is still confusing, consult a classmate or a teacher.

Stuck on You

What are some properties of magnets?

Have you wondered what a magnet is and why all materials are not magnets? The ancient Greeks discovered a mineral, called *magnetite* (MAG•nih•tyt), that would attract things made of iron. Today, we use the term **magnet** to describe any material that attracts iron or objects made of iron. Many magnets are made of iron, nickel, cobalt, or mixtures of these metals.

Inquiry

5 Infer What might be an advantage to making a magnet horseshoe-shaped?

Magnetic Forces

When you bring two magnets together, they exert a push or pull called a **magnetic force** on each other. This force results from spinning electric charges in the magnets. The force can either push the magnets apart or pull them together. Magnetic force is one of only three forces in nature that can act at a distance—electrostatic force and gravity are the other two.

Magnetic force explains why, when you hold a magnet close enough to a paper clip, the paper clip will start to move toward the magnet. You have probably noticed that either end of a magnet can pull on a paper clip. So why is it that when you place two magnets near each other, sometimes they pull together and sometimes they push each other apart?

Active Reading **6 State** Name two things magnetic force can do.

Magnetic Poles

Two magnets can push each other apart because of their ends, or **magnetic poles**. Every magnet has a north pole and a south pole. If you place the north poles of two magnets together, they will repel, or push away. If you place the north pole and the south pole of two magnets near each other, they will attract, or come together. The saying "opposites attract" applies well to magnets.

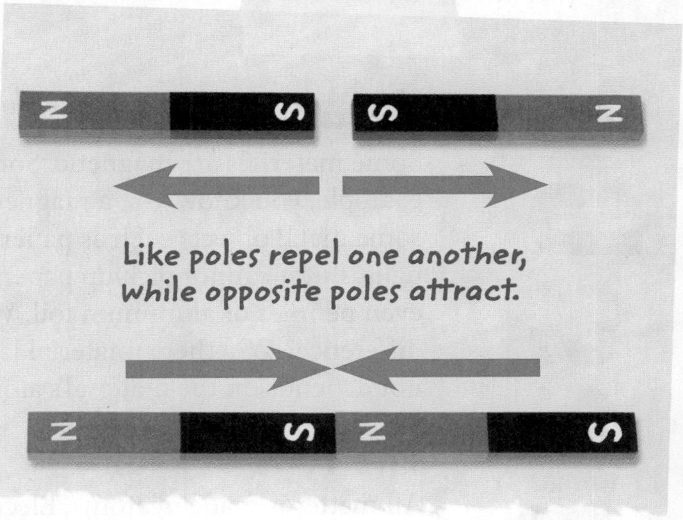

N
S
S
N
Like poles repel one another, while opposite poles attract.
N
S
N
S

Magnetic Fields

The area surrounding a magnet where magnetic forces can be detected is called the **magnetic field**. A magnetic object placed anywhere in the magnetic field will be affected by the magnet.

As you can see in the illustration below, the magnetic field is arranged in lines. Notice that the magnetic field lines enter the magnet at the south pole and exit at the north pole. The magnetic field is strongest near the poles. The greater the distance from the poles, the weaker the magnetic field.

Visualize It!

7 Diagram Draw an *X* on the illustration below to show one location in which a magnetic object would be attracted to the magnet. Draw an *O* to show one location in which a magnetic object would not be attracted to the magnet.

8 Relate Where are the magnetic field lines closest together, and what does that tell you about the strength of the magnetic field?

____

____

____

____

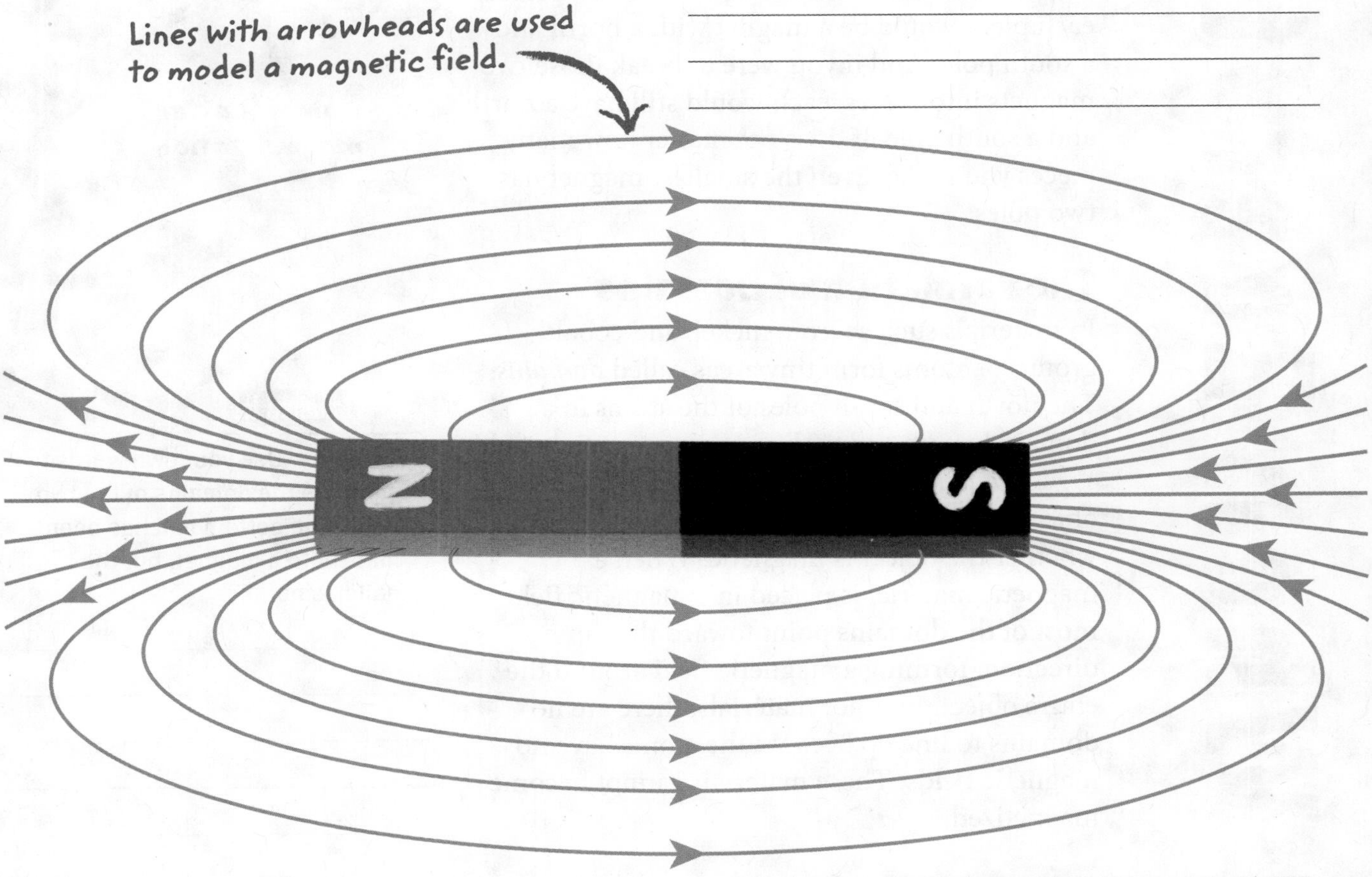

Lines with arrowheads are used to model a magnetic field.
N
S

When Everything Lines Up

What causes magnetism?

Some materials are magnetic. Some are not. For example, you know that a magnet can pick up some metal objects such as paper clips and iron nails. But it cannot pick up paper, plastic, or even pennies or aluminum foil. What causes the difference? Whether a material is magnetic or not depends on the material's atoms.

The Type of Atom

All matter is made of atoms. Electrons are negatively charged particles of atoms. As an electron moves in an atom, it makes, or induces, a magnetic field. The electron will then have a north and a south magnetic pole. In most atoms, such as copper and aluminum, the magnetic fields of the individual electrons cancel each other out. These materials are not magnetic.

But the magnetic fields of the electrons in iron, nickel, and cobalt atoms do not completely cancel each other out. As a result, atoms of these materials have small magnetic fields. These materials are magnetic.

If you were to cut a magnet into two pieces, each piece would be a magnet with a north and a south pole. And if you were to break those two magnets into pieces, each would still have a north and a south pole. It does not matter how many pieces you make. Even the smallest magnet has two poles.

The Formation of Domains

In materials such as iron, nickel, and cobalt, groups of atoms form tiny areas called *domains*. The north and south poles of the atoms in a domain line up and make a strong magnetic field.

Domains are like tiny magnets within an object. The domains in an object determine whether the object is magnetic. When a magnetic material is placed in a magnetic field, most of the domains point toward the same direction, forming a magnetic field around the entire object. In other materials, there are no domains to line up because the atoms have no magnetic fields. These materials cannot become magnetized.

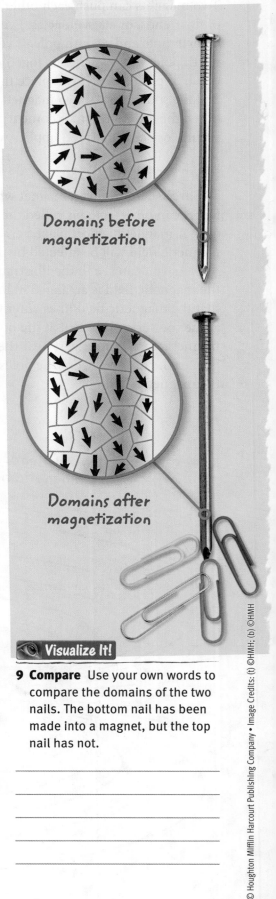

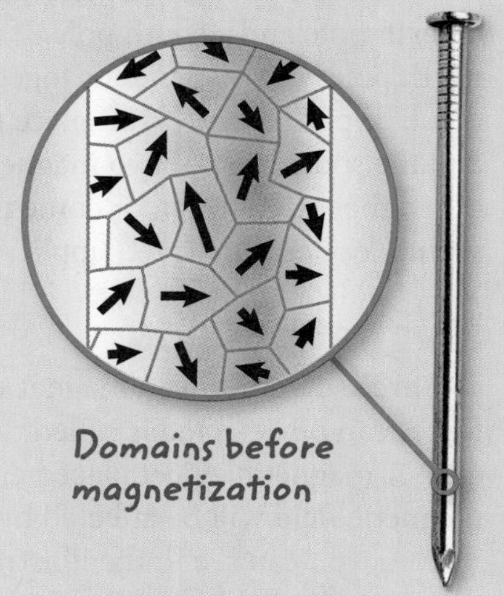
Domains before
magnetization

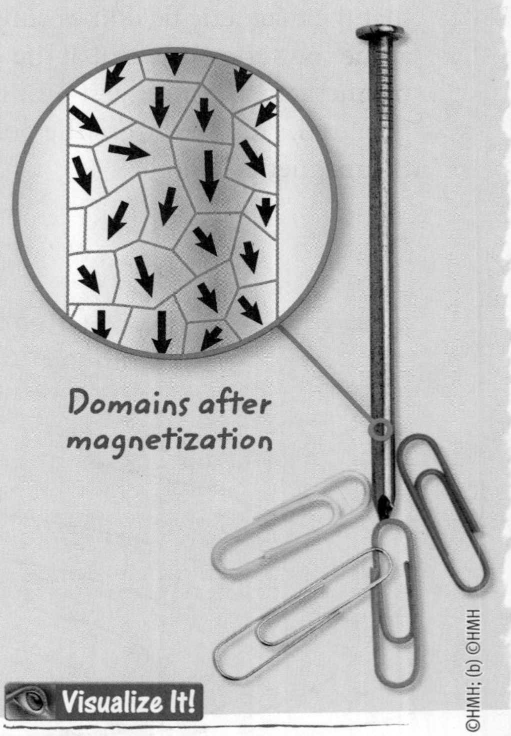
Domains after
magnetization

Visualize It!

9 Compare Use your own words to compare the domains of the two nails. The bottom nail has been made into a magnet, but the top nail has not.

____

____

____

____

____

What are some types of magnets?

There are different types of magnets. Some materials are naturally magnetic, such as the mineral magnetite. Some materials can be turned into either permanent or temporary magnets.

Ferromagnets

A material that can be turned into a magnet is called *ferromagnetic* (fehr•oh•mag•NET•ik). Natural materials such as iron, nickel, cobalt, or mixtures of these materials have strong magnetic properties. They are considered ferromagnets.

A ferromagnetic material can be turned into a permanent magnet when placed in a strong magnetic field. Permanent magnets are difficult to make, but they keep their magnetic properties longer. Magnets can be made into various shapes such as bar magnets, disc magnets, and horseshoe magnets.

Electromagnets

Strong magnets are used to pick up metals in scrap yards, as shown in the photo below. To get a magnet powerful enough to do this, an *electromagnet* is used. An electromagnet is an iron core wrapped with electrical wire. When an electric current is in the wire, a magnetic field forms. When the current is turned off, the magnetic field stops. The strength of an electromagnet depends on the strength of the electric current.

This electromagnet uses electricity to produce a magnetic field.

Temporary Magnets

Some materials, such as soft iron, can be made into magnets temporarily when placed in a strong magnetic field. The material's domains line up, and the material is magnetized. You can make a temporary magnet by rubbing one pole of a strong magnet in one direction on a magnetic material, for example, a pair of scissors. The domains line up in the scissors, and it becomes a temporary magnet. Over time, the domains will lose their alignment. Banging or dropping a temporary magnet can also make it lose its magnetism.

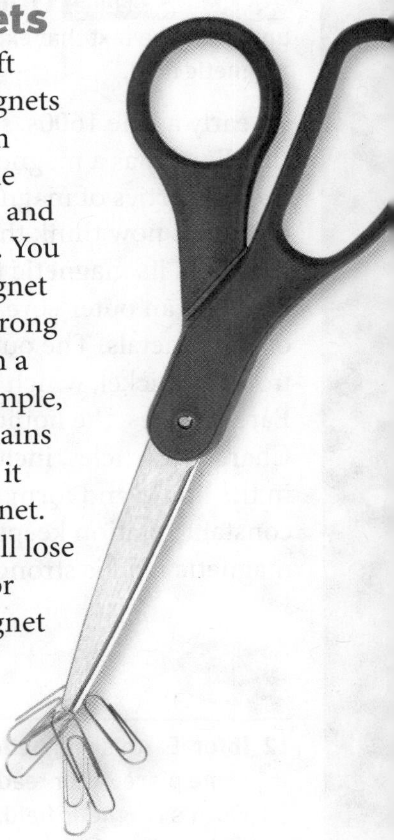

Think Outside the Book **Inquiry**

10 Design Plan an investigation to find out how the strength of a temporary magnet is affected by the number of times you rub the object with a permanent magnet.

Polar Opposites

How is Earth like a giant magnet?

Earth acts like a giant magnet. Like a magnet, Earth has a magnetic field. Earth also has a north magnetic pole and a south magnetic pole. Earth's magnetic poles can attract another magnet, such as the needle of a compass.

It Has a Magnetic Field

Active Reading **11 Identify** As you read, underline the text that explains why Earth has a magnetic field.

As early as the 1600s, scientists hypothesized that Earth has a magnetic field. This was before the properties of magnets were understood. Scientists now think that Earth's inner structure produces its magnetic field. Earth has an inner core and an outer core. The inner core is made of solid metals. The outer core is made of liquid iron and nickel, which are ferromagnetic. As Earth rotates, the liquid outer core moves. Charged particles, including electrons, move in the liquid and form a magnetic field. The constant rotation keeps Earth magnetized. Earth's magnetic field is strongest near its poles.

Inquiry

12 Infer Earth's magnetic poles do not stay in the same place. After reading about what causes Earth's magnetic field, write a possible explanation for why Earth's magnetic poles move.

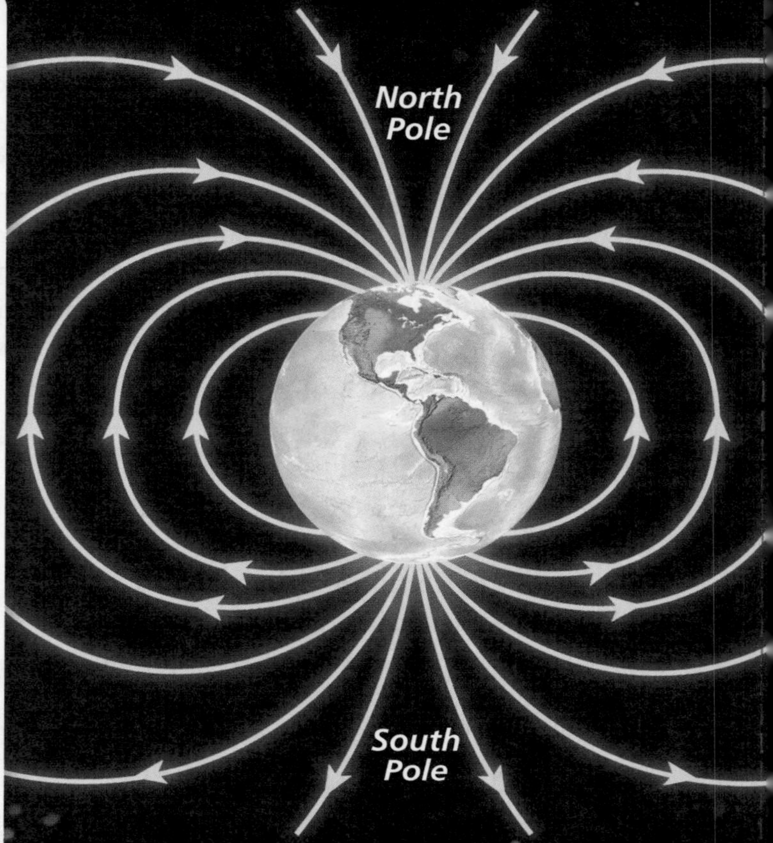
North Pole
South Pole

Like a magnet, Earth has magnetic poles and a magnetic field. Some animals may use Earth's magnetic field to navigate.

It Has Magnetic Poles

Earth's magnetic poles are not the same as Earth's geographic poles. The geographic poles mark the ends of Earth's axis. The geographic poles are near, but not exactly at, the magnetic poles. Navigators on airplanes and ships must take this small difference into account.

How can the north end of a compass point to the north magnetic pole? A compass needle is a magnet. If like poles repel, why do they not repel each other? The "north" pole of a magnet gets its name because it points toward Earth's geographic North Pole. A better term for the north pole of a magnet would be a "north-seeking" pole. Using these terms, the magnetic pole near Earth's North Pole is considered the south pole of a magnet. Likewise, the magnetic pole near Earth's South Pole is considered the north pole of a magnet.

Visualize It!

13 Illustrate Draw a bar magnet on the image o Earth to show Earth's magnetic poles.

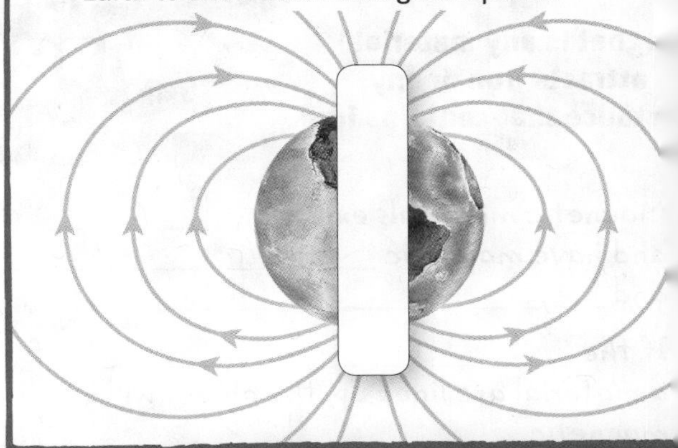

What is an aurora?

The beautiful displays of light that can be seen at northern or southern latitudes are related to Earth's magnetic field. The sun ejects charged particles. When they reach Earth, they are guided by its magnetic field. They enter Earth's upper atmosphere near the magnetic poles. There, the charged particles interact with atoms in the air, causing the atoms to emit visible light. This glow is called an *aurora*. In the Northern Hemisphere, an aurora is called an aurora borealis (bohr•ee•AL•is). In the Southern Hemisphere, it is called an aurora australis (aw•STRAY•lis).

This photo shows an aurora streaming across the night sky in Manitoba, Canada.

Visual Summary

To complete this summary, fill in each blank with the correct word or phrase. Then, use the key below to check your answers. You can use this page to review the main concepts of the lesson.

Magnets and Magnetism

A magnet is any material that attracts iron or any substance that contains iron.

14 Magnetic materials exert ______________ and have magnetic ______________ and ______________

15 If the ______________ of a material are lined up, the object will be magnetic.

There are different types of magnets.

16 A material such as iron is ______________

17 A(n) ______________ is a magnet produced by electricity.

18 An object can become a(n) ______________ magnet by rubbing the object with the end of a magnet.

Earth acts like a magnet because it has properties similar to those of magnets.

19 Earth has a ______________ and north and south ______________

Answers: 14 forces, poles, fields; 15 domains; 16 ferromagnetic; 17 electromagnet; 18 temporary; 19 magnetic field, magnetic poles

20 Synthesis Explain how a compass can be used to find north.

Lesson Review

Vocabulary

Draw a line to connect the following terms to their definitions.

1 magnet

2 magnetic force

3 magnetic pole

4 magnetic field

A a magnet's push or pull

B the end of a magnet where the force is the strongest

C the lines of force surrounding a magnet

D a metal object that attracts iron or nickel

Key Concepts

5 List What are three properties of a magnet?

6 Explain What causes some materials to have magnetic fields?

7 Identify List three types of magnets.

8 Describe How is Earth like a magnet?

9 Describe How do auroras form?

Critical Thinking

Use this drawing to answer the following question.

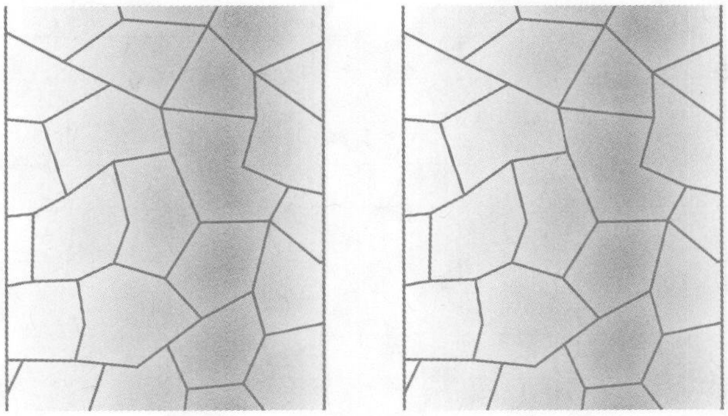

10 Illustrate The metal on the left has been magnetized, and the metal on the right has not. Draw the arrows in the domains of both.

11 Contrast What is the difference between the geographic North Pole and the magnetic north pole?

12 Explain If opposite poles repel each other, why does the north end of a compass point to the North Pole?

13 Apply Food manufacturers want to prevent small bits of metal from entering their product. How might magnets be used?

My Notes

Engineering Design Process

Skills
Identify a need
Conduct research
✔ Brainstorm solutions
✔ Select a solution
✔ Design a prototype
✔ Build a prototype
✔ Test and evaluate
✔ Redesign to improve
✔ Communicate results

Objectives
• Design an electric circuit to provide an answer to a problem.
• Test and modify a prototype circuit to achieve the desired result.

Building an Electric Circuit

Electric circuits are an essential part of many devices and technologies. Automobiles, televisions, digital watches, music players, cell phones, computers, and sports scoreboards all function, in part, because of carefully designed circuits.

This robotic device contains a number of electric circuits.

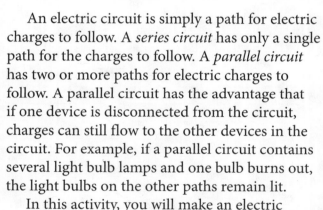

An electric circuit is simply a path for electric charges to follow. A *series circuit* has only a single path for the charges to follow. A *parallel circuit* has two or more paths for electric charges to follow. A parallel circuit has the advantage that if one device is disconnected from the circuit, charges can still flow to the other devices in the circuit. For example, if a parallel circuit contains several light bulb lamps and one bulb burns out, the light bulbs on the other paths remain lit.

In this activity, you will make an electric circuit of conducting wires, batteries, lamps, and switches. A switch can form a break in the circuit to stop the flow of electric charges and turn a device, such as a lamp, on and off.

1 Infer Do you think the lights in your home are wired in series circuits or parallel circuits? Explain.

Modeling an Electric Circuit

Sketching a complex circuit could take a lot of time and expertise. Circuits are often drawn using simple symbols so that models or plans are easier to create and easier to read. You can use symbols like the ones shown below to show parts of a circuit such as wire, lamps, and switches.

2 Apply Compare the series circuit diagram shown on the left to the art of a series circuit on the right. Then, label the symbols in the circuit diagram with *wire, lamp,* or *energy source.*

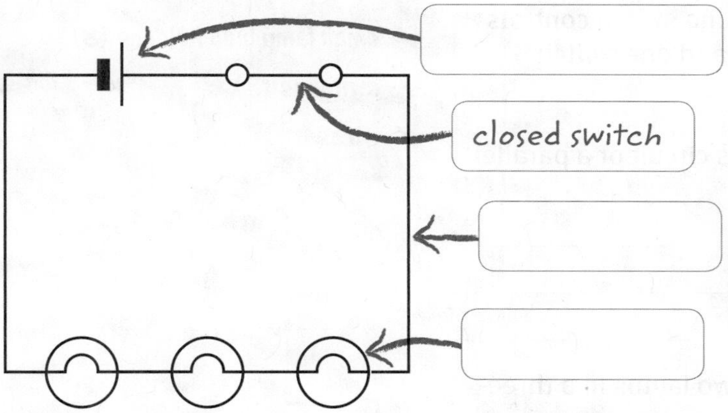

closed switch

BATTERY

3 Apply Complete this parallel circuit diagram by drawing in the symbols for the missing switch and energy source.

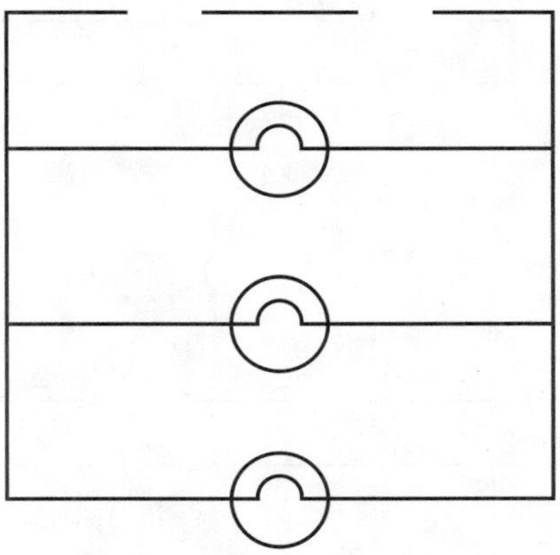

BATTERY

4 Explain What will happen if a light bulb is unscrewed from a lamp in the series circuit? What will happen if a light bulb is unscrewed from a lamp in the parallel circuit?

____

____

____

You Try It!

Now it's your turn to model and build a simple electric circuit.

You Try It!

Now it's your turn to model and build a simple electric circuit with three light bulb lamps and three switches.

You Will Need

- ✔ batteries
- ✔ battery holders
- ✔ masking tape or duct tape
- ✔ small lamp bulbs, 1.5 V (3)
- ✔ small lamp bulb holders (3)
- ✔ switches (3)
- ✔ wires

1 Brainstorm Solutions

Brainstorm ideas for a simple circuit that lights up three light bulbs. The setup must include three switches so that one switch controls only one lamp, one switch controls two lamps, and one switch controls all three lamps.

A How will you decide whether to build a series circuit or a parallel circuit?

____

____

____

B How can a switch turn on or off only one or two lamps in a three-lamp circuit?

____

____

____

2 Select a Solution

Which of your ideas seems to offer the best promise for success?

____

____

3 Design a Prototype

In the space below, draw a circuit diagram for your three-lamp prototype. Be sure to include all the parts you will need, and show how they will be connected.

4 Build a Prototype

Now assemble your three-lamp circuit with the switches in place. Are there some parts of your design that cannot be assembled as you had predicted? What parts did you have to revise?

5 Test and Evaluate

Open and close the switches and see what happens. Did one switch turn all the lamps on and off? Did the other two switches control only one or two lamps as predicted? If not, what parts of your setup could you revise?

6 Redesign to Improve

Keep making revisions until your switches control only the specified number of lamps. What kinds of revisions did you have to make?

7 Communicate Results

In the space below, sketch a diagram of the successful circuit.

Lesson 5

Electromagnetism

When the strings on this guitar vibrate, small magnets in the pickups convert the vibrations into electrical signals.
pickups

ESSENTIAL QUESTION

What is electromagnetism?

By the end of this lesson, you should be able to describe the relationship between electricity and magnetism and how this relationship affects our world.

Lesson Labs

Quick Labs
- Building an Electromagnet
- Making an Electric Generator

S.T.E.M. Lab
- Building a Speaker

Engage Your Brain

1 Predict Check T or F to show whether you think each statement is true or false.

T	F	
☐	☐	A moving magnetic field can produce electricity.
☐	☐	Electricity can produce a magnetic field.
☐	☐	Electricity and magnetism are the same thing.

2 Describe An electromagnet is a magnet produced from electric current. Describe what is happening in the photo.

____

____

Active Reading

3 Apply Many scientific words, such as *induction*, also have everyday meanings. Use context clues to write your own definition for each meaning of *induction*.

Example sentence
There was a party after the baseball star's induction into the Hall of Fame.

induction:

____

____

Example sentence
Induction occurs when a wire moving near a magnet gains an electric current.

induction:

____

____

____

Vocabulary Terms

- **electromagnetism**
- **solenoid**
- **electromagnet**
- **electric motor**
- **electromagnetic induction**
- **transformer**
- **electric generator**

4 Apply As you learn the definition of each vocabulary term in this lesson, create your own definition or sketch to help you remember the meaning of the term.

MAGNETIC ATTRACTION

What is electromagnetism?

Electromagnetism is a relationship between electricity and magnetism. **Electromagnetism** results when electric currents and magnetic fields interact with each other.

The compasses show that an electric current produces a circular magnetic field around the wire.

The Interaction Between Magnets and Electricity

In 1820, physicist Hans Christian Oersted of Denmark made an interesting discovery by accident. He discovered that there is a connection between electricity and magnetism. No one at the time knew that electricity and magnetism were related. One day while preparing for a lecture, he brought a compass close to a wire carrying an electric current. Oersted was surprised to see the compass needle move. A compass needle is a magnet. It usually points north because of Earth's magnetic field. However, the compass moved because it was affected by a magnetic field other than Earth's.

Magnetism Produced by Electricity

Active Reading **5 Identify** As you read, underline what caused Oersted's compass needle to move.

When the current is turned off, the needles align with Earth's magnetic field.

Oersted hypothesized that it was the electric current in the wire that had produced the magnetic field. He then did more experiments with electricity and magnetism. He found that when the wire is carrying a current, a magnetic field is produced around the wire. You can see this in the photograph on the top left. When the current is turned off, as shown in the bottom photograph, the magnetic field disappears. The compasses again point north.

Oersted found that the direction of the electric current also affects the magnetic field. Current in one direction caused a compass needle to move clockwise. Current in the other direction caused the compass needle to move counterclockwise. Oersted's hypothesis was confirmed.

How can you make a magnet using current?

An electric current in a single loop of wire produces a weak magnetic field. You can make a more powerful magnet by making a solenoid or an electromagnet.

With a Solenoid

A coil of wire that carries an electric current, and therefore produces a magnetic field, is called a **solenoid** (SOH•luh•noyd). The more loops, the stronger the magnetic field. A solenoid's magnetic field acts like a bar magnet. Increasing the number of loops or the current increases the strength of the magnetic field.

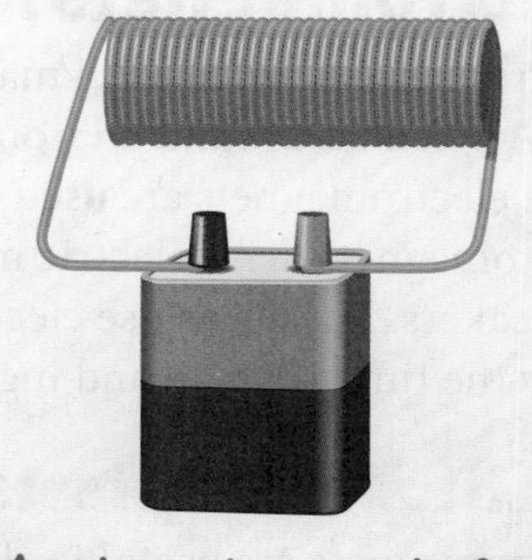

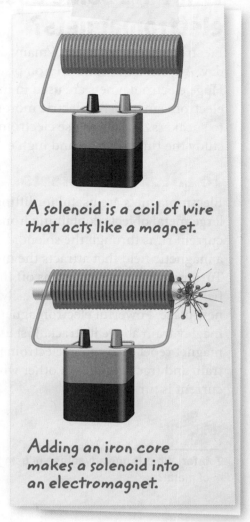

A solenoid is a coil of wire that acts like a magnet.

With an Electromagnet

Wrapping a solenoid around an iron core makes an **electromagnet**. An electromagnet combines the magnetic field of the solenoid with the magnetic field of the magnetized iron core. This combination creates a more powerful magnetic field than the solenoid alone. You can make it stronger by adding loops to the solenoid or increasing the current.

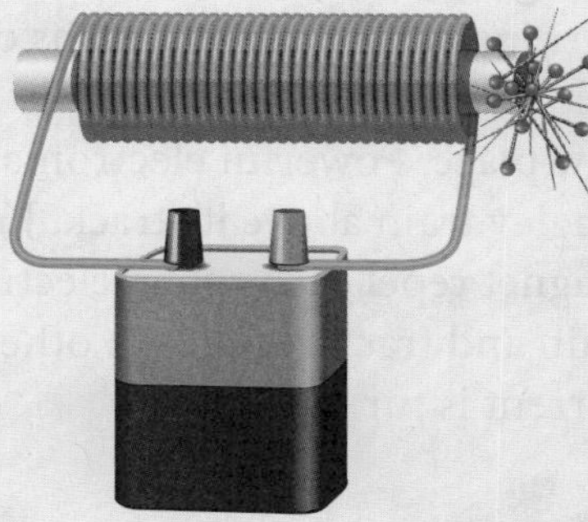

Adding an iron core makes a solenoid into an electromagnet.

Active Reading **6 Solve** What benefit is gained by the addition of the iron core in an electromagnet?

____

____

____

SMT
Shanghai Transrapid

Electromagnets lift this maglev train off the tracks and move it forward.

What are some uses for electromagnets?

Electromagnets are used in many devices that you may use every day. A solenoid around an iron piston makes a doorbell ring. Huge electromagnets are used in industry to move metal. Small electromagnets drive electric motors in objects from hair dryers to speakers. Physicists use electromagnets in "atom smashers" to study the tiny particles and high energies that make up an atom.

To Lift Metal Objects

Electromagnets are useful for lifting and moving large metal objects containing iron. When current runs through the solenoid coils, it creates a magnetic field that attracts the metal objects. Turning off the current turns off the magnetic field so that the metal can be easily dropped in a new place. Powerful electromagnets can raise a maglev train above its track. Just as poles of a bar magnet repel each other, electromagnets in the train and track repel each other when the electric current is turned on.

To Measure Current

A *galvanometer* (gal•vuh•NAHM•ih•ter) is a device that measures the strength and direction of an electric current in a wire. A galvanometer contains an electromagnet between the poles of a permanent magnet, such as a horseshoe magnet. When current is applied to the electromagnet, the two magnetic fields interact and cause the electromagnet to turn. The indicator, attached to the electromagnet, moves to one side of the zero on the scale, indicating the strength and direction of the current. The parts of a simple galvanometer are shown below.

Inquiry

7 Infer What is one advantage of using an electromagnet to move loads of metal?

____

____

Industrial electromagnets can lift tons of metal.

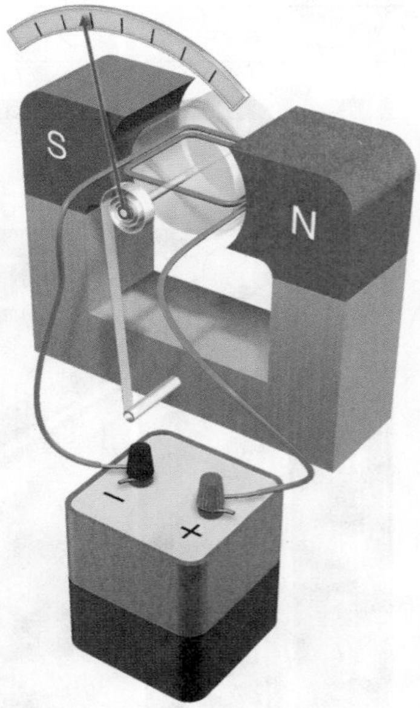
S
N
–
+

The indicator on a galvanometer shows current direction and strength.

Why It Matters

HEALTH WATCH

A Look Inside

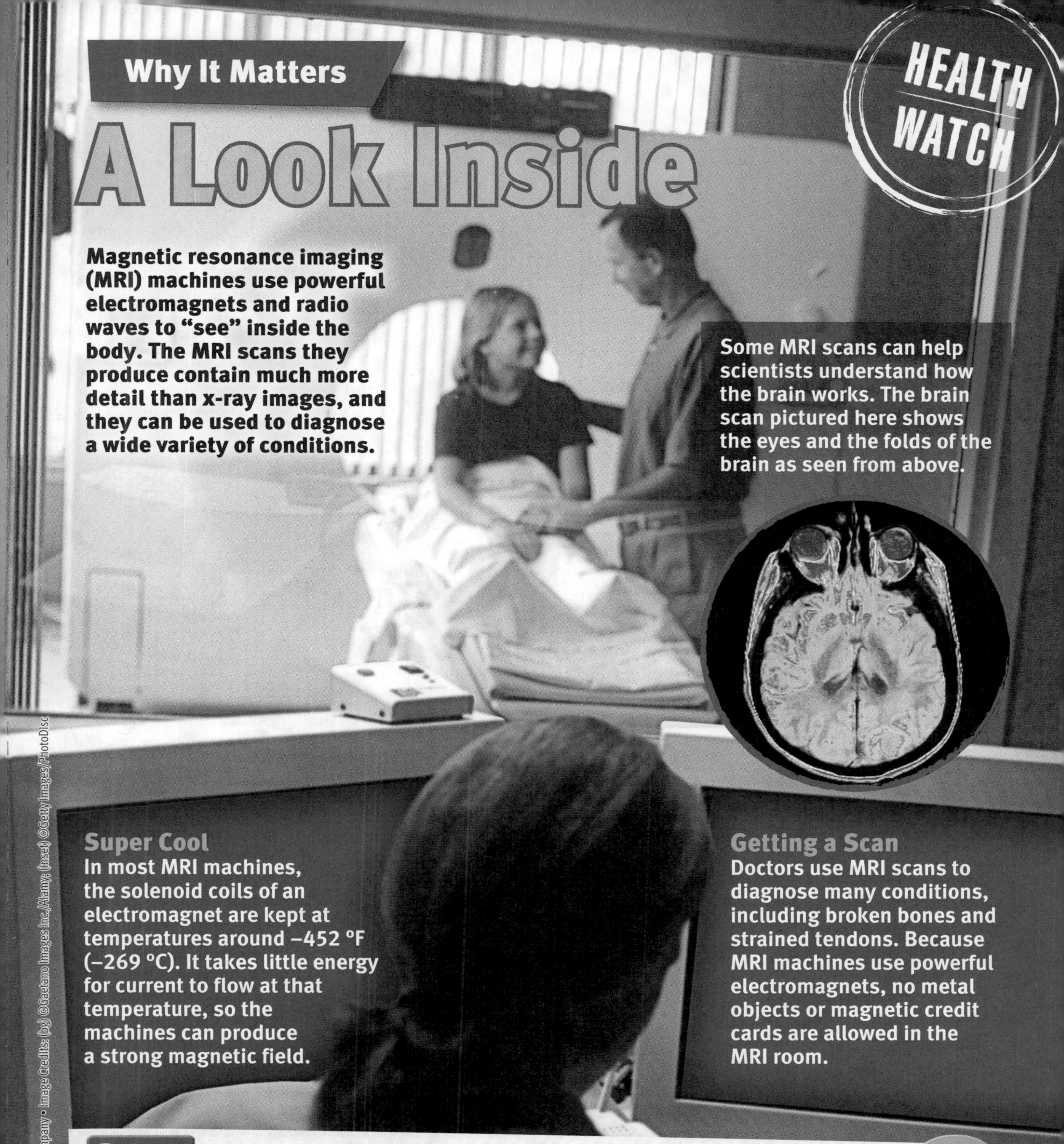

Magnetic resonance imaging (MRI) machines use powerful electromagnets and radio waves to "see" inside the body. The MRI scans they produce contain much more detail than x-ray images, and they can be used to diagnose a wide variety of conditions.

Some MRI scans can help scientists understand how the brain works. The brain scan pictured here shows the eyes and the folds of the brain as seen from above.

Super Cool

In most MRI machines, the solenoid coils of an electromagnet are kept at temperatures around −452 °F (−269 °C). It takes little energy for current to flow at that temperature, so the machines can produce a strong magnetic field.

Getting a Scan

Doctors use MRI scans to diagnose many conditions, including broken bones and strained tendons. Because MRI machines use powerful electromagnets, no metal objects or magnetic credit cards are allowed in the MRI room.

Extend

Inquiry

8 Explain Why are the electromagnets in MRIs kept at very low temperatures?

9 Infer Why are electromagnets, rather than permanent magnets, used in MRIs?

10 Research Investigate *magnetoencephalography* (mag•nee•toh•en•sef•uh•LAHG•ruh•fee), or MEG. Write about one way in which it is being used.

LET'S MOTOR!

How do motors work?

One of the most common places to find an electromagnet is in a motor. An **electric motor** changes electrical energy into mechanical energy. Some electric motors run on direct current (DC), while others are designed to use alternating current (AC). Electric motors range in size from large motors, used to power a Ferris wheel, to small motors used in computer cooling fans. Almost every time a device uses electricity to make something move, there is a motor involved.

Visualize It!

11 List Make a list of all the items in this photo that you think might use motors.

____

____

____

____

Motors Use Electromagnets

Electric motors are very similar to galvanometers. The main difference is that, in a motor, the electromagnet is made to rotate all the way around instead of back and forth in the magnetic field.

A simple motor has a coil or loop of wire called an armature (AR•muh•chur) mounted between the poles of a magnet. The armature becomes an electromagnet when current passes through it. The armature rotates because its poles are pushed and pulled by the opposite poles of the magnet. The armature turns until its north pole is opposite the magnet's south pole. Then, a device called a commutator reverses the direction of the current in the wire, causing the armature to complete its turn.

Visualize It!

Current in the armature causes the magnet to exert force on the armature, making it rotate.

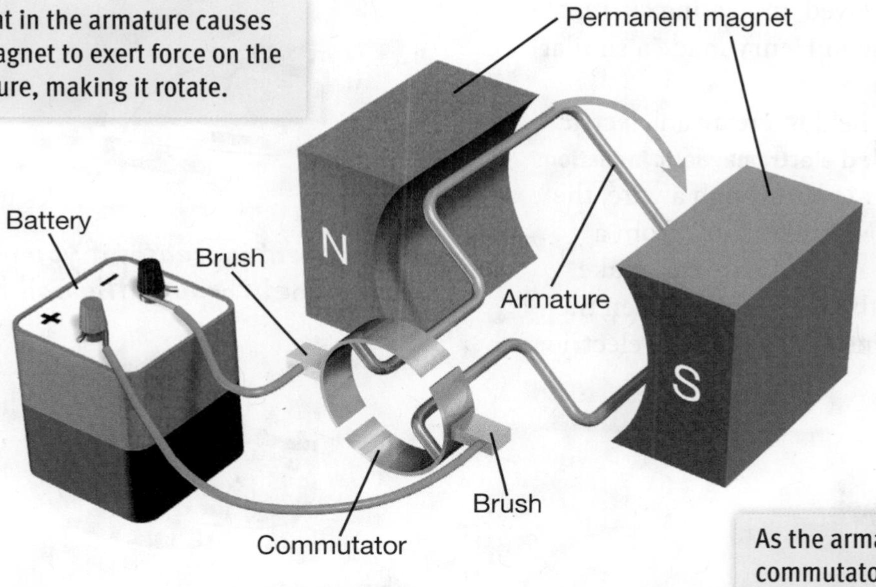
Permanent magnet
Battery
Brush
N
Armature
S
Brush
Commutator

As the armature rotates, the commutator causes the current to change direction. This reverses the direction of force and keeps the armature rotating.

12 Compare Analyze the illustration of the motor, and compare it to the galvanometer on the previous spread. Explain how they are alike.

____

____

____

____

____

____

A NEW GENERATION

What are some uses for induction?

Electric current can produce a magnetic field. In the early 1830s, scientists wondered if the opposite is true. Can a magnetic field create an electric current? English scientist Michael Faraday showed that it could. He connected a galvanometer to a wire coil. When he moved a magnet back and forth inside the coil, the galvanometer needle moved, indicating current. American physicist Joseph Henry made a similar discovery.

Using a magnetic field to create an electric current in a wire is called **electromagnetic induction**. When electric charges move through a wire, the wire carries a current. Magnetic force from a magnet moving inside a coil of wire can make the electric charges in the wire move. When the magnet stops moving inside the coil, the electric current stops.

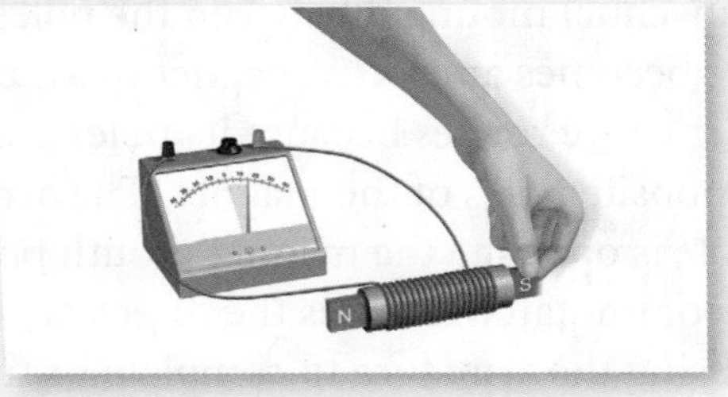

An electric current is induced when you move a magnet through a coil of wire.

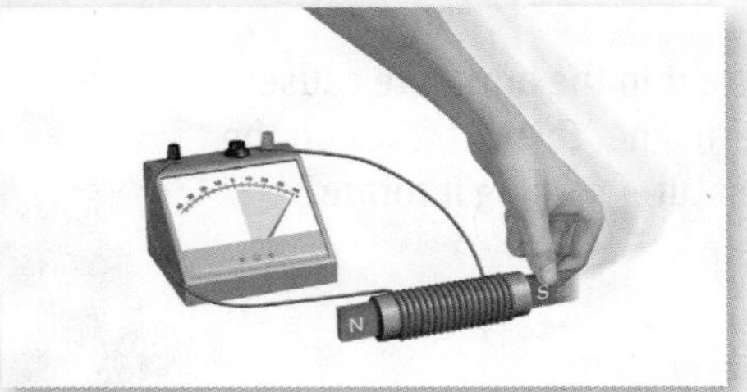

The current increases if you move the magnet through the coil faster.

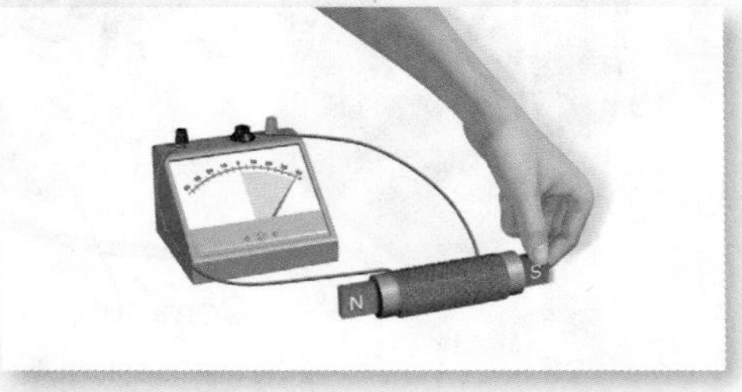

The current also increases if you add more loops of wire.

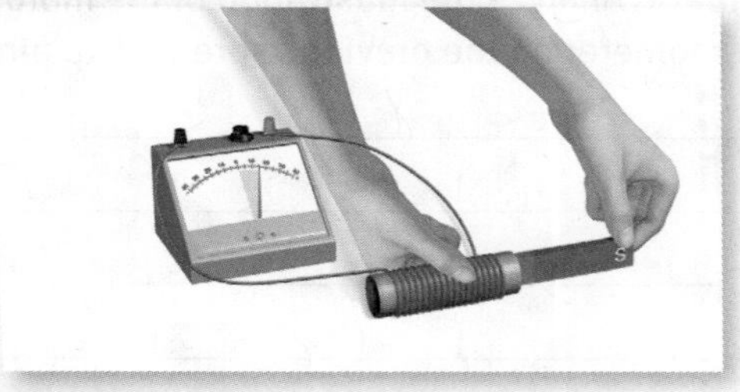

The current can also be induced by reversing the motion—moving the coil over the magnet.

Visualize It!

13 State What are two ways to increase the current in the wire?

____

____

____

____

14 Predict What would happen to the current if the magnet and coil were not moving?

____

____

____

To Change Voltage

Active Reading

15 Identify As you read, underline the sentence that explains the purpose of transformers.

An important device that relies on electromagnetic induction is a transformer. **Transformers** use induction to increase or decrease the voltage of alternating current. For example, transformers on power lines increase voltage to send it miles away and then decrease it for a single home. Most transformers are iron "rings" with two coils of wire. The current in the wire on the primary side makes an electromagnet. Because the current alternates, the magnetic field changes. This induces a current in the wire on the secondary side.

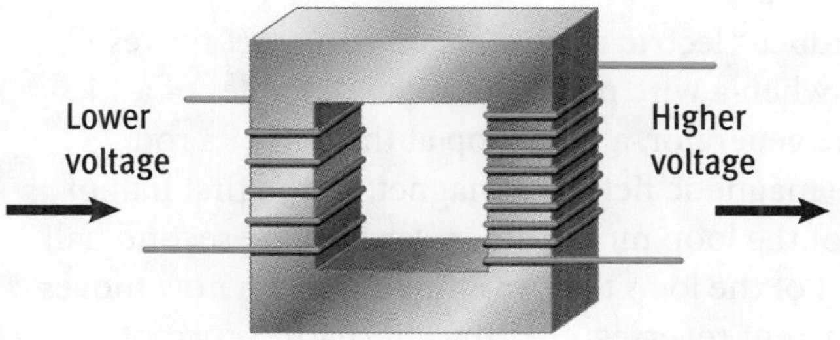
Step-Up Transformer
Lower voltage
Higher voltage

In a step-up transformer, there are more turns of wire on the secondary side.

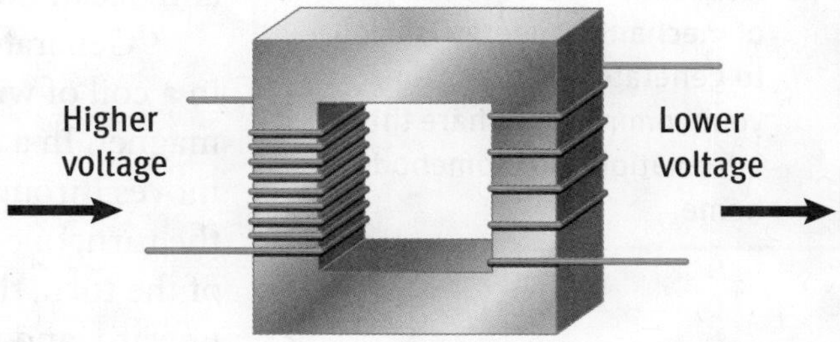
Step-Down Transformer
Higher voltage
Lower voltage

In a step-down transformer, there are more turns of wire on the primary side.

Do the Math

Sample Problem

Imagine the voltage on the primary side of a step-down transformer is 300 volts and the wire has 1,200 turns. The wire on the secondary side has 720 turns. What is the voltage on the secondary side?

The number of volts to wire turns on a transformer coil can be expressed as a ratio. This ratio is equal for both sides of the transformer. Cross-multiply to find the answer to the problem.

$$\frac{\textbf{300}\text{ volts}}{\textbf{1,200}\text{ turns}} = \frac{\textbf{X}\text{ volts}}{\textbf{720}\text{ turns}}$$

$300 \times 720 = 216{,}000$

$216{,}000 / 1{,}200 = 180$

$X = 180$

Answer: 180 volts

You Try It

16 Calculate The voltage on the primary side of a step-down transformer is 500 volts, and the wire has 1,500 turns. The wire on the secondary side has 600 turns. What is the voltage on the secondary side?

To Generate Electricity

Did you know that most of the electricity you use every day comes from electromagnetic induction? **Electric generators** use induction to change mechanical energy into electrical energy. You can think of electric generators as being the "opposite" of electric motors.

In all different types of power plants, mechanical energy is used to rotate turbines. The turbines turn magnets inside coils of wire, generating electricity. Many power plants use rising steam to turn the turbines. The steam is produced from burning fossil fuels or using nuclear reactions to heat water. Other sources of mechanical energy to turn turbines are blowing wind, falling water, and ocean tides and waves.

Generators induce electric current when a magnet moves in a coil of wire or when a wire moves between the poles of a magnet. In a simple generator, a wire loop at the end of a rod moves through the magnetic field of a magnet. In the first half of the turn, one side of the loop moves downward. In the second half of the turn, the part of the loop that was moving down now moves upward, and the current reverses, creating alternating current.

Think Outside the Book

17 Research Find out what type of mechanical energy is used to generate electricity for your community. Share this information with somebody at home.

Active Reading **18 Summarize** How does the function of a generator relate to the function of a motor?

____

____

Generating Electricity

A generator induces electric current in wire that is moving in a magnetic field. A crank would be used to turn the wire in this generator.

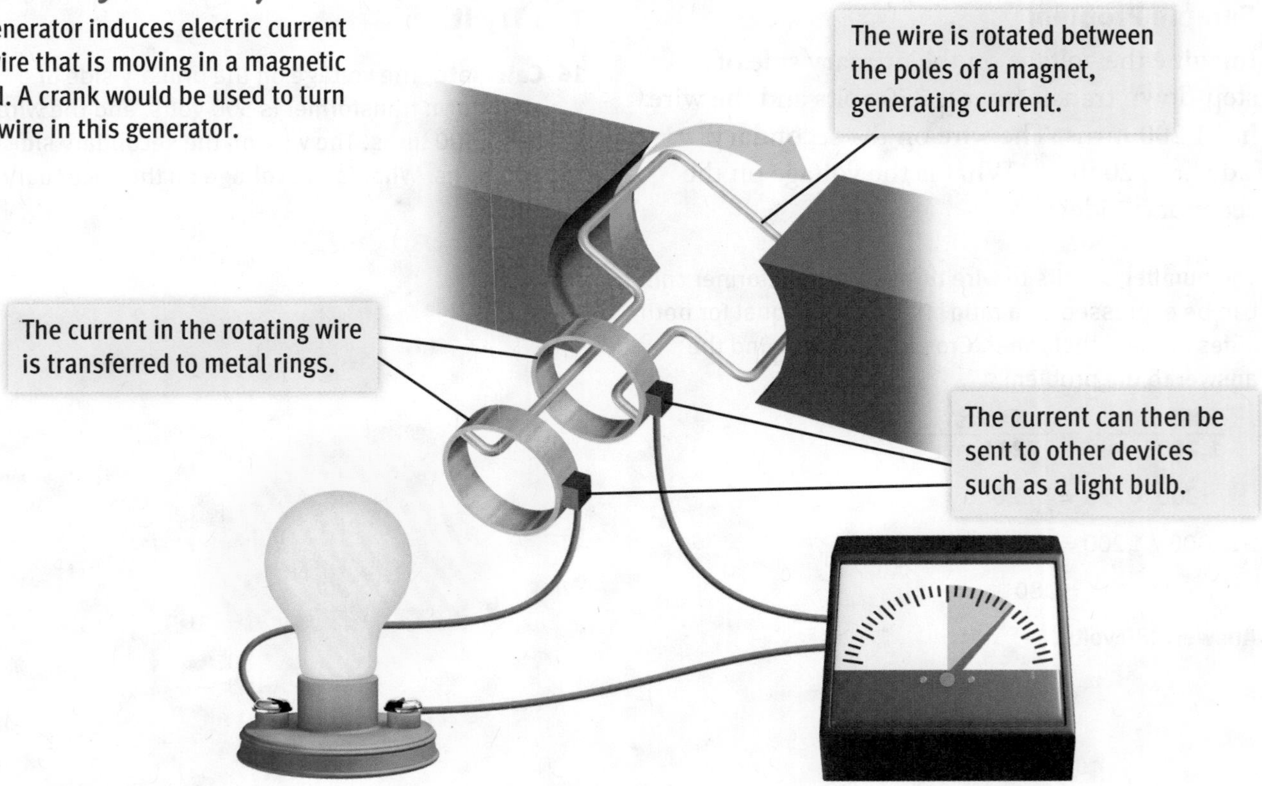
The wire is rotated between the poles of a magnet, generating current.
The current in the rotating wire is transferred to metal rings.
The current can then be sent to other devices such as a light bulb.

19 Diagram Fill in the chart below to help you organize the key concepts from this lesson.

Electromagnetism

Definition:

Uses:
maglev train
motor

Electromagnetic induction

Definition:

Uses:

Visual Summary

To complete this summary, check the box that indicates true or false. Then, use the key below to check your answers. You can use this page to review the main concepts of the lesson.

Electromagnetism is magnetism that results from electric current.

	T	F	
20	☐	☐	Solenoids are magnetic.
21	☐	☐	The strength of an electromagnet decreases when you increase the current.
22	☐	☐	You can increase the number of coils to make an electromagnet stronger.
23	☐	☐	Electromagnets are used to lift heavy metal items.
24	☐	☐	Motors use electromagnets to produce movement.

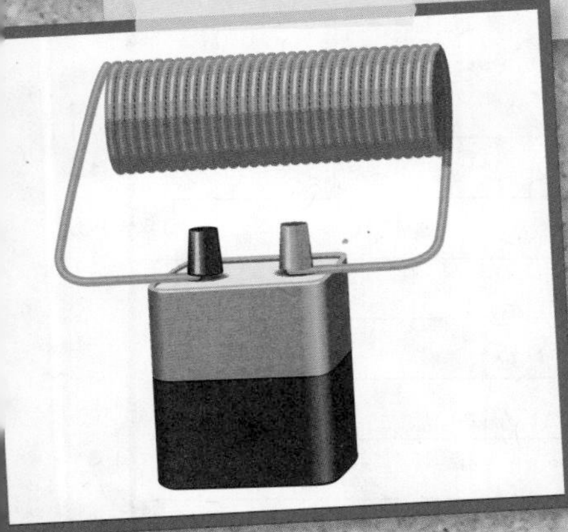

Electromagnetism

Electromagnetic induction is electric current that results from magnetism.

	T	F	
25	☐	☐	Generators use induction to produce electricity.
26	☐	☐	Transformers detect electric current.

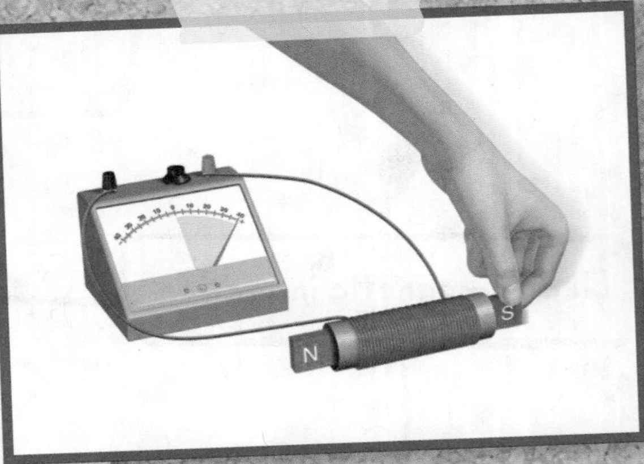
N
S

Answers: 20 True; 21 False; 22 True; 23 True; 24 True; 25 True; 26 False

27 Synthesis Describe how you could use a motor in reverse to generate electricity.

Lesson Review

Vocabulary

Fill in the blank with the term that best completes the following sentences.

1 A(n) ______________________ is a coil of wire that produces a magnetic field when it carries an electric current.

2 A(n) ______________________ changes mechanical energy into electrical energy by means of electromagnetic induction.

3 A(n) ______________________ changes electrical energy into mechanical energy.

Key Concepts

4 Relate How do electricity and magnetism interact?

5 Describe Describe how turning off the electric current in an industrial electromagnet affects its magnetic field.

6 Predict What effect would increasing the number of loops in a coil of wire have on an electromagnet?

7 Summarize How can a magnetic field be used to create an electric current?

8 Identify List three everyday devices that could not have been developed without the discovery of electromagnetism.

Critical Thinking

9 Infer If Faraday had used a more powerful battery in his experiments with electromagnetic induction, what effect would this have had on his galvanometer's measurements of current when the battery was fully connected? Explain your reasoning.

Use the diagram to answer the following questions.

10 Illustrate Draw how the coils would look on a step-up transformer.

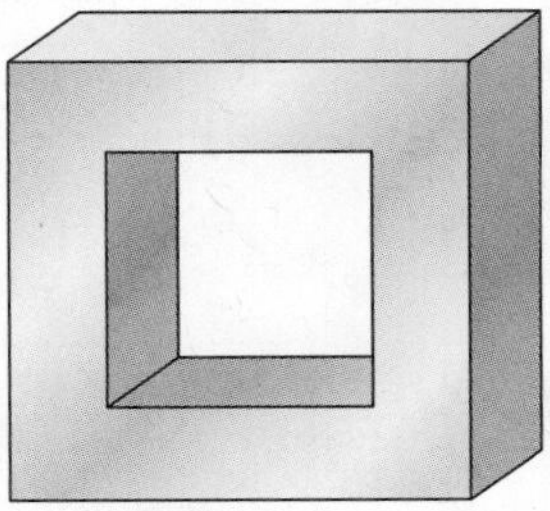

11 Identify On which side would the voltage be higher?

12 Describe How would the illustration look if it were showing a step-down transformer?

My Notes

Lesson 6

Electronic Technology

ESSENTIAL QUESTION

What are electronics, and how have they changed?

By the end of this lesson, you should be able to describe what electronic devices do and how they change as technology changes.

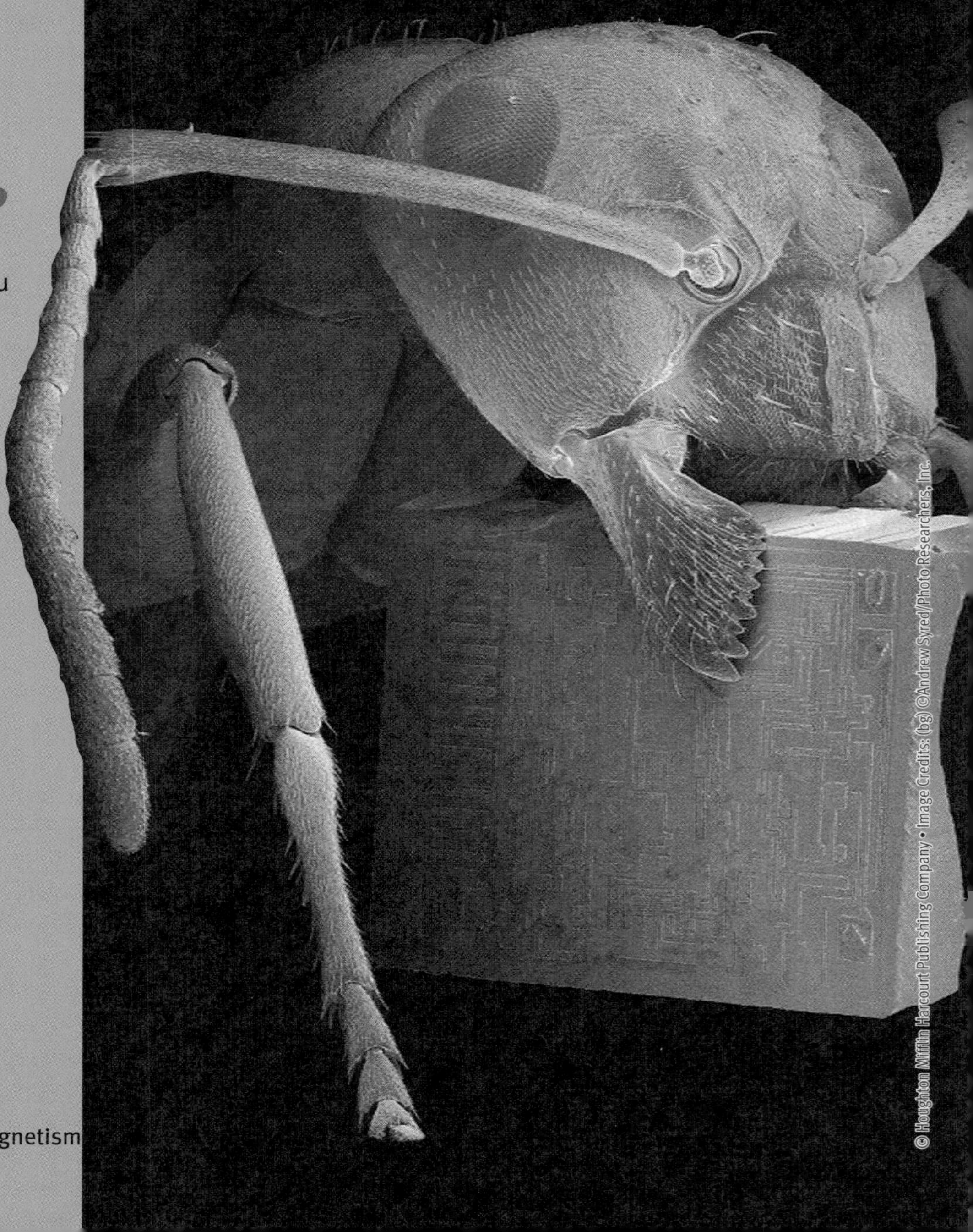

This microchip is small enough to fit inside the mandibles of an ant!

Lesson Labs

Quick Labs
- The Speed of a Simple Computer
- Investigate Satellite Imaging

Engage Your Brain

1 Predict Check T or F to show whether you think each statement is true or false.

T	F	
☐	☐	Electrical devices and electronic devices are the same.
☐	☐	Electronic technology affects the way people work, play, and communicate.
☐	☐	Codes, which used to be an important part of communication between humans, are no longer used.

2 List Make a list of as many electronic devices as you can think of.

Active Reading

3 Apply Many scientific words, such as *digit,* also have everyday meanings. Use context clues to write your own definition for each meaning of *digit.*

Example sentence
She wore a ring on the fourth digit of her left hand.

digit:

Example sentence
I made a mistake when I wrote the last digit of the phone number.

digit:

Vocabulary Terms

- **electronic device**
- **integrated circuit**
- **analog signal**
- **digital signal**
- **computer**

4 Apply As you learn the definition of each vocabulary term in this lesson, write down your own definition or make a sketch to help you remember the meaning of the term.

Speaking in Code

What are electronics?

Electronic devices like computers are not the same as electrical devices like toasters. Both use electrical energy. But electronic devices can perform more sophisticated tasks than electrical devices can. **Electronic devices** are able to control the flow of electrons using *integrated circuits*. An **integrated circuit** is a single, tiny chip of specially treated silicon containing many circuit parts. Integrated circuits carry out instructions, or programs, by controlling current.

A TV remote control is an example of an electronic device. Imagine that you push a button on the remote control to change the channel. A signal goes to integrated circuits inside the remote control. The circuits process the information and send an infrared signal to the TV. The signal tells the TV to change channels.

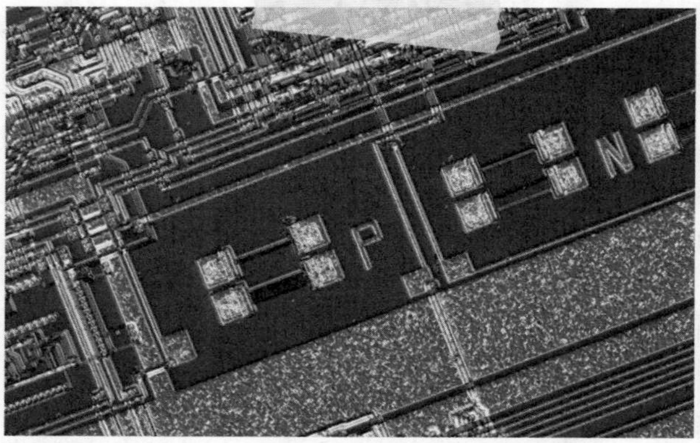

Integrated circuits, or microchips, are tiny silicon-based chips that can process information.

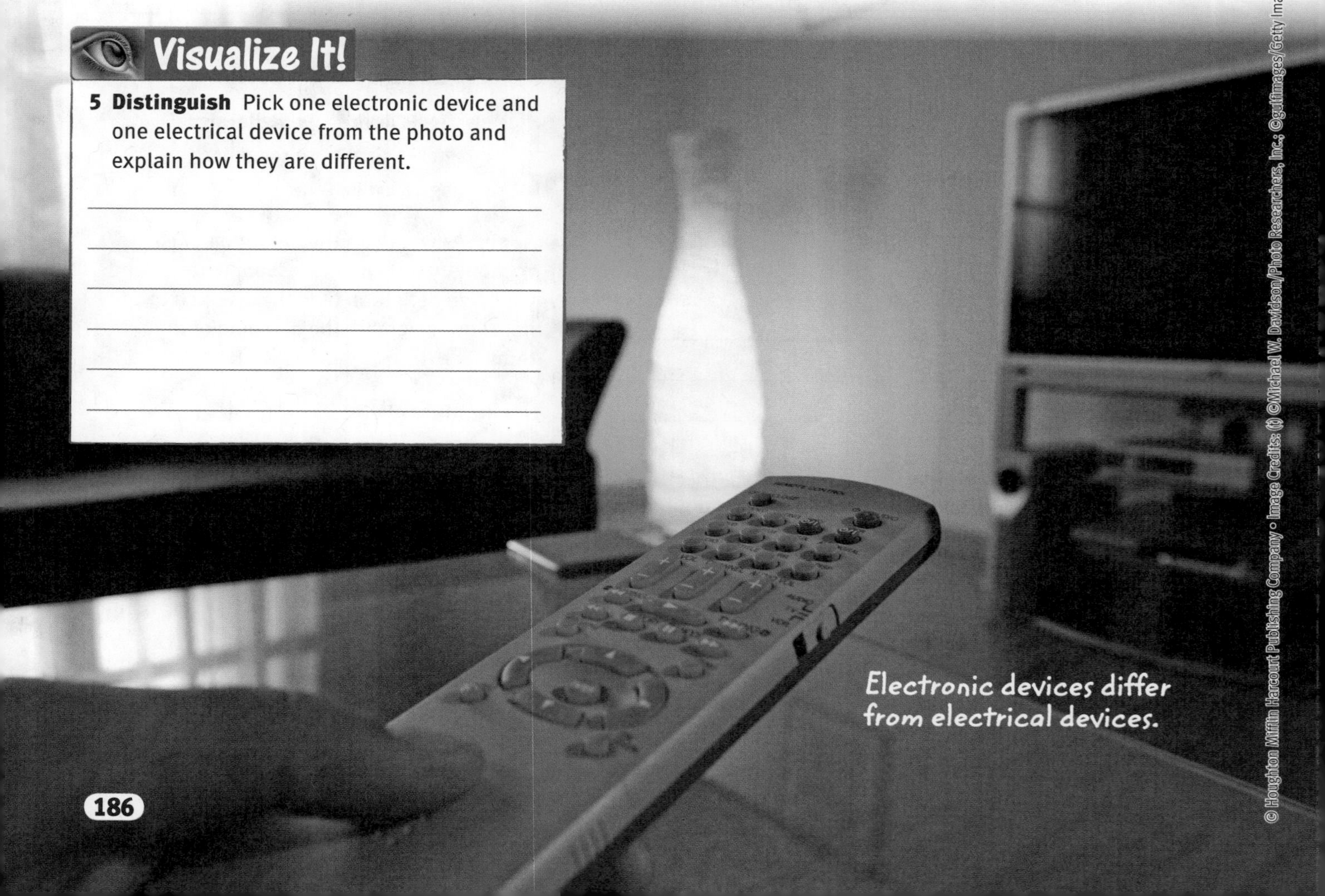

Visualize It!

5 Distinguish Pick one electronic device and one electrical device from the photo and explain how they are different.

Electronic devices differ from electrical devices.

How can information be coded?

A signal is a pattern that contains coded information. For example, when you speak, information is coded in the pattern of sounds you make. Your voice is the carrier of the signal, and a listener interprets it. Morse code is a signal that uses dashes and dots to represent letters of the alphabet. People used to send telegraph messages in Morse code using wires as the carrier. Electronics also use coded signals. The two kinds of signals they use are *analog signals* and *digital signals*.

Morse Code

A •–	B –•••	C –•–•	D –••
E •	F ••–•	G ––•	H ••••
I ••	J •–––	K –•–	L •–••
M ––	N –•	O –––	P •––•
Q ––•–	R •–•	S •••	T –
U ••–	V •••–	W •––	X –••–
	Y –•––	Z ––••	

As an Analog Signal

Signals that change continuously in a given range are called **analog signals**. For example, a dimmer switch sends an analog electrical signal to a light fixture. You slide a dimmer switch up or down in one continuous motion. As you move the switch up or down, the amount of electric current supplied to the lighting goes up or down. If you move the switch just a little bit, the lighting changes just a little bit. A record also produces an analog signal. A record needle moves up and down continuously as it moves over a record's grooves. The up-and-down movements are turned into sound waves by the record player. As the record groove changes, the sound changes.

Think Outside the Book *Inquiry*

7 Apply With a classmate, come up with a carrier that you can use to send Morse code. Then use the Morse code chart to send each other a short message.

Visualize It!

6 Identify What are the carriers of the analog signals in the examples shown below?

____

____

A dimmer switch is an example of a device that sends an analog signal.

Recording Company
Long Playing
High Fidelity
side
1

Some people think the analog signals used by records and record players produce a richer sound than digital media.

CDs and DVDs use digital signals.

As a Digital Signal

Unlike an analog signal, such as the one used by the dimmer switch, a digital signal does not change continuously. A **digital signal** is a sequence of separate values. Like a regular light switch, it goes back and forth between on or off. Information in a digital signal is represented using a pattern called the *binary code* (BY•nuh•ree KOHD). Binary means "two." The digital binary code is made up of the two digits 1 and 0. In computers and other digital electronics, digital signals are carried by a series of on-off electric pulses. A 1 is encoded as a pulse. A 0 is encoded as no pulse.

An analog signal, like music, can be converted to a digital signal and stored on a compact disc (CD). The flat, reflecting layer of a CD is called the *land*. Data is recorded on the land in a spiral-shaped series of bumps called *pits*. Inside a computer or CD player, a laser shines light on a spinning CD. Pits are read as dark areas because they reflect light differently than the land does. The patterns of light and dark are interpreted as a digital signal that can be converted into your favorite song.

Active Reading **8 Contrast** How do digital signals differ from analog signals?

Binary Code

The binary code for the numbers 1 through 16 is shown below.

9 Predict What is the binary code for 17?

Number		Binary Code
0	=	0
1	=	1
2	=	10
3	=	11
4	=	100
5	=	101
6	=	110
7	=	111
8	=	1000
9	=	1001
10	=	1010
11	=	1011
12	=	1100
13	=	1101
14	=	1110
15	=	1111
16	=	10000

17 =

Think of how much information a computer can process. And it's all processed using only two digits!

Do the Math

Digital images, like this picture of a giraffe, are created using digital signals. The lens of a digital camera focuses light onto a computer chip inside the camera. The chip stores digital data about the light in binary code.

You Try It

10 Calculate In computer terms, a *bit* is a binary digit, either a one or a zero. A *byte* is a string of 8 bits, and there are 1,000,000 bytes in a megabyte (MB). Suppose you are sending a picture that is 2.6 MB. How many 1s and 0s (bits) is that? *(Hint: Use multiplication.)*

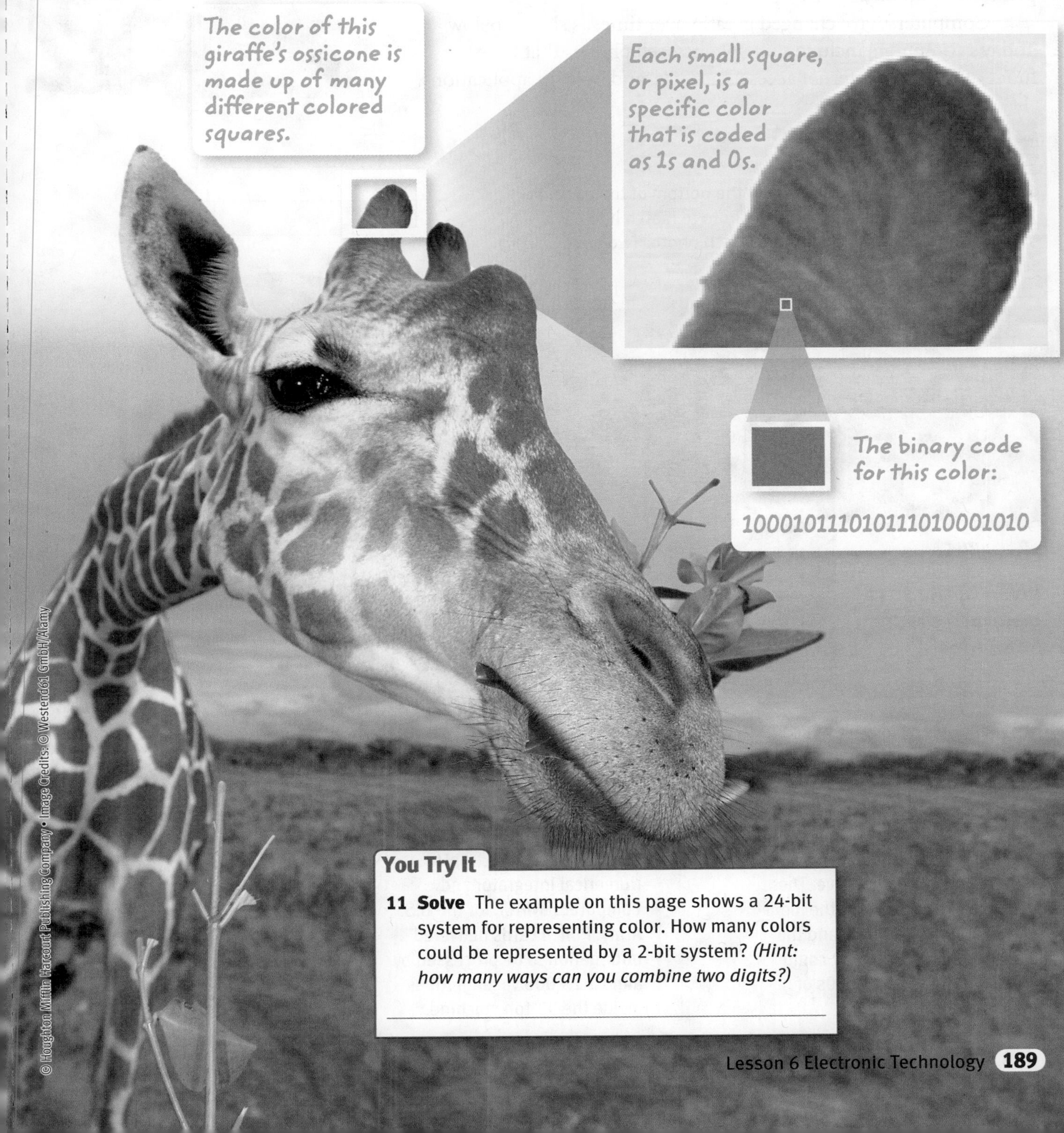

The color of this giraffe's ossicone is made up of many different colored squares.
Each small square, or pixel, is a specific color that is coded as 1s and 0s.
The binary code for this color:
100010111010111010001010

You Try It

11 Solve The example on this page shows a 24-bit system for representing color. How many colors could be represented by a 2-bit system? *(Hint: how many ways can you combine two digits?)*

____

The Incredible

How have computers changed?

A **computer** is any electronic device that performs tasks by following instructions given to it. Computers receive information, called *input*, through keyboards, touchscreens, or other devices. The input can be processed through a central processor or stored in memory. Computers output information through monitors, printers, or other devices.

Computers have changed greatly over time, as shown below. Today's computers include *smartphones*, cell phones that have functions such as Internet access, cameras, and built-in applications.

____

____

____

____

Visualize It!

12 Sequence Read the timeline at the bottom of the page. Write a letter and year on each photo to match it to its description. Write a label for each photo. Two have been completed for you.

B 1945

ENIAC, the first general-purpose computer

____

____

____

____

1800

A In 1801, French weaver Joseph Marie Jacquard invented wooden punch cards to program which pattern a loom would weave. The presence of a hole meant the loom needle could go through, and the absence of a hole meant it could not, similar to the 1s and 0s of modern software.

1945

B In 1945, engineers completed one of the first general-purpose computers, the Electronic Numerical Integrator and Computer (ENIAC), for the U.S. Army. Punch cards delivered information to be processed by almost 18,000 vacuum tubes inside the 33-ton machine.

C In 1958, developers introduced the integrated circuit, which allowed the development of much smaller computers.

Shrinking Computer

C 1958

The first integrated circuit

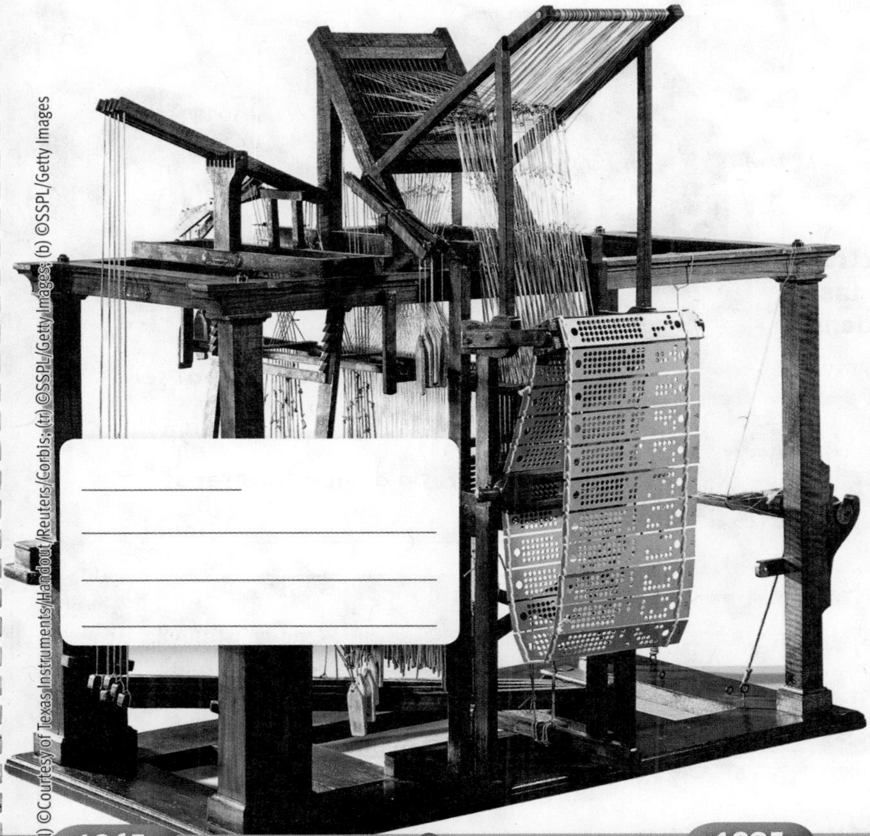

Think Outside the Book **Inquiry**

13 Create Design a new electronic device for tomorrow's classrooms. Create a poster describing the advantages of your technology.

1965 — 1985 — 2005

D In 1965, the first commercially successful tabletop computer came on the market. It could sit on a table, but it was too expensive for home computing. It cost what the average person might earn in 15 years!

E In the mid-1970s, personal computers like those used today first appeared. They had monitors, keyboards, and hard drives. These computers could store, process, and output information for people in their homes or businesses.

F In the early 2000s, the first touchscreen smartphones came on the market. Smartphones combined the features of a telephone with a computer. People could make phone calls, send e-mail or messages, and surf the Internet from almost anywhere.

Visual Summary

To complete this summary, fill in each blank with the correct word or phrase. Then, use the key below to check your answers. You can use this page to review the main concepts of the lesson.

Electronic Technology

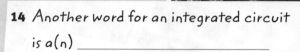

Electronic devices use integrated circuits to process information.

14 Another word for an integrated circuit is a(n) ______________________

15 A signal is carried by a(n) ______________________

Analog signals change continuously. Digital signals use the binary code, which is a pattern of 1s and 0s.

Recording Company

16 A dimmer switch is a device that sends a(n) ______________ signal.

17 A computer is a device that sends a(n) ______________ signal.

A computer is an electronic device that performs tasks by following instructions given to it.

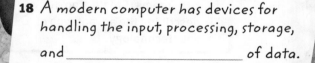

18 A modern computer has devices for handling the input, processing, storage, and ______________ of data.

Answers: 14 microchip; 15 carrier; 16 analog; 17 digital; 18 output

19 Synthesize Compare the dots and dashes of Morse code with the 1s and 0s of digital binary code. How are they alike and how are they different?

Lesson Review

Vocabulary

Draw a line to connect the following terms to their definitions.

1 electronic device

2 integrated circuit

3 computer

A a tiny circuit with many parts

B device for storing and processing data in binary form

C something that uses electrical energy to process information

Key Concepts

4 Describe Explain the difference between how a lamp and a TV use electrical energy.

5 Identify What device enabled computers to shrink from early models, such as ENIAC, to smartphones that fit in your hand?

6 Compare How do the components that processed information in the ENIAC compare with the components that process information in a modern laptop computer?

7 List What are the four basic functions of a modern computer?

Critical Thinking

8 Relate If water could be used to create digital signals using a drip into a pond as a 1 and no drip as a 0, what would the carrier be?

9 Explain Are digital signals the only signals that use binary code? Explain.

Use this photo to answer the following question.

10 Explain Identify the items shown above and explain the function of each item.

My Notes

Unit 3 Big Idea

An electric current can produce a magnetic field, and a magnetic field can produce an electric current.

Lesson 1
ESSENTIAL QUESTION
What makes something electrically charged?

Describe electric charges in objects and distinguish between electrical conductors and insulators.

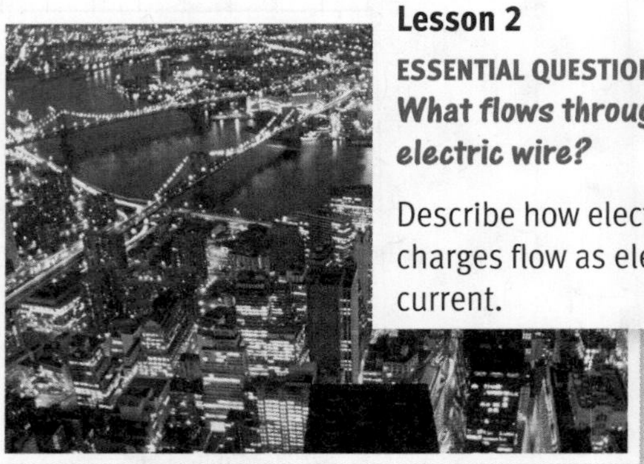

Lesson 2
ESSENTIAL QUESTION
What flows through an electric wire?

Describe how electric charges flow as electric current.

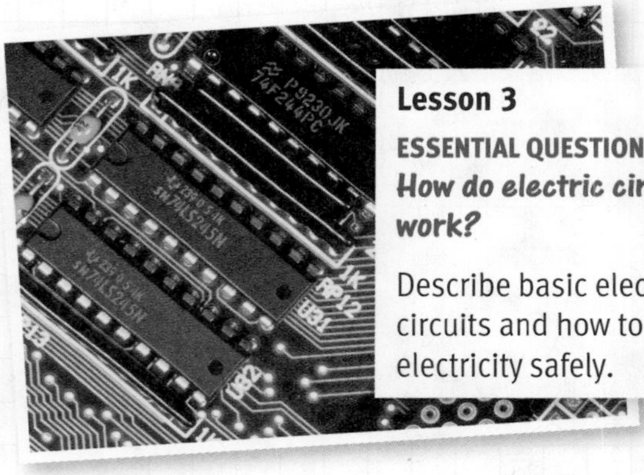

Lesson 3
ESSENTIAL QUESTION
How do electric circuits work?

Describe basic electric circuits and how to use electricity safely.

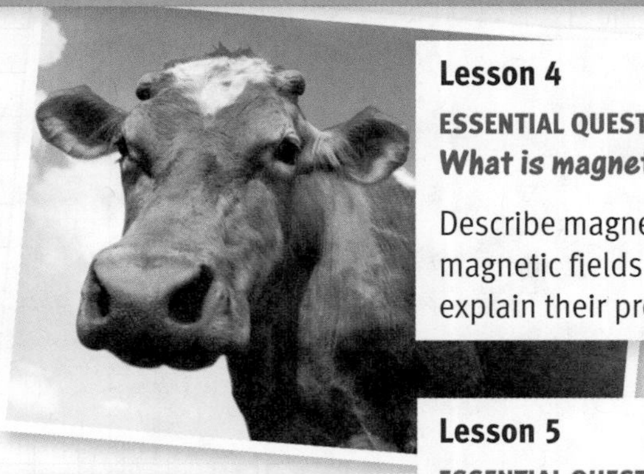

Lesson 4
ESSENTIAL QUESTION
What is magnetism?

Describe magnets and magnetic fields and explain their properties.

Lesson 5
ESSENTIAL QUESTION
What is electromagnetism?

Describe the relationship between electricity and magnetism and how this relationship affects our world.

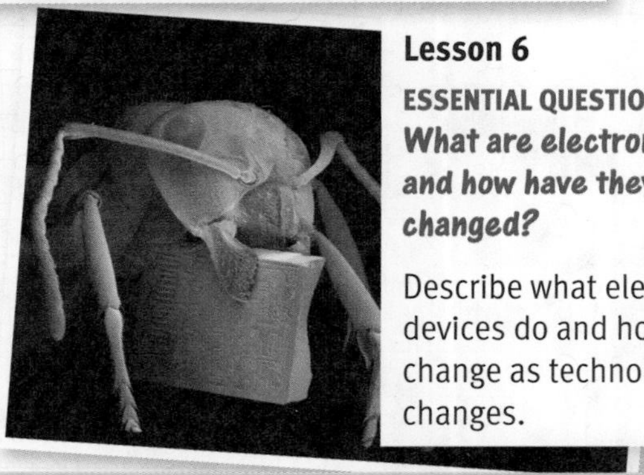

Lesson 6
ESSENTIAL QUESTION
What are electronics, and how have they changed?

Describe what electronic devices do and how they change as technology changes.

Connect ESSENTIAL QUESTIONS
Lessons 4 and 5

1 Synthesize Could a stationary magnet be used to generate an electric current? Explain.

____

____

____

Think Outside the Book

2 Synthesize Choose one of these activities to help synthesize what you have learned in this unit.

☐ Using what you learned in lessons 1 and 4, describe similarities between electricity and magnetism by making a poster presentation. Include captions and labels.

☐ Using what you learned in lessons 2, 3, 5, and 6, explain how electric current, electric circuits, and electromagnetism have affected telecommunication by creating a timeline. Include specific examples from the lessons, your own experience, and history.

Unit 3 Review

Name ______________________________

Vocabulary

Fill in each blank with the term that best completes the following sentences.

1 A(n) ______________________________ allows electrical charges to move freely.

2 The amount of work required to move a unit electric charge between two points is called ______________________.

3 A(n) ___________________________ is an electric circuit in which all the parts are connected in a single loop.

4 Magnets exert forces on each other and are surrounded by a(n) ______________________________.

5 A(n) ______________________________ is a signal that is represented as a sequence of separate values made up of zeroes and ones.

Key Concepts

Read each question below, and circle the best answer.

6 Objects can be charged in many ways. In the image below, a student is rubbing a balloon on his head.

What method is he using to charge the balloon?

A friction

B repulsion

C induction

D conduction

7 Which of the following is an electrical insulator?

A copper

B rubber

C aluminum

D iron

8 Which of the following wires has the lowest resistance?

A a short, thick copper wire at 25 °C

B a long, thick copper wire at 35 °C

C a long, thin copper wire at 35 °C

D a short, thin iron wire at 25 °C

9 There are many devices in the home that use electricity. Below is a diagram of four common electrical devices.

Device 1

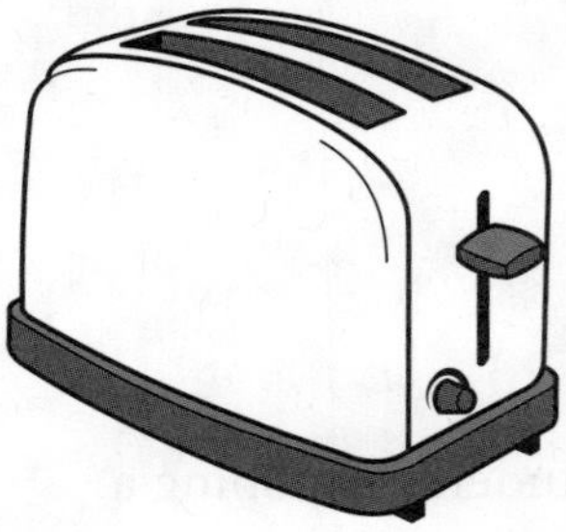

Device 3

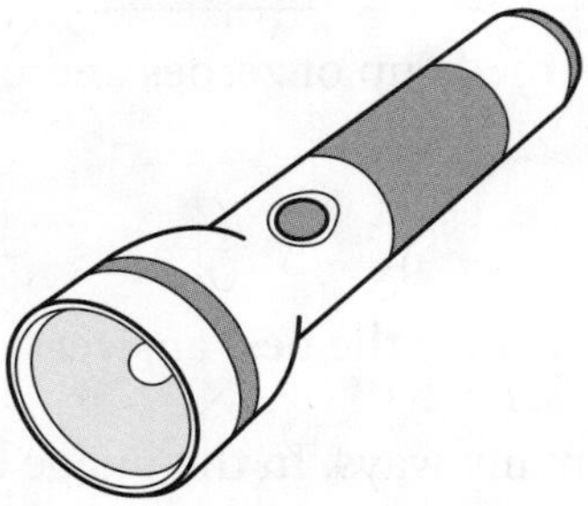

Device 2

Device 4

Which electrical device runs on direct current?

A Device 1

B Device 2

C Device 3

D Device 4

Name ______________________________

10 The diagram below shows two examples of electrical circuits.

Circuit 1

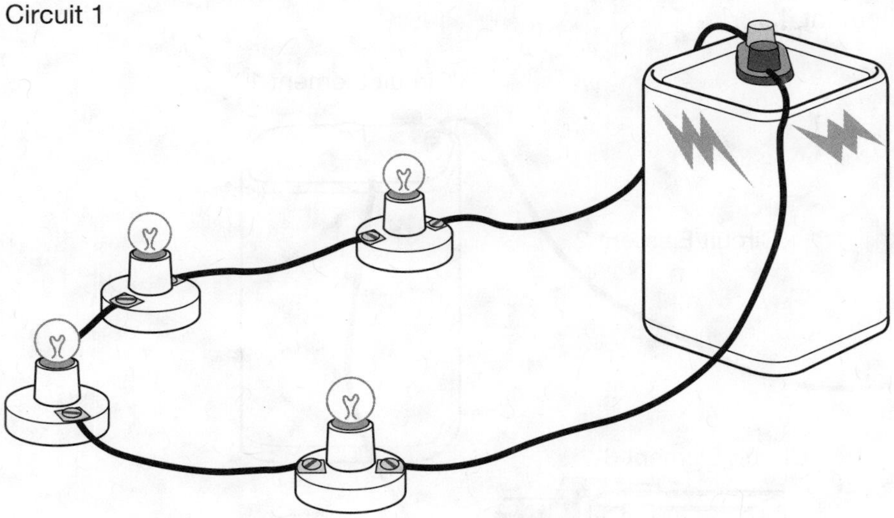

Circuit 2

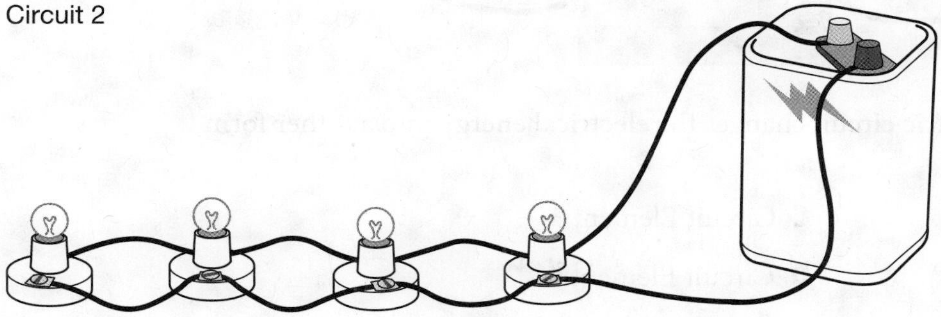

Which of the following statements about the circuits is correct?

A Circuit 1 is a parallel circuit, and Circuit 2 is a parallel circuit.

B Circuit 1 is a series circuit, and Circuit 2 is a parallel circuit.

C Circuit 1 is a parallel circuit, and Circuit 2 is a series circuit.

D Circuit 1 is a series circuit, and Circuit 2 is a series circuit.

11 It is important to practice electrical safety. Which of the following choices is unsafe?

A only using electrical cords that have proper insulation

B seeking shelter on a beach or under a tree during a lightning storm

C keeping electrical appliances away from sinks and bathtubs

D using ground fault circuit interrupters (GFCIs) in the home

12 Here is a diagram of a simple electric circuit. There are four elements to the circuit. They are labeled Circuit Element 1, Circuit Element 2, Circuit Element 3, and Circuit Element 4.

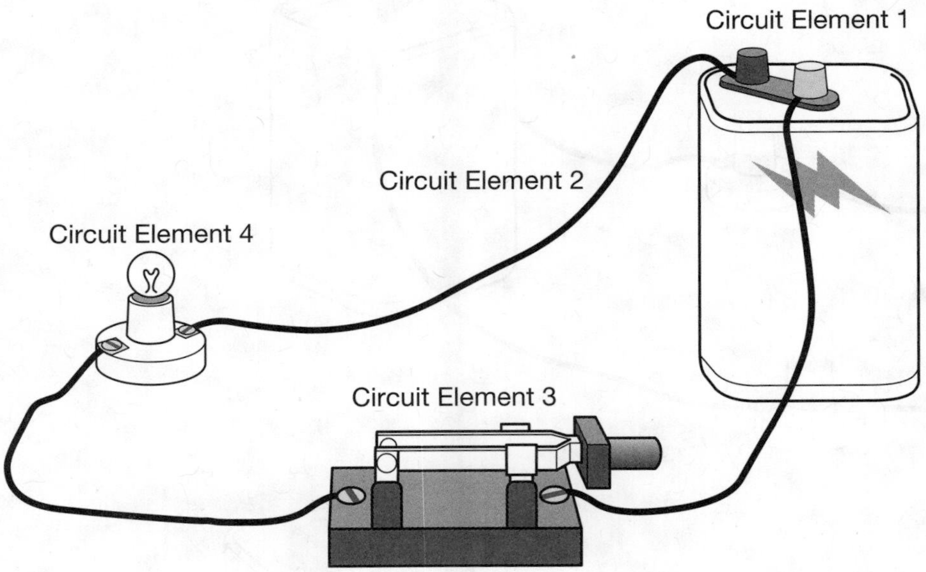
Circuit Element 1
Circuit Element 2
Circuit Element 4
Circuit Element 3

What part of an electric circuit changes the electrical energy into another form of energy?

A Circuit Element 1 **C** Circuit Element 3

B Circuit Element 2 **D** Circuit Element 4

13 Which of the following does not use an electromagnet?

A electric motor **C** hand-held compass

B galvanometer **D** doorbell

14 An object can become electrically charged if it gains or loses which particles?

A volts **C** atoms

B neutrons **D** electrons

15 Over time, computer size has been greatly reduced because of the introduction of which component?

A memory device **C** monitor

B microprocessor chip **D** mouse

Name ______________________

16 Binary code is an example of which of the following?

A an analog system

B a digital signal

C an electronic device

D an integrated circuit

17 Below is an image of a magnet showing the magnetic field.

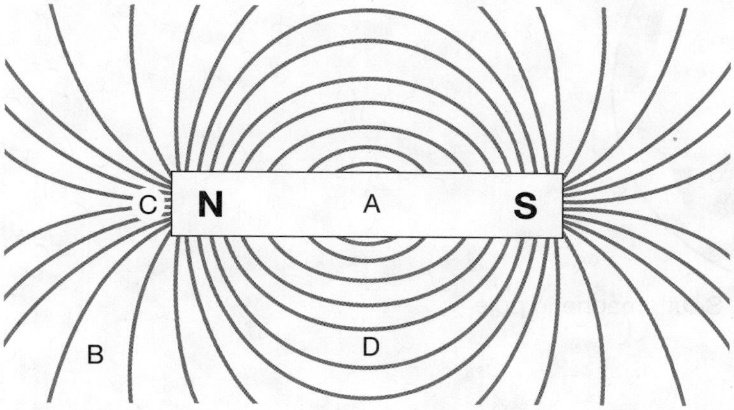
C
N
A
S
B
D

Where is the magnetic force the strongest?

A Position A

B Position B

C Position C

D Position D

Critical Thinking

Answer the following questions in the space provided.

18 Describe three properties of magnets.

____

____

____

____

____

19 List two ways in which the strength of an electromagnet can be increased.

____

____

____

____

20 The image below shows Earth and its magnetic field.

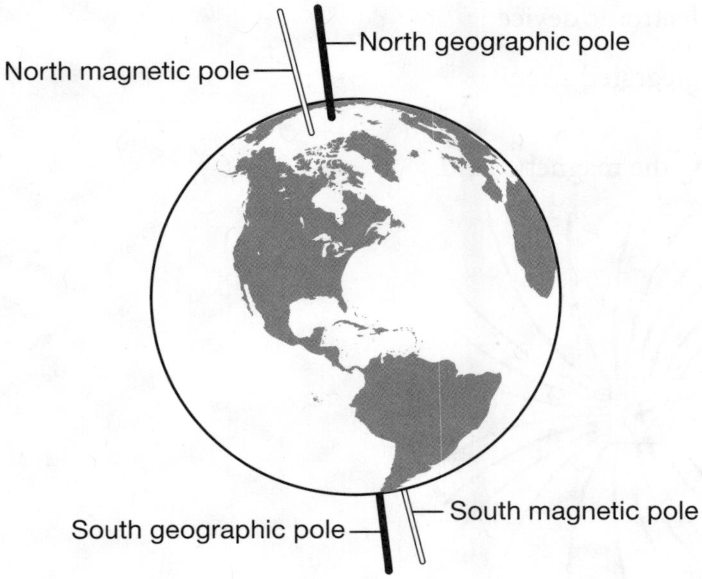
North geographic pole
North magnetic pole
South magnetic pole
South geographic pole

What is the difference between Earth's magnetic and geographic poles? How do navigators take advantage of this?

____

____

____

____

____

Connect ESSENTIAL QUESTIONS
Lessons 4 and 5

Answer the following question in the space provided.

21 There is a close relationship between magnetic forces and the generation of electricity. Explain how magnets can be used to generate electricity and how electric current can be used to create electromagnets. For each process, give an example of a device you would find around the home.

____

____

____

____

____

Look It Up!

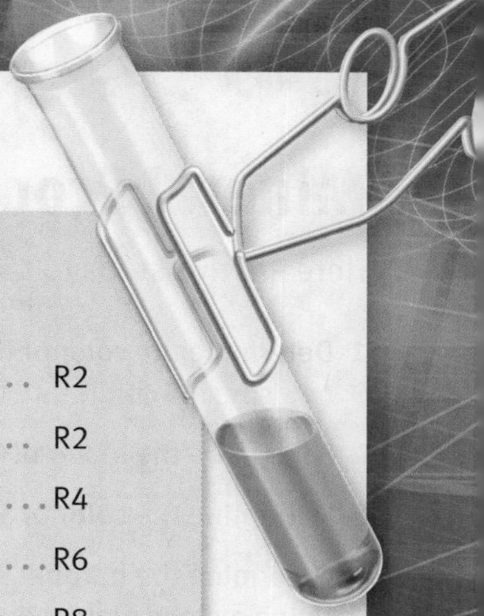

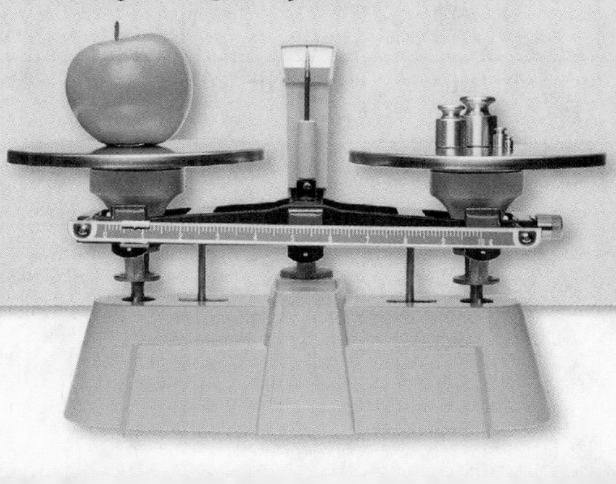

Mineral Properties

Here are five steps to take in mineral identification:

1 Determine the color of the mineral. Is it light-colored, dark-colored, or a specific color?

2 Determine the luster of the mineral. Is it metallic or non-metallic?

3 Determine the color of any powder left by its streak.

4 Determine the hardness of your mineral. Is it soft, hard, or very hard? Using a glass plate, see if the mineral scratches it.

5 Determine whether your sample has cleavage or any special properties.

TERMS TO KNOW	DEFINITION
adamantine	a non-metallic luster like that of a diamond
cleavage	how a mineral breaks when subject to stress on a particular plane
luster	the state or quality of shining by reflecting light
streak	the color of a mineral when it is powdered
submetallic	between metallic and nonmetallic in luster
vitreous	glass-like type of luster

Silicate Minerals					
Mineral	**Color**	**Luster**	**Streak**	**Hardness**	**Cleavage and Special Properties**
Beryl	deep green, pink, white, bluish green, or yellow	vitreous	white	7.5–8	1 cleavage direction; some varieties fluoresce in ultraviolet light
Chlorite	green	vitreous to pearly	pale green	2–2.5	1 cleavage direction
Garnet	green, red, brown, black	vitreous	white	6.5–7.5	no cleavage
Hornblende	dark green, brown, or black	vitreous	none	5–6	2 cleavage directions
Muscovite	colorless, silvery white, or brown	vitreous or pearly	white	2–2.5	1 cleavage direction
Olivine	olive green, yellow	vitreous	white or none	6.5–7	no cleavage
Orthoclase	colorless, white, pink, or other colors	vitreous	white or none	6	2 cleavage directions
Plagioclase	colorless, white, yellow, pink, green	vitreous	white	6	2 cleavage directions
Quartz	colorless or white; any color when not pure	vitreous or waxy	white or none	7	no cleavage

Nonsilicate Minerals					
Mineral	**Color**	**Luster**	**Streak**	**Hardness**	**Cleavage and Special Properties**
Native Elements					
Copper	copper-red	metallic	copper-red	2.5–3	no cleavage
Diamond	pale yellow or colorless	adamantine	none	10	4 cleavage directions
Graphite	black to gray	submetallic	black	1–2	1 cleavage direction
Carbonates					
Aragonite	colorless, white, or pale yellow	vitreous	white	3.5–4	2 cleavage directions; reacts with hydrochloric acid
Calcite	colorless or white to tan	vitreous	white	3	3 cleavage directions; reacts with weak acid; double refraction
Halides					
Fluorite	light green, yellow, purple, bluish green, or other colors	vitreous	none	4	4 cleavage directions; some varieties fluoresce
Halite	white	vitreous	white	2.0–2.5	3 cleavage directions
Oxides					
Hematite	reddish brown to black	metallic to earthy	dark red to red-brown	5.6–6.5	no cleavage; magnetic when heated
Magnetite	iron-black	metallic	black	5.5–6.5	no cleavage; magnetic
Sulfates					
Anhydrite	colorless, bluish, or violet	vitreous to pearly	white	3–3.5	3 cleavage directions
Gypsum	white, pink, gray, or colorless	vitreous, pearly, or silky	white	2.0	3 cleavage directions
Sulfides					
Galena	lead-gray	metallic	lead-gray to black	2.5–2.8	3 cleavage directions
Pyrite	brassy yellow	metallic	greenish, brownish, or black	6–6.5	no cleavage

Geologic Time Scale

Geologists developed the geologic time scale to represent the 4.6 billion years of Earth's history that have passed since Earth formed. This scale divides Earth's history into blocks of time. The boundaries between these time intervals (shown in millions of years ago or mya in the table below), represent major changes in Earth's history. Some boundaries are defined by mass extinctions, major changes in Earth's surface, and/or major changes in Earth's climate.

The four major divisions that encompass the history of life on Earth are Precambrian time, the Paleozoic era, the Mesozoic era, and the Cenozoic era. The largest divisions are eons. **Precambrian time** is made up of the first three eons, over 4 billion years of Earth's history.

The **Paleozoic era** lasted from 542 mya to 251 mya. All major plant groups, except flowering plants, appeared during this era. By the end of the era, reptiles, winged insects, and fishes had also appeared. The largest known mass extinction occurred at the end of this era.

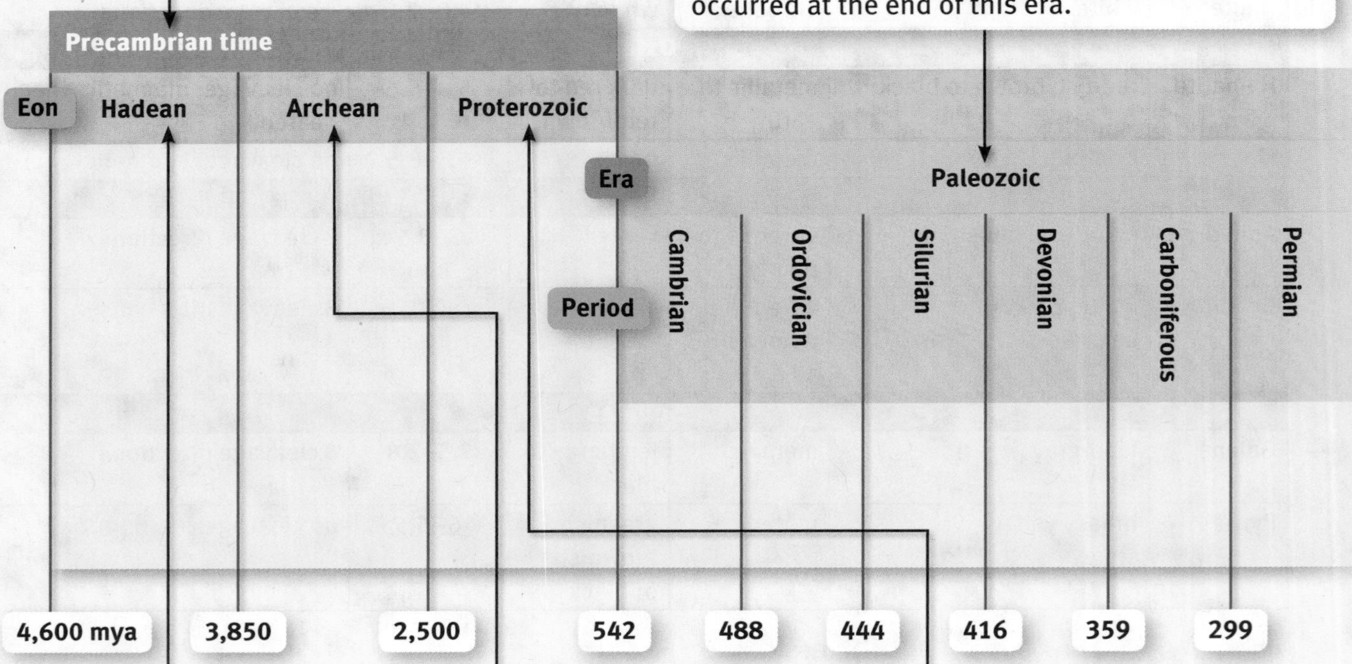
Precambrian time
Eon
Hadean
Archean
Proterozoic
Era
Paleozoic
Period
Cambrian
Ordovician
Silurian
Devonian
Carboniferous
Permian
4,600 mya
3,850
2,500
542
488
444
416
359
299

The **Hadean eon** lasted from about 4.6 billion years ago (bya) to 3.85 bya. It is described based on evidence from meterorites and rocks from the moon.

The **Archean eon** lasted from 3.85 bya to 2.5 bya. The earliest rocks from Earth that have been found and dated formed at the start of this eon.

The **Proterozoic eon** lasted from 2.5 bya to 542 mya. The first organisms, which were single-celled organisms, appeared during this eon. These organisms produced so much oxygen that they changed Earth's oceans and Earth's atmosphere.

Divisions of Time

The divisions of time shown here represent major changes in Earth's surface and when life developed and changed significantly on Earth. As new evidence is found, the boundaries of these divisions may shift. The Phanerozoic eon is divided into three eras. The beginning of each of these eras represents a change in the types of organisms that dominated Earth. And, each era is commonly characterized by the types of organisms that dominated the era. These eras are divided into periods, and periods are divided into epochs.

The **Mesozoic era** lasted from 251 mya to 65.5 mya. During this era, many kinds of dinosaurs dominated land, and giant lizards swam in the ocean. The first birds, mammals, and flowering plants also appeared during this time. About two-thirds of all land species went extinct at the end of this era.

The **Phanerozoic eon** began 542 mya. We live in this eon.

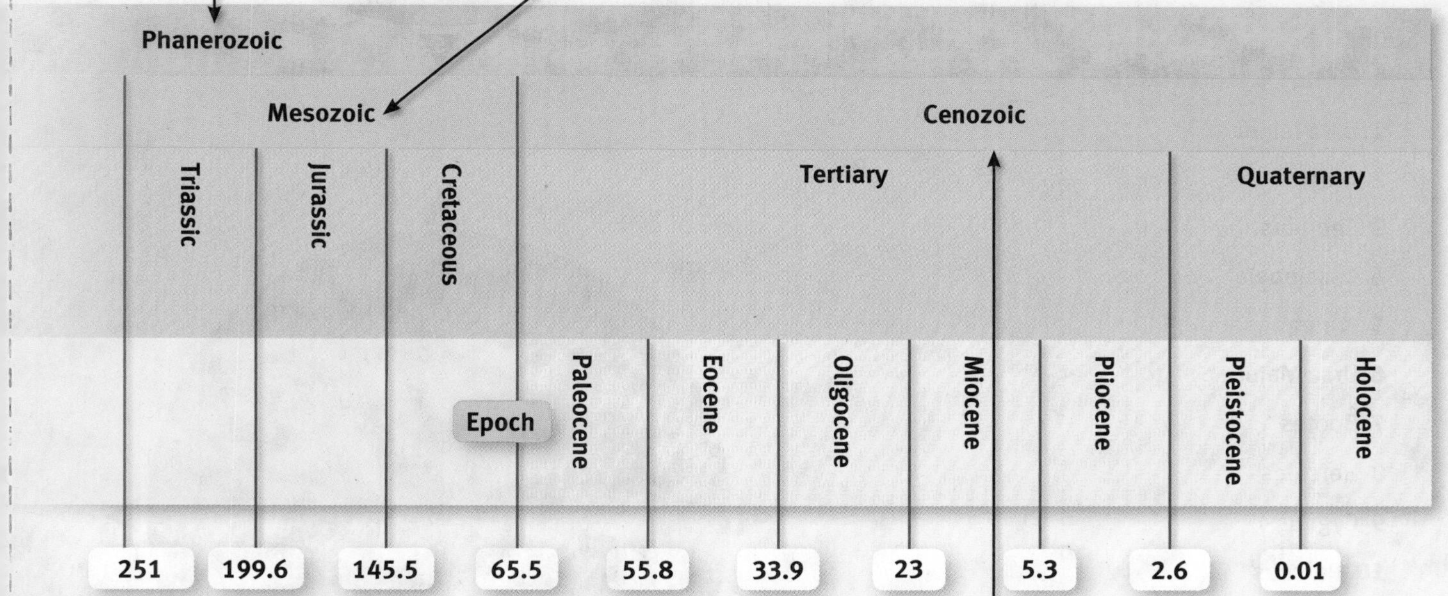

Phanerozoic
Mesozoic
Cenozoic
Triassic
Jurassic
Cretaceous
Tertiary
Quaternary
Epoch
Paleocene
Eocene
Oligocene
Miocene
Pliocene
Pleistocene
Holocene
251
199.6
145.5
65.5
55.8
33.9
23
5.3
2.6
0.01

The **Cenozoic era** began 65.5 mya and continues today. Mammals dominate this era. During the Mesozoic era, mammals were small in size but grew much larger during the Cenozoic era. Primates, including humans, appeared during this era.

Star Charts for the Northern Hemisphere

A star chart is a map of the stars in the night sky. It shows the names and positions of constellations and major stars. Star charts can be used to identify constellations and even to orient yourself using Polaris, the North Star.

Because Earth moves through space, different constellations are visible at different times of the year. The star charts on these pages show the constellations visible during each season in the Northern Hemisphere.

Spring

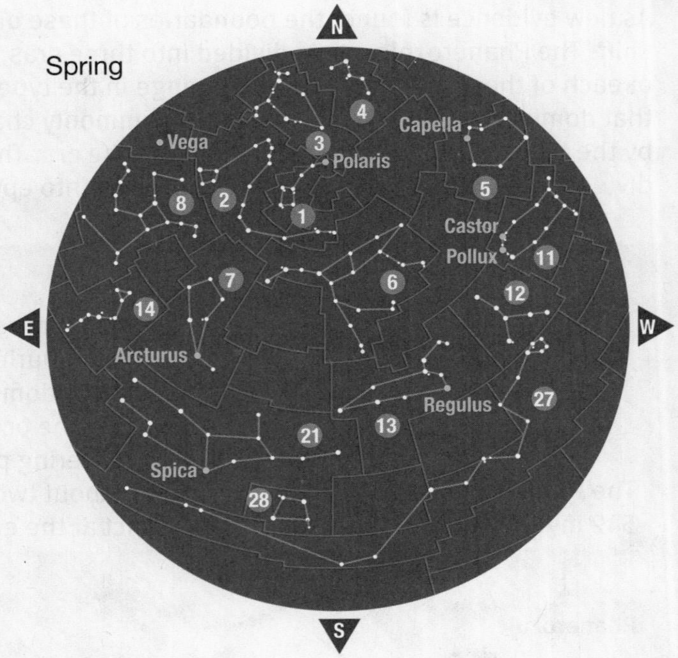
N
E
W
S
Vega
Polaris
Capella
Castor
Pollux
Arcturus
Regulus
Spica
1
2
3
4
5
6
7
8
11
12
13
14
21
27
28

Summer

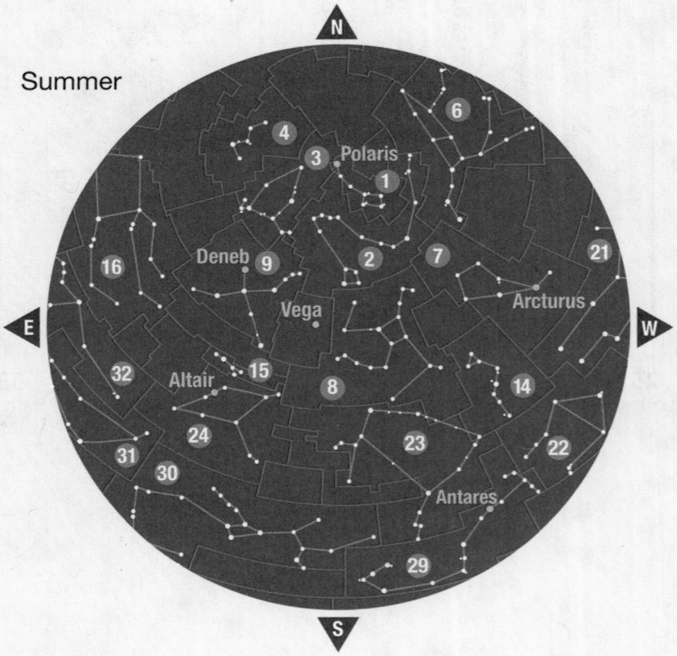
N
E
W
S
Polaris
Deneb
Vega
Arcturus
Altair
Antares
1
2
3
4
6
7
8
9
14
15
16
21
22
23
24
29
30
31
32

Constellations

1 Ursa Minor
2 Draco
3 Cepheus
4 Cassiopeia
5 Auriga
6 Ursa Major
7 Boötes
8 Hercules
9 Cygnus
10 Perseus
11 Gemini
12 Cancer
13 Leo
14 Serpens
15 Sagitta
16 Pegasus
17 Pisces

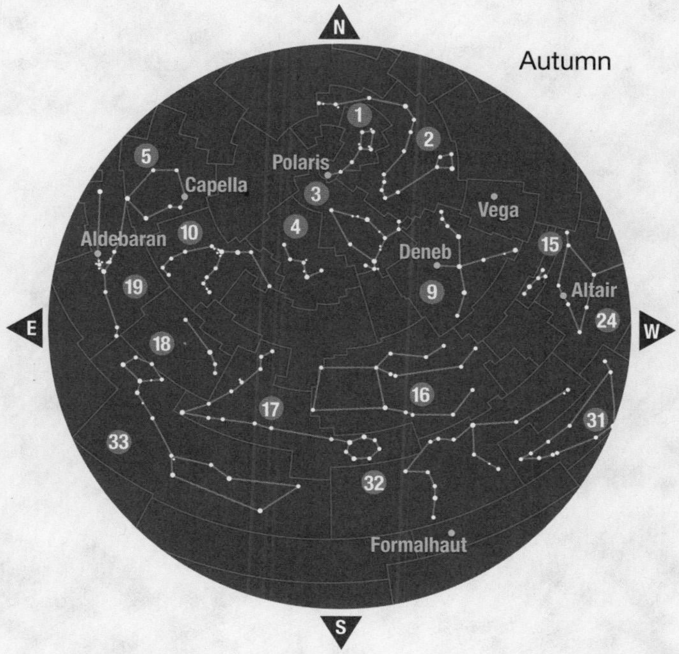
N
Autumn
1
2
5
Polaris
Capella
3
Vega
4
Aldebaran
10
Deneb
15
9
Altair
19
E
24
W
18
16
17
31
33
32
Formalhaut
S

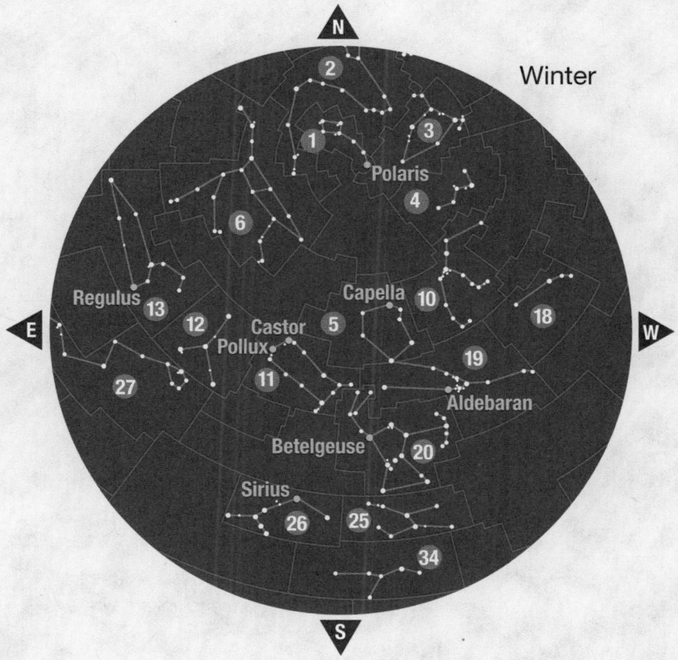
N
2
Winter
1
3
Polaris
4
6
Capella
Regulus
10
13
18
12
Castor
5
E
W
Pollux
19
11
27
Aldebaran
Betelgeuse
20
Sirius
26
25
34
S

Constellations

18 Aries
19 Taurus
20 Orion
21 Virgo
22 Libra
23 Ophiuchus
24 Aquila
25 Lepus
26 Canis Major
27 Hydra
28 Corvus
29 Scorpius
30 Sagittarius
31 Capricornus
32 Aquarius
33 Cetus
34 Columba

World Map

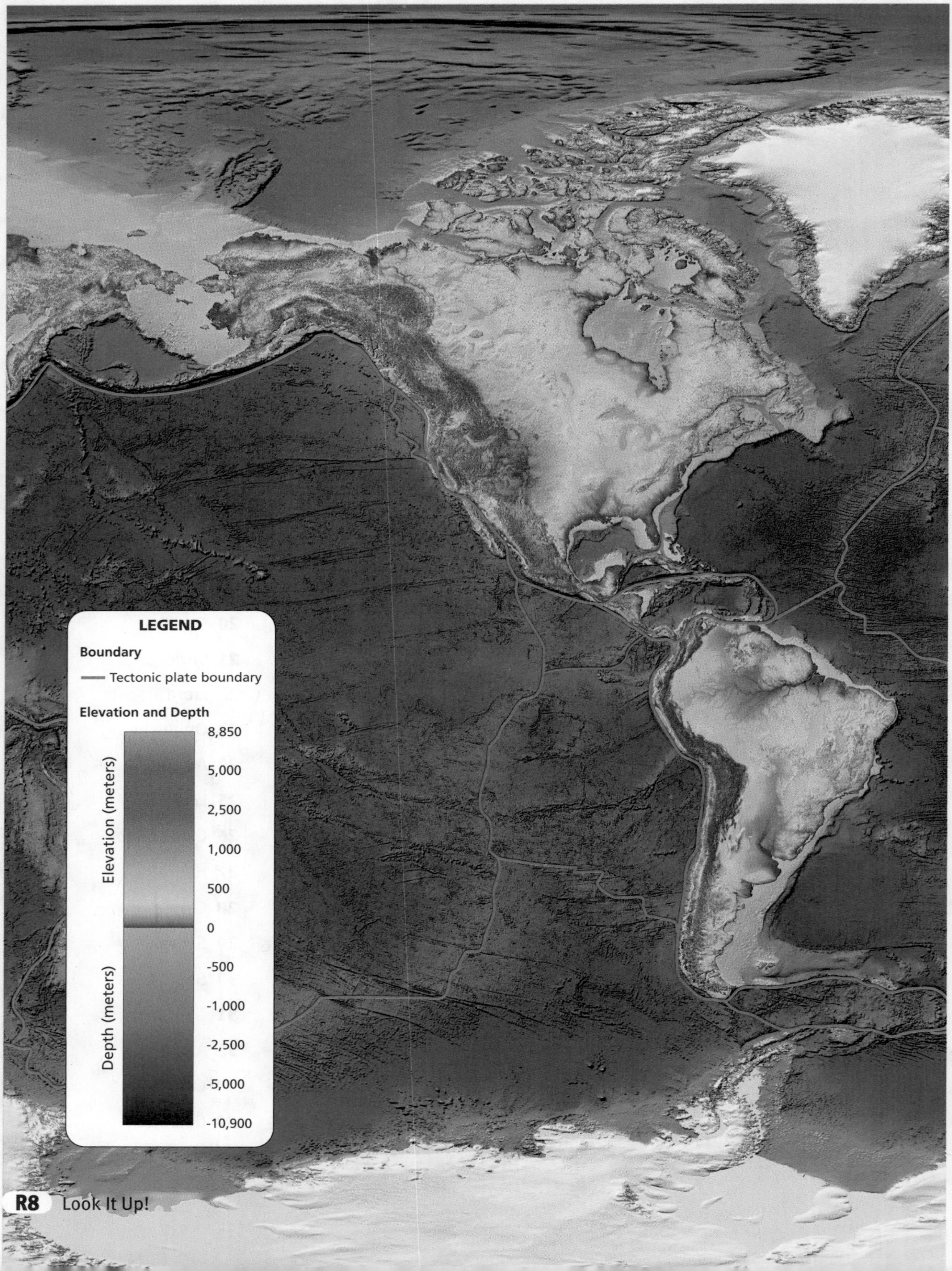
LEGEND
Boundary
Tectonic plate boundary
Elevation and Depth
8,850
5,000
2,500
1,000
500
0
-500
-1,000
-2,500
-5,000
-10,900
Elevation (meters)
Depth (meters)

Classification of Living Things

Domains and Kingdoms

All organisms belong to one of three domains: Domain Archaea, Domain Bacteria, or Domain Eukarya. Some of the groups within these domains are shown below. (Remember that genus names are italicized.)

Domain Archaea

The organisms in this domain are single-celled prokaryotes, many of which live in extreme environments.

Archaea		
Group	**Example**	**Characteristics**
Methanogens	*Methanococcus*	produce methane gas; can't live in oxygen
Thermophiles	*Sulpholobus*	require sulphur; can't live in oxygen
Halophiles	*Halococcus*	live in very salty environments; most can live in oxygen

Domain Bacteria

Organisms in this domain are single-celled prokaryotes and are found in almost every environment on Earth.

Bacteria		
Group	**Example**	**Characteristics**
Bacilli	*Escherichia*	rod shaped; some bacilli fix nitrogen; some cause disease
Cocci	*Streptococcus*	spherical shaped; some cause disease; can form spores
Spirilla	*Treponema*	spiral shaped; cause diseases such as syphilis and Lyme disease

Domain Eukarya

Organisms in this domain are single-celled or multicellular eukaryotes.

Kingdom Protista Many protists resemble fungi, plants, or animals, but are smaller and simpler in structure. Most are single celled.

Protists		
Group	**Example**	**Characteristics**
Sarcodines	*Amoeba*	radiolarians; single-celled consumers
Ciliates	*Paramecium*	single-celled consumers
Flagellates	*Trypanosoma*	single-celled parasites
Sporozoans	*Plasmodium*	single-celled parasites
Euglenas	*Euglena*	single celled; photosynthesize
Diatoms	*Pinnularia*	most are single celled; photosynthesize
Dinoflagellates	*Gymnodinium*	single celled; some photosynthesize
Algae	*Volvox*	single celled or multicellular; photosynthesize
Slime molds	*Physarum*	single celled or multicellular; consumers or decomposers
Water molds	powdery mildew	single celled or multicellular; parasites or decomposers

Kingdom Fungi Most fungi are multicellular. Their cells have thick cell walls. Fungi absorb food from their environment.

Fungi		
Group	**Examples**	**Characteristics**
Threadlike fungi	bread mold	spherical; decomposers
Sac fungi	yeast; morels	saclike; parasites and decomposers
Club fungi	mushrooms; rusts; smuts	club shaped; parasites and decomposers
Lichens	British soldier	a partnership between a fungus and an alga

Kingdom Plantae Plants are multicellular and have cell walls made of cellulose. Plants make their own food through photosynthesis. Plants are classified into divisions instead of phyla.

Plants		
Group	**Examples**	**Characteristics**
Bryophytes	mosses; liverworts	no vascular tissue; reproduce by spores
Club mosses	*Lycopodium;* ground pine	grow in wooded areas; reproduce by spores
Horsetails	rushes	grow in wetland areas; reproduce by spores
Ferns	spleenworts; sensitive fern	large leaves called fronds; reproduce by spores
Conifers	pines; spruces; firs	needlelike leaves; reproduce by seeds made in cones
Cycads	*Zamia*	slow growing; reproduce by seeds made in large cones
Gnetophytes	*Welwitschia*	only three living families; reproduce by seeds
Ginkgoes	*Ginkgo*	only one living species; reproduce by seeds
Angiosperms	all flowering plants	reproduce by seeds made in flowers; fruit

Kingdom Animalia Animals are multicellular. Their cells do not have cell walls. Most animals have specialized tissues and complex organ systems. Animals get food by eating other organisms.

Animals		
Group	**Examples**	**Characteristics**
Sponges	glass sponges	no symmetry or specialized tissues; aquatic
Cnidarians	jellyfish; coral	radial symmetry; aquatic
Flatworms	planaria; tapeworms; flukes	bilateral symmetry; organ systems
Roundworms	*Trichina;* hookworms	bilateral symmetry; organ systems
Annelids	earthworms; leeches	bilateral symmetry; organ systems
Mollusks	snails; octopuses	bilateral symmetry; organ systems
Echinoderms	sea stars; sand dollars	radial symmetry; organ systems
Arthropods	insects; spiders; lobsters	bilateral symmetry; organ systems
Chordates	fish; amphibians; reptiles; birds; mammals	bilateral symmetry; complex organ systems

Periodic Table of the Elements

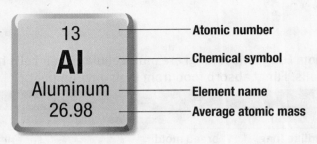

13 — Atomic number
Al — Chemical symbol
Aluminum — Element name
26.98 — Average atomic mass

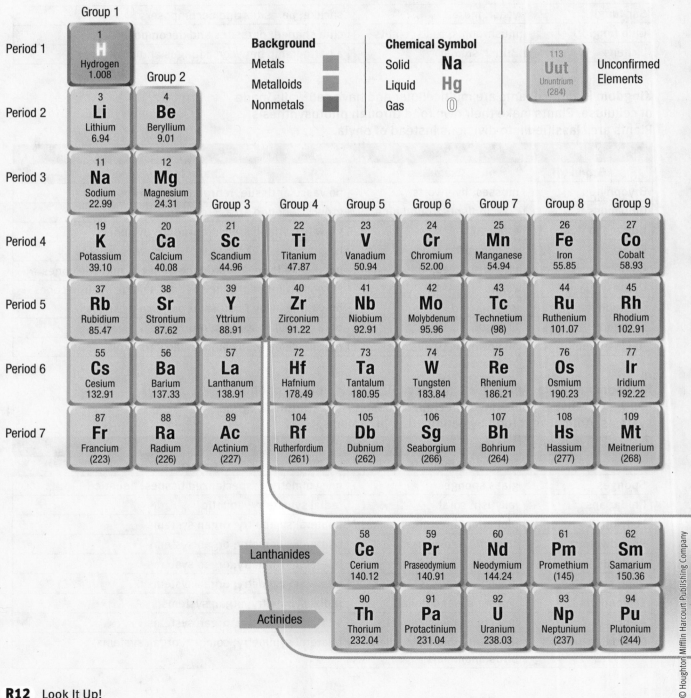

Background
Metals
Metalloids
Nonmetals

Chemical Symbol
Solid — Na
Liquid — Hg
Gas — O

113 Uut Ununtrium (284) — Unconfirmed Elements

	Group 1	Group 2	Group 3	Group 4	Group 5	Group 6	Group 7	Group 8	Group 9
Period 1	1 H Hydrogen 1.008								
Period 2	3 Li Lithium 6.94	4 Be Beryllium 9.01							
Period 3	11 Na Sodium 22.99	12 Mg Magnesium 24.31							
Period 4	19 K Potassium 39.10	20 Ca Calcium 40.08	21 Sc Scandium 44.96	22 Ti Titanium 47.87	23 V Vanadium 50.94	24 Cr Chromium 52.00	25 Mn Manganese 54.94	26 Fe Iron 55.85	27 Co Cobalt 58.93
Period 5	37 Rb Rubidium 85.47	38 Sr Strontium 87.62	39 Y Yttrium 88.91	40 Zr Zirconium 91.22	41 Nb Niobium 92.91	42 Mo Molybdenum 95.96	43 Tc Technetium (98)	44 Ru Ruthenium 101.07	45 Rh Rhodium 102.91
Period 6	55 Cs Cesium 132.91	56 Ba Barium 137.33	57 La Lanthanum 138.91	72 Hf Hafnium 178.49	73 Ta Tantalum 180.95	74 W Tungsten 183.84	75 Re Rhenium 186.21	76 Os Osmium 190.23	77 Ir Iridium 192.22
Period 7	87 Fr Francium (223)	88 Ra Radium (226)	89 Ac Actinium (227)	104 Rf Rutherfordium (261)	105 Db Dubnium (262)	106 Sg Seaborgium (266)	107 Bh Bohrium (264)	108 Hs Hassium (277)	109 Mt Meitnerium (268)

Lanthanides	58 Ce Cerium 140.12	59 Pr Praseodymium 140.91	60 Nd Neodymium 144.24	61 Pm Promethium (145)	62 Sm Samarium 150.36
Actinides	90 Th Thorium 232.04	91 Pa Protactinium 231.04	92 U Uranium 238.03	93 Np Neptunium (237)	94 Pu Plutonium (244)

The International Union of Pure and Applied Chemistry (IUPAC) has determined that, because of isotopic variance, the average atomic mass is best represented by a range of values for each of the following elements: hydrogen, lithium, boron, carbon, nitrogen, oxygen, silicon, sulfur, chlorine, and thallium. However, the values in this table are appropriate for everyday calculations.

Group 10	Group 11	Group 12	Group 13	Group 14	Group 15	Group 16	Group 17	Group 18
								2 He Helium 4.003
			5 B Boron 10.81	6 C Carbon 12.01	7 N Nitrogen 14.01	8 O Oxygen 16.00	9 F Fluorine 19.00	10 Ne Neon 20.18
			13 Al Aluminum 26.98	14 Si Silicon 28.09	15 P Phosphorus 30.97	16 S Sulfur 32.06	17 Cl Chlorine 35.45	18 Ar Argon 39.95
28 Ni Nickel 58.69	29 Cu Copper 63.55	30 Zn Zinc 65.38	31 Ga Gallium 69.72	32 Ge Germanium 72.63	33 As Arsenic 74.92	34 Se Selenium 78.96	35 Br Bromine 79.90	36 Kr Krypton 83.80
46 Pd Palladium 106.42	47 Ag Silver 107.87	48 Cd Cadmium 112.41	49 In Indium 114.82	50 Sn Tin 118.71	51 Sb Antimony 121.76	52 Te Tellurium 127.60	53 I Iodine 126.90	54 Xe Xenon 131.29
78 Pt Platinum 195.08	79 Au Gold 196.97	80 Hg Mercury 200.59	81 Tl Thallium 204.38	82 Pb Lead 207.2	83 Bi Bismuth 208.98	84 Po Polonium (209)	85 At Astatine (210)	86 Rn Radon (222)
110 Ds Darmstadtium (271)	111 Rg Roentgenium (272)	112 Cn Copernicium (285)	113 Uut Ununtrium (284)	114 Uuq Ununquadium (289)	115 Uup Ununpentium (288)	116 Uuh Ununhexium (292)	117 Uus Ununseptium (294)	118 Uuo Ununoctium (294)

63 Eu Europium 151.96	64 Gd Gadolinium 157.25	65 Tb Terbium 158.93	66 Dy Dysprosium 162.50	67 Ho Holmium 164.93	68 Er Erbium 167.26	69 Tm Thulium 168.93	70 Yb Ytterbium 173.05	71 Lu Lutetium 174.97
95 Am Americium (243)	96 Cm Curium (247)	97 Bk Berkelium (247)	98 Cf Californium (251)	99 Es Einsteinium (252)	100 Fm Fermium (257)	101 Md Mendelevium (258)	102 No Nobelium (259)	103 Lr Lawrencium (262)

Physical Science Refresher

Atoms and Elements

Every object in the universe is made of matter. **Matter** is anything that takes up space and has mass. All matter is made of atoms. An **atom** is the smallest particle into which an element can be divided and still be the same element. An **element**, in turn, is a substance that cannot be broken down into simpler substances by chemical means. Each element consists of only one kind of atom. An element may be made of many atoms, but they are all the same kind of atom.

Atomic Structure

Atoms are made of smaller particles called **electrons**, **protons**, and **neutrons**. Electrons have a negative electric charge, protons have a positive charge, and neutrons have no electric charge. Together, protons and neutrons form the **nucleus**, or small dense center, of an atom. Because protons are positively charged and neutrons are neutral, the nucleus has a positive charge. Electrons move within an area around the nucleus called the **electron cloud**. Electrons move so quickly that scientists cannot determine their exact speeds and positions at the same time.

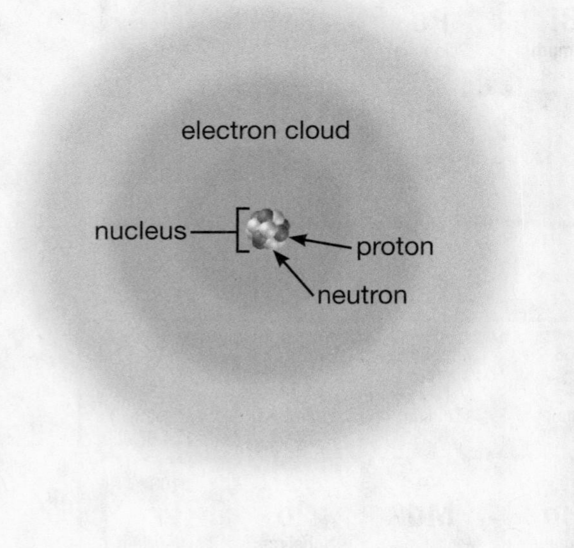
electron cloud
nucleus
proton
neutron

Atomic Number

To help distinguish one element from another, scientists use the atomic numbers of atoms. The **atomic number** is the number of protons in the nucleus of an atom. The atoms of a certain element always have the same number of protons.

When atoms have an equal number of protons and electrons, they are uncharged, or electrically neutral. The atomic number equals the number of electrons in an uncharged atom. The number of neutrons, however, can vary for a given element. Atoms of the same element that have different numbers of neutrons are called **isotopes**.

Periodic Table of the Elements

In the periodic table, each element in the table is in a separate box. And the elements are arranged from left to right in order of increasing atomic number. That is, an uncharged atom of each element has one more electron and one more proton than an uncharged atom of the element to its left. Each horizontal row of the table is called a **period**. Changes in chemical properties of elements across a period correspond to changes in the electron arrangements of their atoms.

Each vertical column of the table is known as a **group**. A group lists elements with similar physical and chemical properties. For this reason, a group is also sometimes called a family. The elements in a group have similar properties because their atoms have the same number of electrons in their outer energy level. For example, the elements helium, neon, argon, krypton, xenon, and radon all have similar properties and are known as the noble gases.

Molecules and Compounds

When two or more elements join chemically, they form a **compound**. A compound is a new substance with properties different from those of the elements that compose it. For example, water, H_2O, is a compound formed when hydrogen (H) and oxygen (O) combine. The smallest complete unit of a compound that has the properties of that compound is called a **molecule**. A chemical formula indicates the elements in a compound. It also indicates the relative number of atoms of each element in the compound. The chemical formula for water is H_2O. So, each water molecule consists of two atoms of hydrogen and one atom of oxygen. The subscript number after the symbol for an element shows how many atoms of that element are in a single molecule of the compound.

Chemical Equations

A chemical reaction occurs when a chemical change takes place. A chemical equation describes a chemical reaction using chemical formulas. The equation indicates the substances that react and the substances that are produced. For example, when carbon and oxygen combine, they can form carbon dioxide, shown in the equation below: $C + O_2 \longrightarrow CO_2$

Acids, Bases, and pH

An **ion** is an atom or group of chemically bonded atoms that has an electric charge because it has lost or gained one or more electrons. When an acid, such as hydrochloric acid, HCl, is mixed with water, it separates into ions. An **acid** is a compound that produces hydrogen ions, H^+, in water. The hydrogen ions then combine with a water molecule to form a hydronium ion, H_3O^+. A **base**, on the other hand, is a substance that produces hydroxide ions, OH^-, in water.

To determine whether a solution is acidic or basic, scientists use pH. The **pH** of a solution is a measure of the hydronium ion concentration in a solution. The pH scale ranges from 0 to 14. Acids have a pH that is less than 7. The lower the number, the more acidic the solution. The middle point, pH = 7, is neutral, neither acidic nor basic. Bases have a pH that is greater than 7. The higher the number is, the more basic the solution.

The pH of Some Common Materials

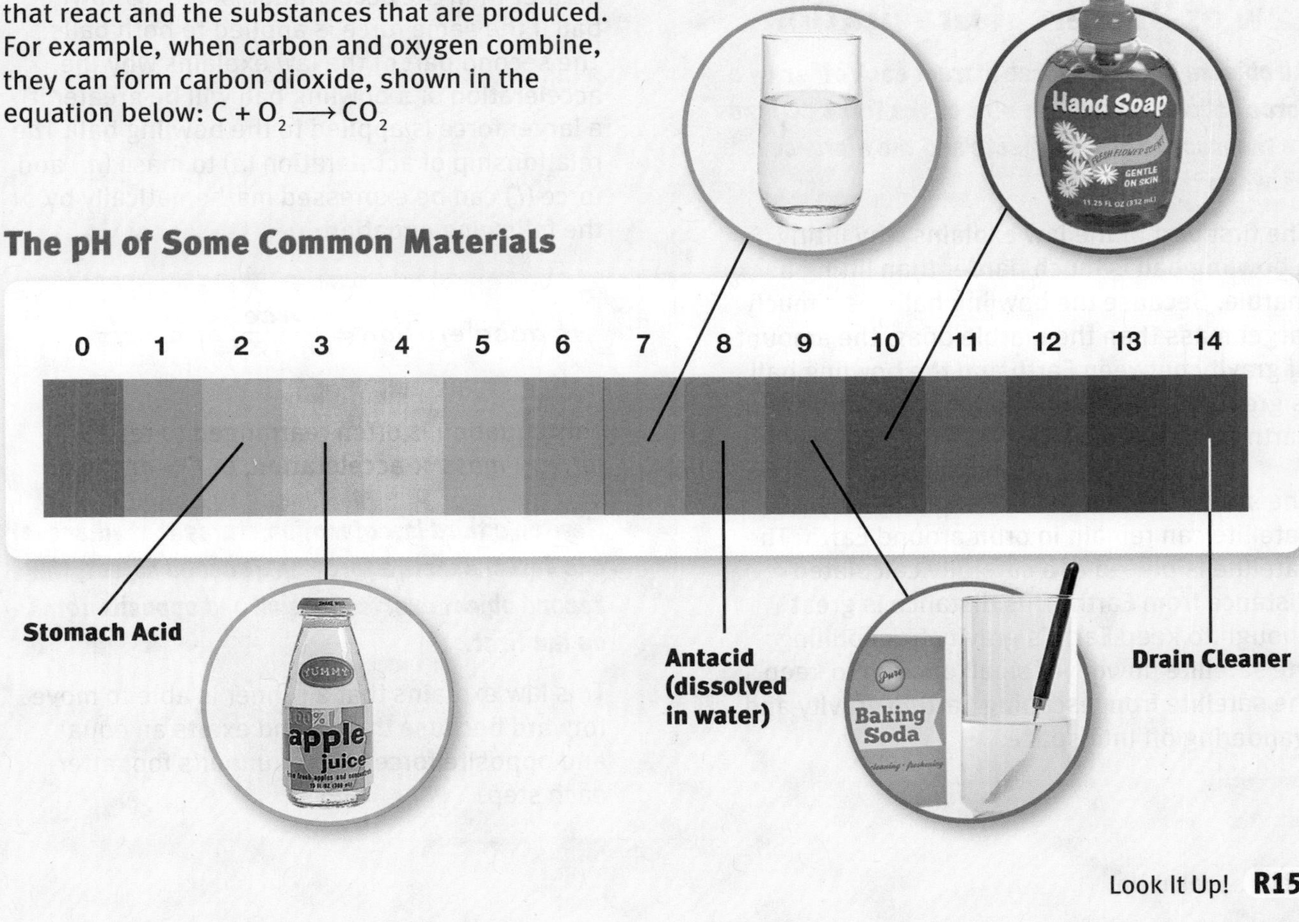

0
1
2
3
4
5
6
7
8
9
10
11
12
13
14
Stomach Acid
apple juice
Antacid (dissolved in water)
Baking Soda
Hand Soap
Drain Cleaner

Physical Laws and Useful Equations

Law of Conservation of Mass

Mass cannot be created or destroyed during ordinary chemical or physical changes.

The total mass in a closed system is always the same no matter how many physical changes or chemical reactions occur.

Law of Conservation of Energy

Energy can be neither created nor destroyed.

The total amount of energy in a closed system is always the same. Energy can be changed from one form to another, but all of the different forms of energy in a system always add up to the same total amount of energy, no matter how many energy conversions occur.

Law of Universal Gravitation

All objects in the universe attract each other by a force called gravity. The size of the force depends on the masses of the objects and the distance between the objects.

The first part of the law explains why lifting a bowling ball is much harder than lifting a marble. Because the bowling ball has a much larger mass than the marble does, the amount of gravity between Earth and the bowling ball is greater than the amount of gravity between Earth and the marble.

The second part of the law explains why a satellite can remain in orbit around Earth. The satellite is placed at a carefully calculated distance from Earth. This distance is great enough to keep Earth's gravity from pulling the satellite down, yet small enough to keep the satellite from escaping Earth's gravity and wandering off into space.

Newton's Laws of Motion

Newton's first law of motion states that an object at rest remains at rest, and an object in motion remains in motion at constant speed and in a straight line unless acted on by an unbalanced force.

The first part of the law explains why a football will remain on a tee until it is kicked off or until a gust of wind blows it off. The second part of the law explains why a bike rider will continue moving forward after the bike comes to an abrupt stop. Gravity and the friction of the sidewalk will eventually stop the rider.

Newton's second law of motion states that the acceleration of an object depends on the mass of the object and the amount of force applied.

The first part of the law explains why the acceleration of a 4 kg bowling ball will be greater than the acceleration of a 6 kg bowling ball if the same force is applied to both balls. The second part of the law explains why the acceleration of a bowling ball will be greater if a larger force is applied to the bowling ball. The relationship of acceleration (*a*) to mass (*m*) and force (*F*) can be expressed mathematically by the following equation:

$$\text{acceleration} = \frac{\text{force}}{\text{mass}}, \text{ or } a = \frac{F}{m}$$

This equation is often rearranged to read *force* = *mass* × acceleration, or $F = m \times a$

Newton's third law of motion states that whenever one object exerts a force on a second object, the second object exerts an equal and opposite force on the first.

This law explains that a runner is able to move forward because the ground exerts an equal and opposite force on the runner's foot after each step.

Average speed

$$\text{average speed} = \frac{\text{total distance}}{\text{total time}}$$

Example:
A bicycle messenger traveled a distance of 136 km in 8 h. What was the messenger's average speed?

$$\frac{136\ \text{km}}{8\ \text{h}} = 17\ \text{km/h}$$

The messenger's average speed was **17 km/h**.

Average acceleration

$$\text{average acceleration} = \frac{\text{final velocity} - \text{starting velocity}}{\text{time it takes to change velocity}}$$

Example:
Calculate the average acceleration of an Olympic 100 m dash sprinter who reached a velocity of 20 m/s south at the finish line. The race was in a straight line and lasted 10 s.

$$\frac{20\ \text{m/s} - 0\ \text{m/s}}{10\ \text{s}} = 2\ \text{m/s/s}$$

The sprinter's average acceleration was **2 m/s/s south.**

Net force

Forces in the Same Direction

When forces are in the same direction, add the forces together to determine the net force.

Example:
Calculate the net force on a stalled car that is being pushed by two people. One person is pushing with a force of 13 N northwest, and the other person is pushing with a force of 8 N in the same direction.

$$13\ \text{N} + 8\ \text{N} = 21\ \text{N}$$

The net force is **21 N northwest.**

Forces in Opposite Directions

When forces are in opposite directions, subtract the smaller force from the larger force to determine the net force. The net force will be in the direction of the larger force.

Example:
Calculate the net force on a rope that is being pulled on each end. One person is pulling on one end of the rope with a force of 12 N south. Another person is pulling on the opposite end of the rope with a force of 7 N north.

$$12\ \text{N} - 7\ \text{N} = 5\ \text{N}$$

The net force is **5 N south.**

Pressure

Pressure is the force exerted over a given area. The SI unit for pressure is the pascal. Its symbol is Pa.

$$\text{pressure} = \frac{\text{force}}{\text{area}}$$

Example:
Calculate the pressure of the air in a soccer ball if the air exerts a force of 10 N over an area of 0.5 m^2.

$$\text{pressure} = \frac{10N}{0.5\ m^2} = \frac{20N}{m^2} = 20\ Pa$$

The pressure of the air inside the soccer ball is **20 Pa**.

A How-To Manual for Active Reading

This book belongs to you, and you are invited to write in it. In fact, the book won't be complete until you do. Sometimes you'll answer a question or follow directions to mark up the text. Other times you'll write down your own thoughts. And when you're done reading and writing in the book, the book will be ready to help you review what you learned and prepare for tests.

Active Reading Annotations

Before you read, you'll often come upon an Active Reading prompt that asks you to underline certain words or number the steps in a process. Here's an example.

> **Active Reading**
>
> **12 Identify** In this paragraph, number the sequence of sentences that describe replication.

Marking the text this way is called **annotating,** and your marks are called **annotations.** Annotating the text can help you identify important concepts while you read.

There are other ways that you can annotate the text. You can draw an asterisk (*) by vocabulary terms, mark unfamiliar or confusing terms and information with a question mark (?), and mark main ideas with a double underline. And you can even invent your own marks to annotate the text!

Other Annotating Opportunities

Keep your pencil, pen, or highlighter nearby as you read, so you can make a note or highlight an important point at any time. Here are a few ideas to get you started.

- Notice the headings in red and blue. The blue headings are questions that point to the main idea of what you're reading. The red headings are answers to the questions in the blue ones. Together these headings outline the content of the lesson. After reading a lesson, you could write your own answers to the questions.

- Notice the bold-faced words that are highlighted in yellow. They are highlighted so that you can easily find them again on the page where they are defined. As you read or as you review, challenge yourself to write your own sentence using the bold-faced term.
- Make a note in the margin at any time. You might
  - Ask a “What if” question
  - Comment on what you read
  - Make a connection to something you read elsewhere
  - Make a logical conclusion from the text

Use your own language and abbreviations. Invent a code, such as using circles and boxes around words to remind you of their importance or relation to each other. Your annotations will help you remember your questions for class discussions, and when you go back to the lesson later, you may be able to fill in what you didn’t understand the first time you read it. Like a scientist in the field or in a lab, you will be recording your questions and observations for analysis later.

Active Reading Questions

After you read, you’ll often come upon Active Reading questions that ask you to think about what you’ve just read. You’ll write your answer underneath the question. Here’s an example.

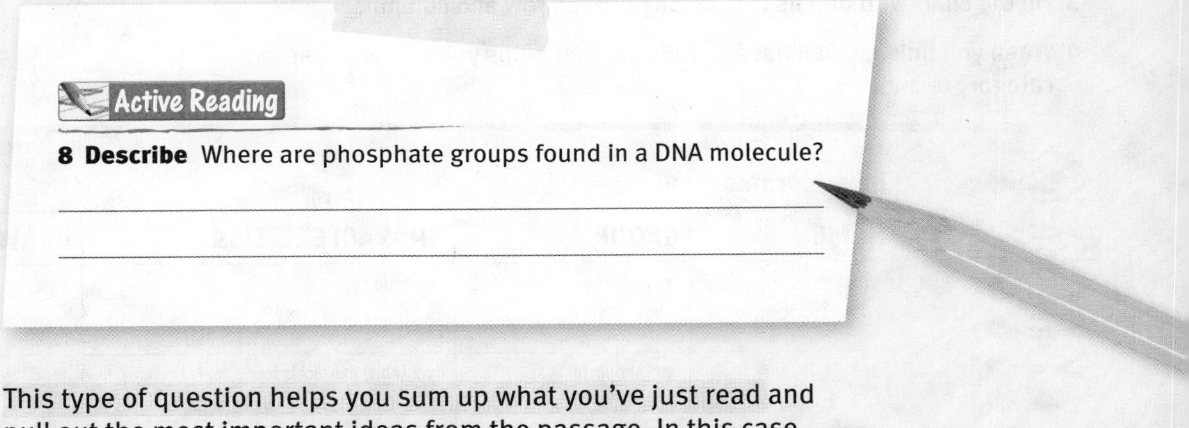
Active Reading
8 Describe Where are phosphate groups found in a DNA molecule?

This type of question helps you sum up what you’ve just read and pull out the most important ideas from the passage. In this case the question asks you to **describe** the structure of a DNA molecule that you have just read about. Other times you may be asked to do such things as **apply** a concept, **compare** two concepts, **summarize** a process, or **identify a cause-and-effect** relationship. You’ll be strengthening those critical thinking skills that you’ll use often in learning about science.

Using Graphic Organizers to Take Notes

Graphic organizers help you remember information as you read it for the first time and as you study it later. There are dozens of graphic organizers to choose from, so the first trick is to choose the one that's best suited to your purpose. Following are some graphic organizers to use for different purposes.

To remember lots of information	To relate a central idea to subordinate details	To describe a process	To make a comparison
• Arrange data in a Content Frame • Use Combination Notes to describe a concept in words and pictures	• Show relationships with a Mind Map or a Main Idea Web • Sum up relationships among many things with a Concept Map	• Use a Process Diagram to explain a procedure • Show a chain of events and results in a Cause-and-Effect Chart	• Compare two or more closely related things in a Venn Diagram

Content Frame

1 Make a four-column chart.

2 Fill the first column with categories (e.g., snail, ant, earthworm) and the first row with descriptive information (e.g., group, characteristic, appearance).

3 Fill the chart with details that belong in each row and column.

4 When you finish, you'll have a study aid that helps you compare one category to another.

Invertebrates

NAME	GROUP	CHARACTERISTICS	DRAWING
snail	mollusks	mangle	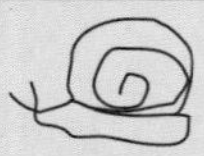
ant	arthropods	six legs, exoskeleton	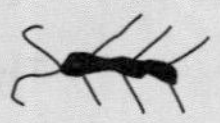
earthworm	segmented worms	segmented body, circulatory and digestive systems	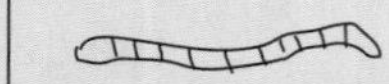
heartworm	roundworms	digestive system	
sea star	echinoderms	spiny skin, tube feet	
jellyfish	cnidarians	stinging cells	

Combination Notes

1 Make a two-column chart.
2 Write descriptive words and definitions in the first column.
3 Draw a simple sketch that helps you remember the meaning of the term in the second column.

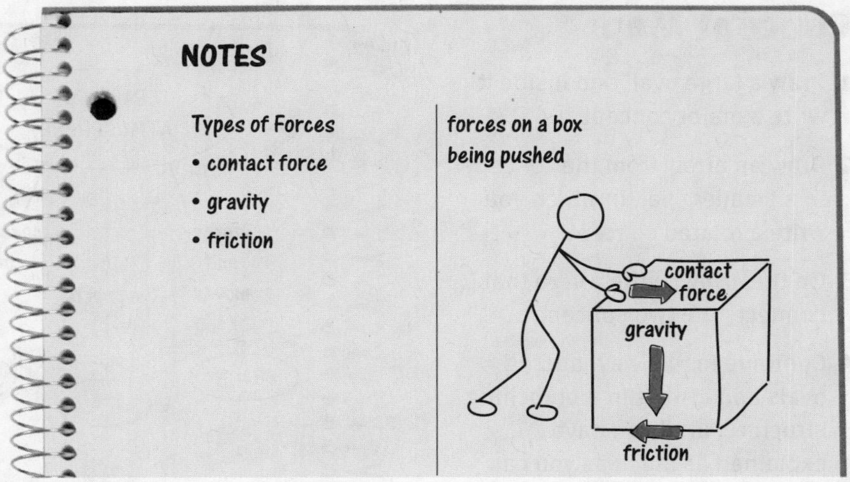
NOTES
Types of Forces
• contact force
• gravity
• friction
forces on a box being pushed
contact force
gravity
friction

Mind Map

1 Draw an oval, and inside it write a topic to analyze.
2 Draw two or more arms extending from the oval. Each arm represents a main idea about the topic.
3 Draw lines from the arms on which to write details about each of the main ideas.

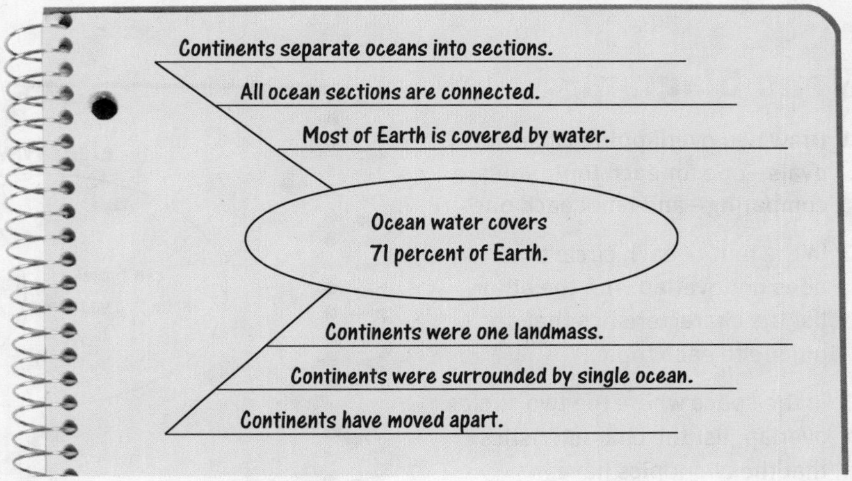
Continents separate oceans into sections.
All ocean sections are connected.
Most of Earth is covered by water.
Ocean water covers 71 percent of Earth.
Continents were one landmass.
Continents were surrounded by single ocean.
Continents have moved apart.

Main Idea Web

1 Make a box and write a concept you want to remember inside it.
2 Draw boxes around the central box, and label each one with a category of information about the concept (e.g., definition, formula, descriptive details).
3 Fill in the boxes with relevant details as you read.

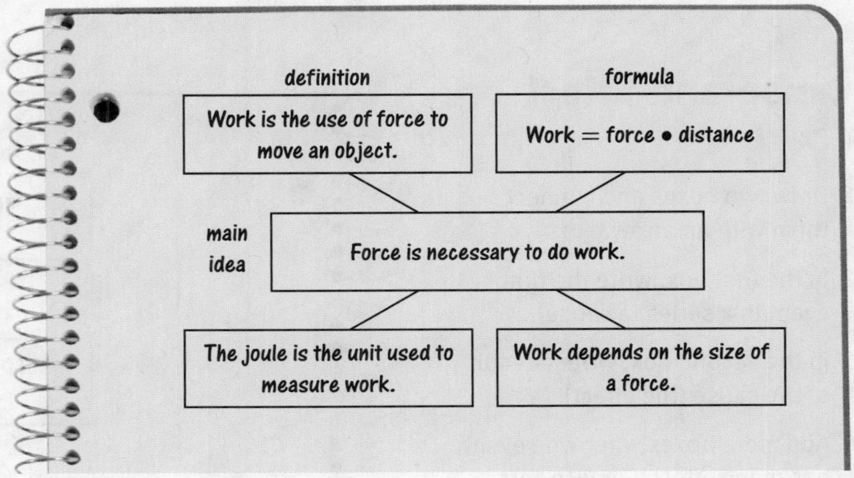
definition
Work is the use of force to move an object.
formula
Work = force • distance
main idea
Force is necessary to do work.
The joule is the unit used to measure work.
Work depends on the size of a force.

Reading and Study Skills

Concept Map

1 Draw a large oval, and inside it write a major concept.

2 Draw an arrow from the concept to a smaller oval, in which you write a related concept.

3 On the arrow, write a verb that connects the two concepts.

4 Continue in this way, adding ovals and arrows in a branching structure, until you have explained as much as you can about the main concept.

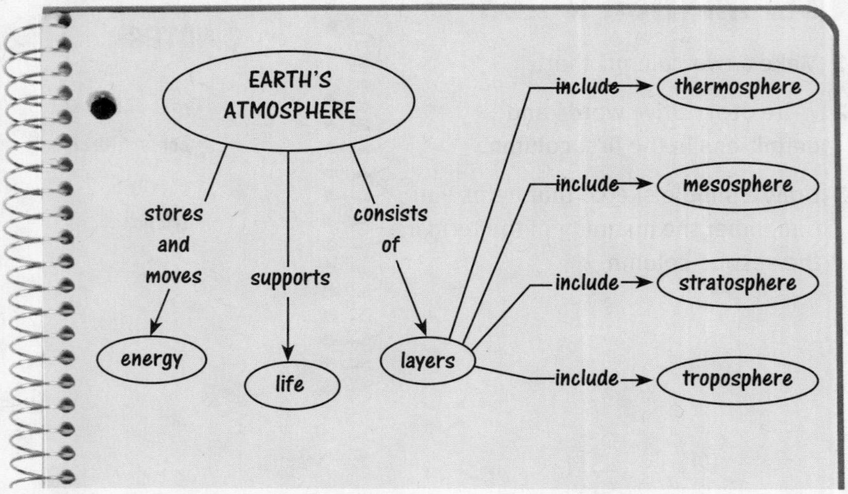

EARTH'S ATMOSPHERE
stores and moves
supports
consists of
energy
life
layers
include
include
include
include
thermosphere
mesosphere
stratosphere
troposphere

Venn Diagram

1 Draw two overlapping circles or ovals—one for each topic you are comparing—and label each one.

2 In the part of each circle that does not overlap with the other, list the characteristics that are unique to each topic.

3 In the space where the two circles overlap, list the characteristics that the two topics have in common.

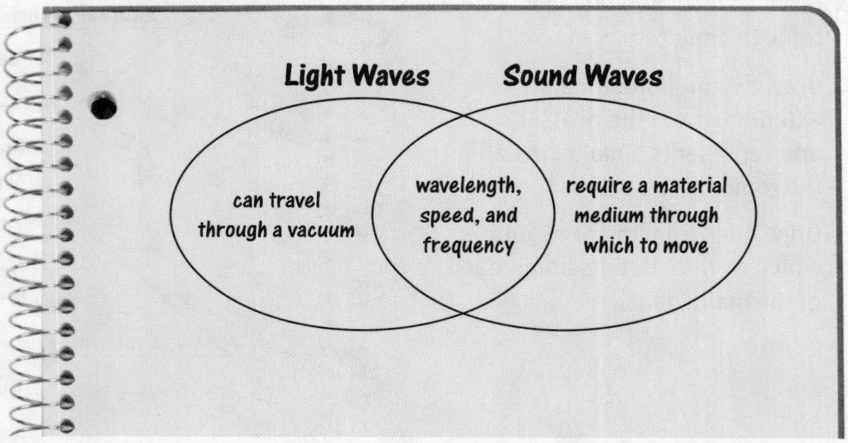

Light Waves
Sound Waves
can travel through a vacuum
wavelength, speed, and frequency
require a material medium through which to move

Cause-and-Effect Chart

1 Draw two boxes and connect them with an arrow.

2 In the first box, write the first event in a series (a cause).

3 In the second box, write a result of the cause (the effect).

4 Add more boxes when one event has many effects, or vice versa.

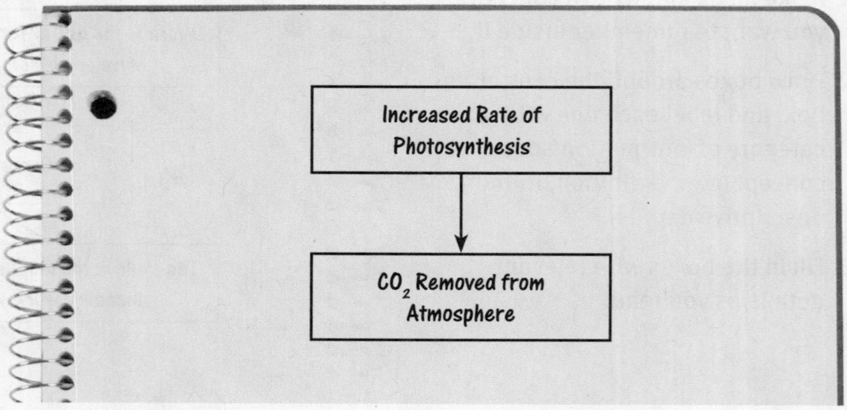

Increased Rate of Photosynthesis
CO_2 Removed from Atmosphere

Process Diagram

A process can be a never-ending cycle. As you can see in this technology design process, engineers may backtrack and repeat steps, they may skip steps entirely, or they may repeat the entire process before a useable design is achieved.

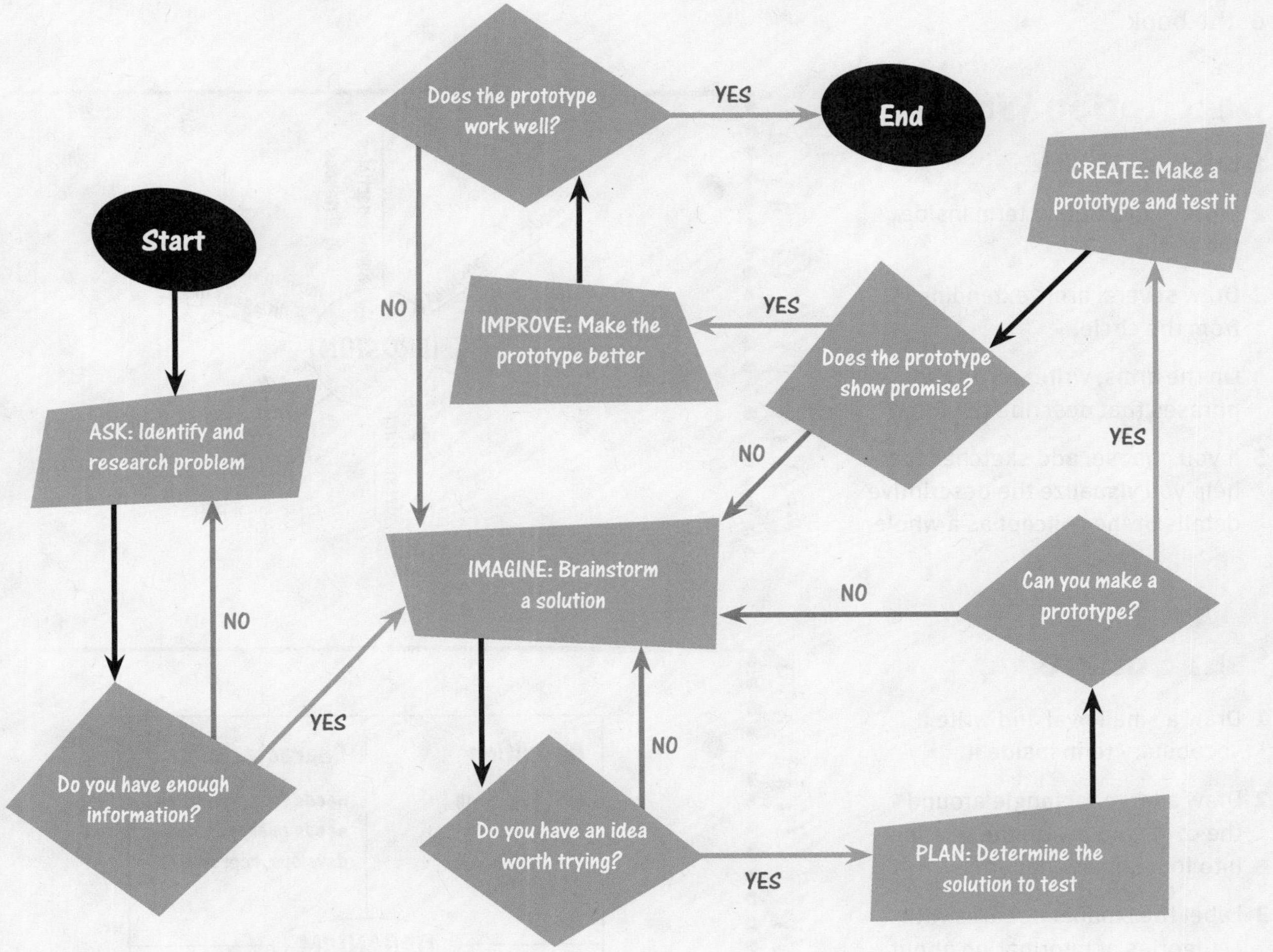

Start
ASK: Identify and research problem
NO
Do you have enough information?
YES
IMAGINE: Brainstorm a solution
NO
Do you have an idea worth trying?
YES
PLAN: Determine the solution to test
Can you make a prototype?
NO
YES
CREATE: Make a prototype and test it
Does the prototype show promise?
NO
YES
IMPROVE: Make the prototype better
Does the prototype work well?
NO
YES
End

Using Vocabulary Strategies

Important science terms are highlighted where they are first defined in this book. One way to remember these terms is to take notes and make sketches when you come to them. Use the strategies on this page and the next for this purpose. You will also find a formal definition of each science term in the Glossary at the end of the book.

Description Wheel

1 Draw a small circle.

2 Write a vocabulary term inside the circle.

3 Draw several arms extending from the circle.

4 On the arms, write words and phrases that describe the term.

5 If you choose, add sketches that help you visualize the descriptive details or the concept as a whole.

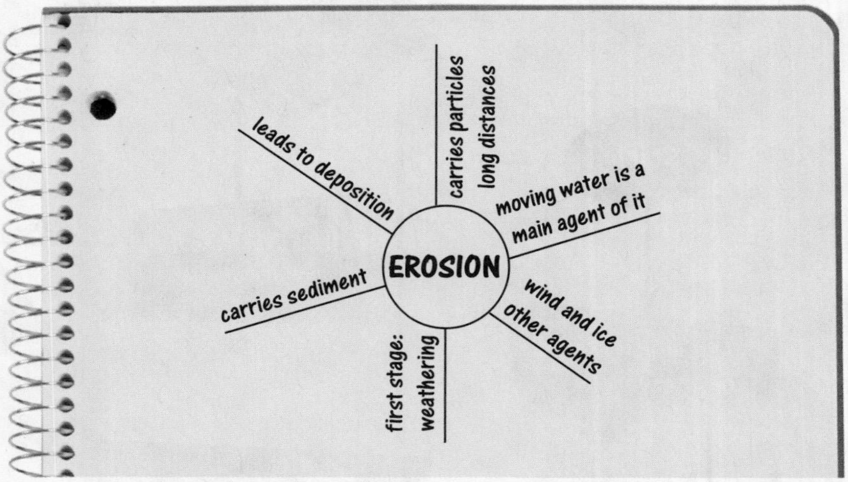

EROSION
leads to deposition
carries particles long distances
moving water is a main agent of it
wind and ice other agents
first stage: weathering
carries sediment

Four Square

1 Draw a small oval and write a vocabulary term inside it.

2 Draw a large rectangle around the oval, and divide the rectangle into four smaller squares.

3 Label the smaller squares with categories of information about the term, such as: definition, characteristics, examples, non-examples, appearance, and root words.

4 Fill the squares with descriptive words and drawings that will help you remember the overall meaning of the term and its essential details.

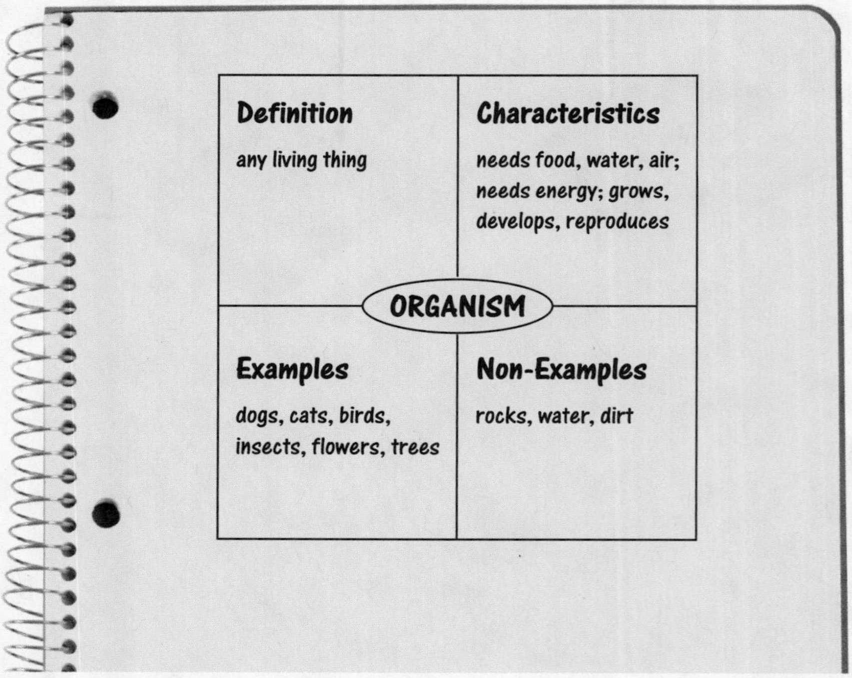

Definition
any living thing
Characteristics
needs food, water, air; needs energy; grows, develops, reproduces
ORGANISM
Examples
dogs, cats, birds, insects, flowers, trees
Non-Examples
rocks, water, dirt

Frame Game

1. Draw a small rectangle, and write a vocabulary term inside it.
2. Draw a larger rectangle around the smaller one. Connect the corners of the larger rectangle to the corners of the smaller one, creating four spaces that frame the word.
3. In each of the four parts of the frame, draw or write details that help define the term. Consider including a definition, essential characteristics, an equation, examples, and a sentence using the term.

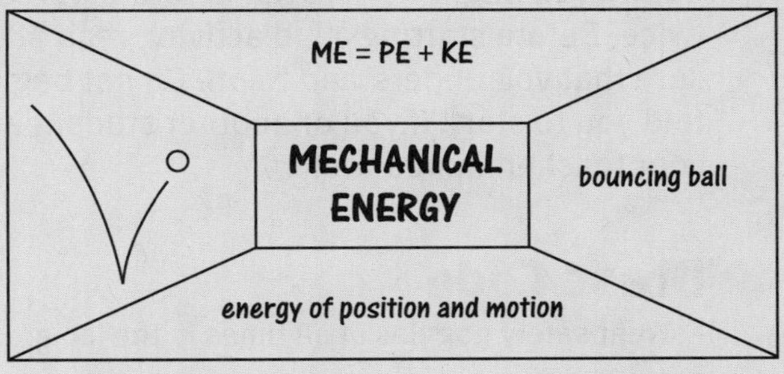
ME = PE + KE
MECHANICAL ENERGY
bouncing ball
energy of position and motion

Magnet Word

1. Draw horseshoe magnet, and write a vocabulary term inside it.
2. Add lines that extend from the sides of the magnet.
3. Brainstorm words and phrases that come to mind when you think about the term.
4. On the lines, write the words and phrases that describe something essential about the term.

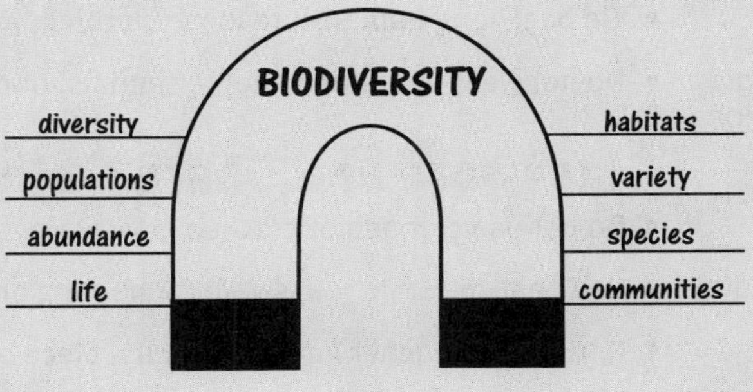
BIODIVERSITY
diversity
populations
abundance
life
habitats
variety
species
communities

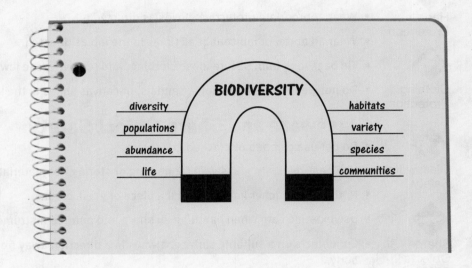

Word Triangle

1. Draw a triangle, and add lines to divide it into three parts.
2. Write a term and its definition in the bottom section of the triangle.
3. In the middle section, write a sentence in which the term is used correctly.
4. In the top section, draw a small picture to illustrate the term.

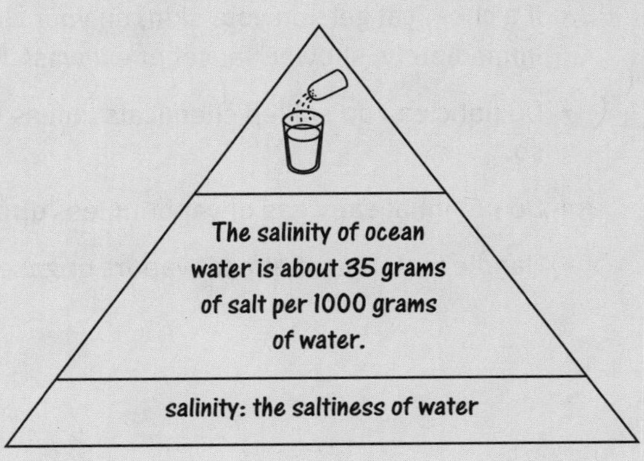
The salinity of ocean water is about 35 grams of salt per 1000 grams of water.
salinity: the saltiness of water

Science Skills

Safety in the Lab

Before you begin work in the laboratory, read these safety rules twice. Before starting a lab activity, read all directions and make sure that you understand them. Do not begin until your teacher has told you to start. If you or another student are injured in any way, tell your teacher immediately.

Dress Code

Eye Protection

Hand Protection

Clothing Protection

- Wear safety goggles at all times in the lab as directed.
- If chemicals get into your eyes, flush your eyes immediately.
- Do not wear contact lenses in the lab.
- Do not look directly at the sun or any intense light source or laser.
- Do not cut an object while holding the object in your hand.
- Wear appropriate protective gloves as directed.
- Wear an apron or lab coat at all times in the lab as directed.
- Tie back long hair, secure loose clothing, and remove loose jewelry.
- Do not wear open-toed shoes, sandals, or canvas shoes in the lab.

Glassware and Sharp Object Safety

Glassware Safety

Sharp Objects Safety

- Do not use chipped or cracked glassware.
- Use heat-resistant glassware for heating or storing hot materials.
- Notify your teacher immediately if a piece of glass breaks.
- Use extreme care when handling all sharp and pointed instruments.
- Cut objects on a suitable surface, always in a direction away from your body.

Chemical Safety

Chemical Safety

- If a chemical gets on your skin, on your clothing, or in your eyes, rinse it immediately (shower, faucet or eyewash fountain) and alert your teacher.
- Do not clean up spilled chemicals unless your teacher directs you to do so.
- Do not inhale any gas or vapor unless directed to do so by your teacher.
- Handle materials that emit vapors or gases in a well-ventilated area.

Electrical Safety

Electrical Safety

- Do not use equipment with frayed electrical cords or loose plugs.
- Do not use electrical equipment near water or when clothing or hands are wet.
- Hold the plug housing when you plug in or unplug equipment.

Heating and Fire Safety

Heating Safety

- Be aware of any source of flames, sparks, or heat (such as flames, heating coils, or hot plates) before working with any flammable substances.
- Know the location of lab fire extinguishers and fire-safety blankets.
- Know your school's fire-evacuation routes.
- If your clothing catches on fire, walk to the lab shower to put out the fire.
- Never leave a hot plate unattended while it is turned on or while it is cooling.
- Use tongs or appropriate insulated holders when handling heated objects.
- Allow all equipment to cool before storing it.

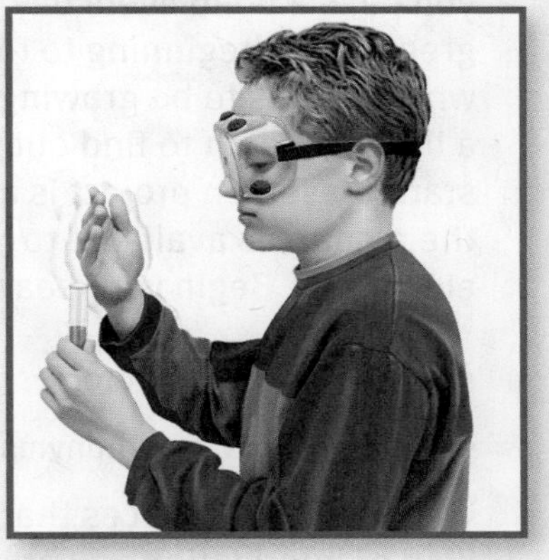

Wafting

Plant and Animal Safety

Plant Safety

Animal Safety

- Do not eat any part of a plant.
- Do not pick any wild plants unless your teacher instructs you to do so.
- Handle animals only as your teacher directs.
- Treat animals carefully and respectfully.
- Wash your hands thoroughly after handling any plant or animal.

Cleanup

Proper Waste Disposal

Hygienic Care

- Clean all work surfaces and protective equipment as directed by your teacher.
- Dispose of hazardous materials or sharp objects only as directed by your teacher.
- Keep your hands away from your face while you are working on any activity.
- Wash your hands thoroughly before you leave the lab or after any activity.

Designing, Conducting, and Reporting an Experiment

An experiment is an organized procedure to study something under specific conditions. Use the following steps of the scientific method when designing or conducting a controlled experiment.

1 Identify a Research Problem

Every day, you make observations by using your senses to gather information. Careful observations lead to good questions, and good questions can lead you to an experiment. Imagine, for example, that you pass a pond every day on your way to school, and you notice green scum beginning to form on top of it. You wonder what it is and why it seems to be growing. You list your questions, and then you do a little research to find out what is already known. A good place to start a research project is at the library. A library catalog lists all of the resources available to you at that library and often those found elsewhere. Begin your search by using:

- keywords or main topics.
- similar words, or synonyms, of your keyword.

The types of resources that will be helpful to you will depend on the kind of information you are interested in. And, some resources are more reliable for a given topic than others. Some different kinds of useful resources are:

- magazines and journals (or periodicals)—articles on a topic.
- encyclopedias—a good overview of a topic.
- books on specific subjects—details about a topic.
- newspapers—useful for current events.

The Internet can also be a great place to find information. Some of your library's reference materials may even be online. When using the Internet, however, it is especially important to make sure you are using appropriate and reliable sources. Websites of universities and government agencies are usually more accurate and reliable than websites created by individuals or businesses. Decide which sources are relevant and reliable for your topic. If in doubt, check with your teacher.

Take notes as you read through the information in these resources. You will probably come up with many questions and ideas for which you can do more research as needed. Once you feel you have enough information, think about the questions you have on the topic. Then, write down the problem that you want to investigate. Your notes might look like these.

Research Questions	Research Problem	Library and Internet Resources
• How do algae grow? • How do people measure algae? • What kind of fertilizer would affect the growth of algae? • Can fertilizer and algae be used safely in a lab? How?	How does fertilizer affect the algae in a pond?	Pond fertilization: initiating an algal bloom - from University of California Davis website. Blue-Green algae in Wisconsin waters-from the Department of Natural Resources of Wisconsin website.

As you gather information from reliable sources, record details about each source, including author name(s), title, date of publication, and/or web address. Make sure to also note the specific information that you use from each source. Staying organized in this way will be important when you write your report and create a bibliography or works cited list. Recording this information and staying organized will help you credit the appropriate author(s) for the information that you have gathered.

Representing someone else's ideas or work as your own, (without giving the original author credit), is known as plagiarism. Plagiarism can be intentional or unintentional. The best way to make sure that you do not commit plagiarism is to always do your own work and to always give credit to others when you use their words or ideas.

Current scientific research is built on scientific research and discoveries that have happened in the past. This means that scientists are constantly learning from each other and combining ideas to learn more about the natural world through investigation. But, a good scientist always credits the ideas and research that they have gathered from other people to those people. There are more details about crediting sources and creating a bibliography under step 9.

2 Make a Prediction

A prediction is a statement of what you expect will happen in your experiment. Before making a prediction, you need to decide in a general way what you will do in your procedure. You may state your prediction in an if-then format.

Prediction

If the amount of fertilizer in the pond water is increased, then the amount of algae will also increase.

3 Form a Hypothesis

Many experiments are designed to test a hypothesis. A hypothesis is a tentative explanation for an expected result. You have predicted that additional fertilizer will cause additional algae growth in pond water; your hypothesis should state the connection between fertilizer and algal growth.

Hypothesis

The addition of fertilizer to pond water will affect the amount of algae in the pond.

4 Identify Variables to Test the Hypothesis

The next step is to design an experiment to test the hypothesis. The experimental results may or may not support the hypothesis. Either way, the information that results from the experiment may be useful for future investigations.

Experimental Group and Control Group

An experiment to determine how two factors are related has a control group and an experimental group. The two groups are the same, except that the investigator changes a single factor in the experimental group and does not change it in the control group.

Experimental Group: two containers of pond water with one drop of fertilizer solution added to each

Control Group: two containers of the same pond water sampled at the same time but with no fertilizer solution added

Variables and Constants

In a controlled experiment, a variable is any factor that can change. Constants are all of the variables that are kept the same in both the experimental group and the control group.

The independent variable is the factor that is manipulated or changed in order to test the effect of the change on another variable. The dependent variable is the factor the investigator measures to gather data about the effect.

Independent Variable	Dependent Variable	Constants
Amount of fertilizer in pond water	Growth of algae in the pond water	• Where and when the pond water is obtained • The type of container used • Light and temperature conditions where the water is stored

5 Write a Procedure

Write each step of your procedure. Start each step with a verb, or action word, and keep the steps short. Your procedure should be clear enough for someone else to use as instructions for repeating your experiment.

Procedure

1. Use the masking tape and the marker to label the containers with your initials, the date, and the identifiers "Jar 1 with Fertilizer," "Jar 2 with Fertilizer," "Jar 1 without Fertilizer," and "Jar 2 without Fertilizer."
2. Put on your gloves. Use the large container to obtain a sample of pond water.
3. Divide the water sample equally among the four smaller containers.
4. Use the eyedropper to add one drop of fertilizer solution to the two containers labeled, "Jar 1 with Fertilizer," and "Jar 2 with Fertilizer".
5. Cover the containers with clear plastic wrap. Use the scissors to punch ten holes in each of the covers.
6. Place all four containers on a window ledge. Make sure that they all receive the same amount of light.
7. Observe the containers every day for one week.
8. Use the ruler to measure the diameter of the largest clump of algae in each container, and record your measurements daily.

DR May 3
Jar 1 with Fertilizer
DR May 3
Jar 2 with Fertilizer
DR May 3
Jar 1 without Fertilizer
DR May 3
Jar 2 without Fertilizer

6 Experiment and Collect Data

Once you have all of your materials and your procedure has been approved, you can begin to experiment and collect data. Record both quantitative data (measurements) and qualitative data (observations), as shown below.

Algal Growth and Fertilizer

	Experimental Group		Control Group		
Date and Time	Jar 1 with Fertilizer (diameter of algal clump in mm)	Jar 2 with Fertilizer (diameter of algal clump in mm)	Jar 1 without Fertilizer (diameter of algal clump in mm)	Jar 2 without Fertilizer (diameter of algal clump in mm)	Observations
5/3 4:00 p.m.	0	0	0	0	condensation in all containers
5/4 4:00 p.m.	0	3	0	0	tiny green blobs in Jar 2 with fertilizer
5/5 4:15 p.m.	4	5	0	3	green blobs in Jars 1 and 2 with fertilizer and Jar 2 without fertilizer
5/6 4:00 p.m.	5	6	0	4	water light green in Jar 2 with fertilizer
5/7 4:00 p.m.	8	10	0	6	water light green in Jars 1 and 2 with fertilizer and Jar 2 without fertilizer
5/8 3:30 p.m.	10	18	0	6	cover off of Jar 2 with fertilizer
5/9 3:30 p.m.	14	23	0	8	drew sketches of each container

Drawings of Samples Viewed Under Microscope on 5/9 at 100x

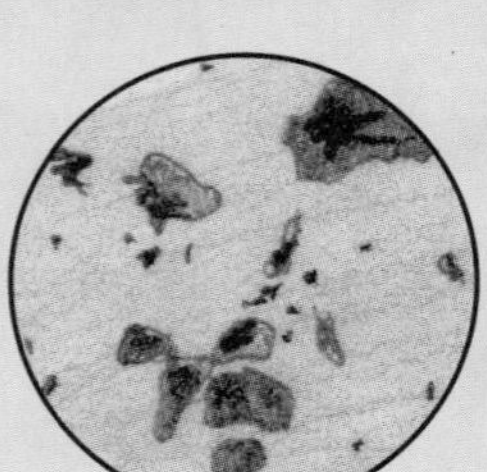
Jar 1 with Fertilizer

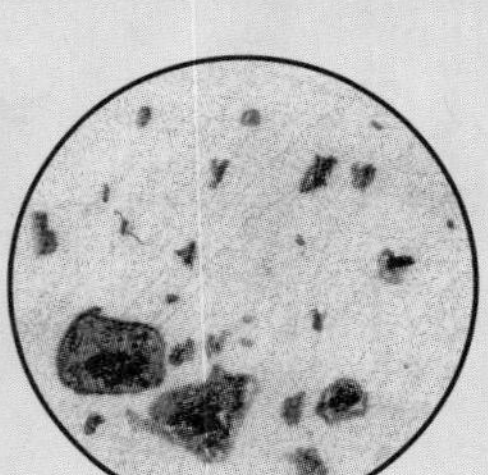
Jar 2 with Fertilizer

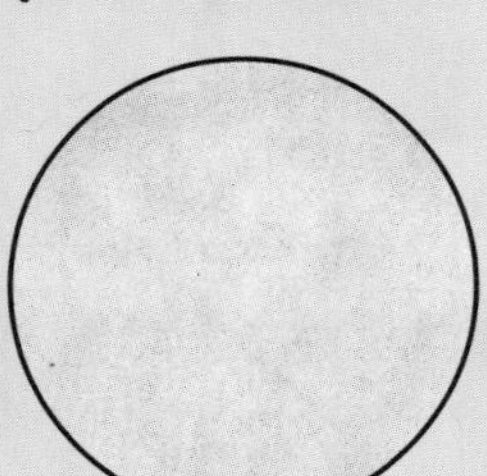
Jar 1 without Fertilizer

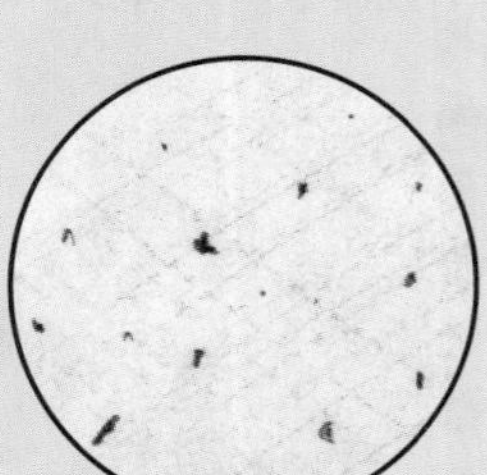
Jar 2 without Fertilizer

7 Analyze Data

After you complete your experiment, you must analyze all of the data you have gathered. Tables, statistics, and graphs are often used in this step to organize and analyze both the qualitative and quantitative data. Sometimes, your qualitative data are best used to help explain the relationships you see in your quantitative data.

Computer graphing software is useful for creating a graph from data that you have collected. Most graphing software can make line graphs, pie charts, or bar graphs from data that has been organized in a spreadsheet. Graphs are useful for understanding relationships in the data and for communicating the results of your experiment.

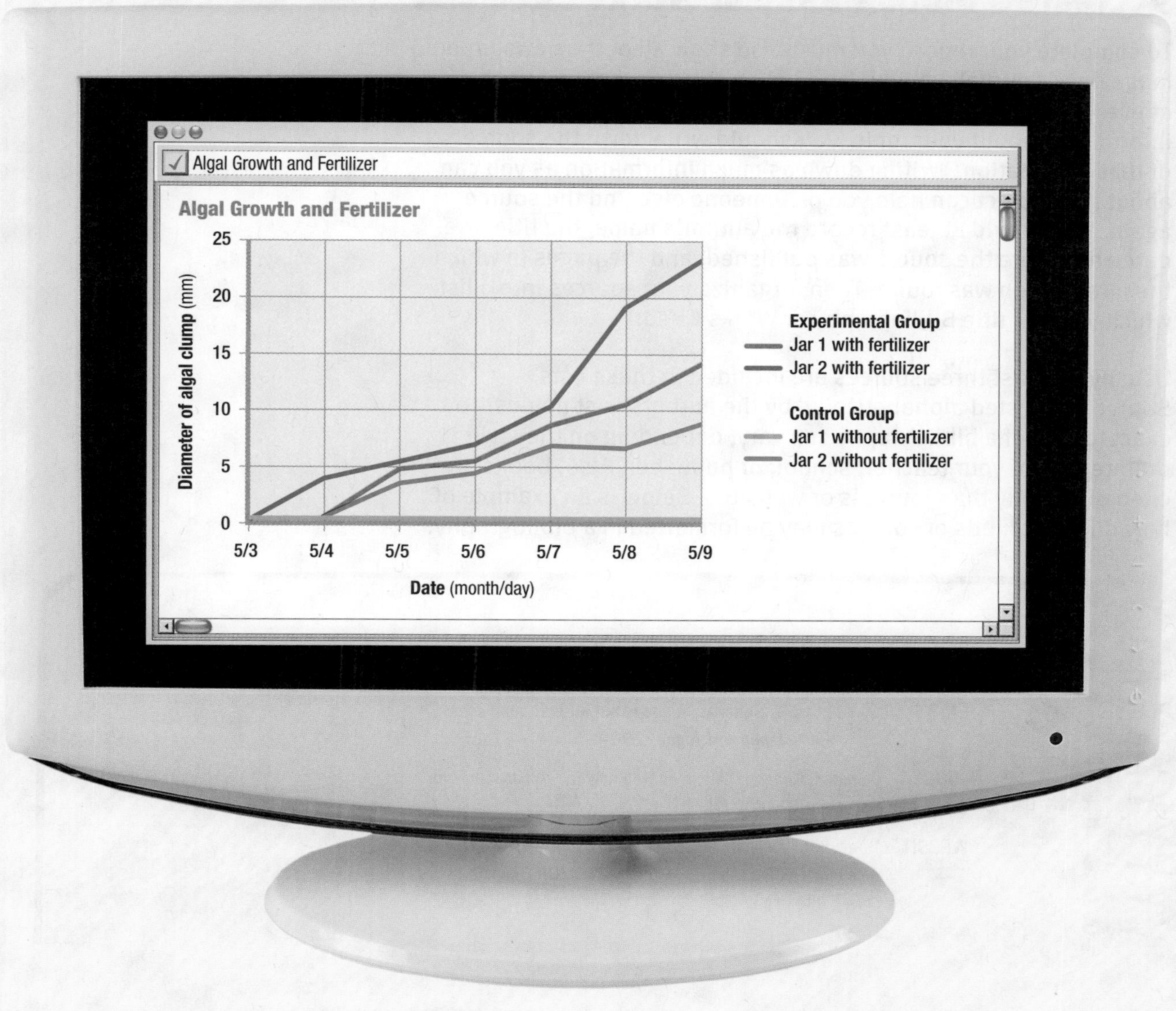

Algal Growth and Fertilizer
Algal Growth and Fertilizer
Diameter of algal clump (mm)
0
5
10
15
20
25
5/3
5/4
5/5
5/6
5/7
5/8
5/9
Date (month/day)
Experimental Group
Jar 1 with fertilizer
Jar 2 with fertilizer
Control Group
Jar 1 without fertilizer
Jar 2 without fertilizer

8 Make Conclusions

To draw conclusions from your experiment, first, write your results. Then, compare your results with your hypothesis. Do your results support your hypothesis? What have you learned?

Conclusion

More algae grew in the pond water to which fertilizer had been added than in the pond water to which fertilizer had not been added. My hypothesis was supported. I conclude that it is possible that the growth of algae in ponds can be influenced by the input of fertilizer.

9 Create a Bibliography or Works Cited List

To complete your report, you must also show all of the newspapers, magazines, journals, books, and online sources that you used at every stage of your investigation. Whenever you find useful information about your topic, you should write down the source of that information. Writing down as much information as you can about the subject can help you or someone else find the source again. You should at least record the author's name, the title, the date and where the source was published, and the pages in which the information was found. Then, organize your sources into a list, which you can title Bibliography or Works Cited.

Usually, at least three sources are included in these lists. Sources are listed alphabetically, by the authors' last names. The exact format of a bibliography can vary, depending on the style preferences of your teacher, school, or publisher. Also, books are cited differently than journals or websites. Below is an example of how different kinds of sources may be formatted in a bibliography.

BOOK: Hauschultz, Sara. Freshwater Algae. Brainard, Minnesota: Northwoods Publishing, 2011.

ENCYCLOPEDIA: Lasure, Sedona. "Algae is not all just pond scum." Encyclopedia of Algae. 2009.

JOURNAL: Johnson, Keagan. "Algae as we know it." Sci Journal, vol 64. (September 2010): 201-211.

WEBSITE: Dout, Bill. "Keeping algae scum out of birdbaths." Help Keep Earth Clean. News. January 26, 2011. <www.SaveEarth.org>.

Using a Microscope

Scientists use microscopes to see very small objects that cannot easily be seen with the eye alone. A microscope magnifies the image of an object so that small details may be observed. A microscope that you may use can magnify an object 400 times—the object will appear 400 times larger than its actual size.

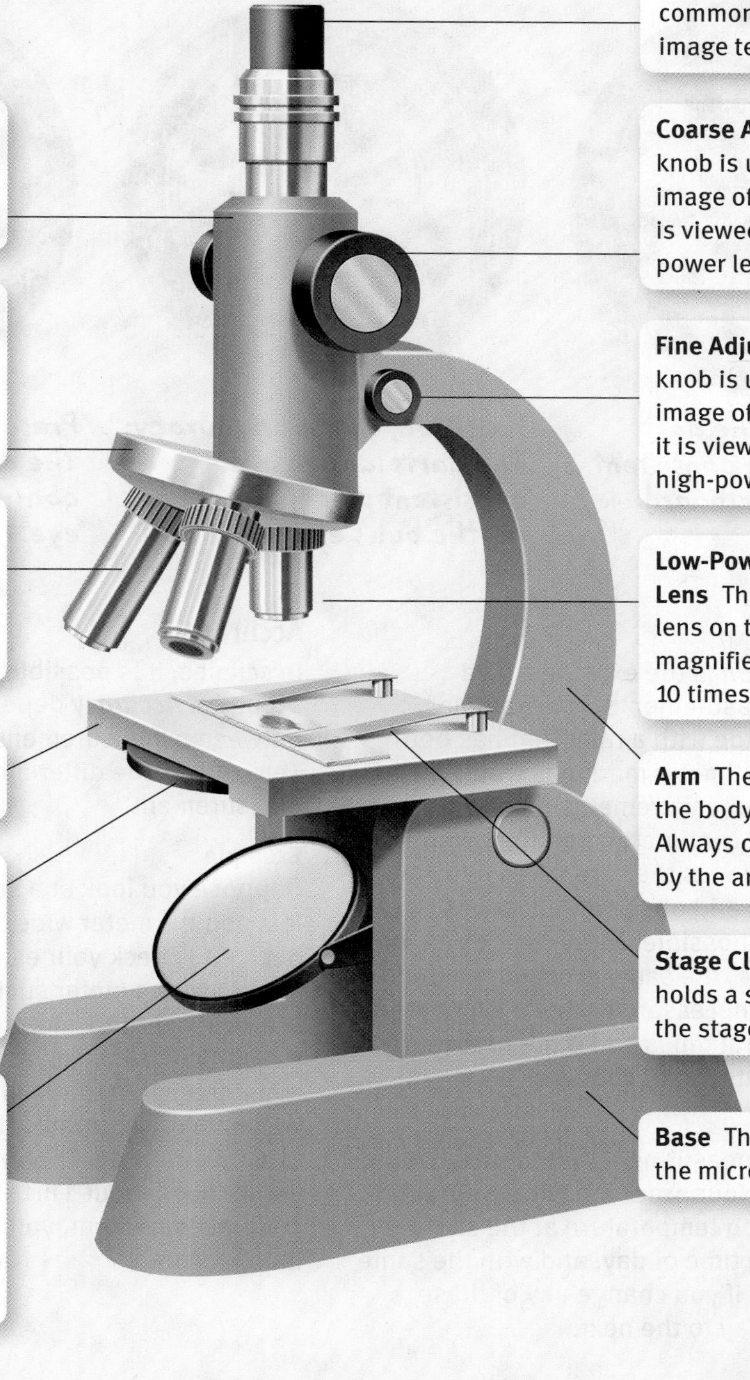

Eyepiece Objects are viewed through the eyepiece. The eyepiece contains a lens that commonly magnifies an image ten times.

Body The body separates the lens in the eyepiece from the objective lenses below.

Coarse Adjustment This knob is used to focus the image of an object when it is viewed through the low-power lens.

Nosepiece The nosepiece holds the objective lenses above the stage and rotates so that all lenses may be used.

Fine Adjustment This knob is used to focus the image of an object when it is viewed through the high-power lens.

High-Power Objective Lens This is the largest lens on the nosepiece. It magnifies an image approximately 40 times.

Low-Power Objective Lens This is the smallest lens on the nosepiece. It magnifies images about 10 times.

Stage The stage supports the object being viewed.

Arm The arm supports the body above the stage. Always carry a microscope by the arm and base.

Diaphragm The diaphragm is used to adjust the amount of light passing through the slide and into an objective lens.

Stage Clip The stage clip holds a slide in place on the stage.

Mirror or Light Source Some microscopes use light that is reflected through the stage by a mirror. Other microscopes have their own light sources.

Base The base supports the microscope.

Measuring Accurately

Precision and Accuracy

When you do a scientific investigation, it is important that your methods, observations, and data be both precise and accurate.

20 1 18 4 13 6 10 15 2 17 3 19 7 16 8 11 14 9 12 5

Low precision: The darts did not land in a consistent place on the dartboard.

20 1 18 4 13 6 10 15 2 17 3 19 7 16 8 11 14 9 12 5

Precision, but not accuracy: The darts landed in a consistent place, but did not hit the bull's eye.

20 1 18 4 13 6 10 15 2 17 3 19 7 16 8 11 14 9 12 5

Prescision and accuracy: The darts landed consistently on the bull's eye.

Precision

In science, *precision* is the exactness and consistency of measurements. For example, measurements made with a ruler that has both centimeter and millimeter markings would be more precise than measurements made with a ruler that has only centimeter markings. Another indicator of precision is the care taken to make sure that methods and observations are as exact and consistent as possible. Every time a particular experiment is done, the same procedure should be used. Precision is necessary because experiments are repeated several times and if the procedure changes, the results might change.

Example

Suppose you are measuring temperatures over a two-week period. Your precision will be greater if you measure each temperature at the same place, at the same time of day, and with the same thermometer than if you change any of these factors from one day to the next.

Accuracy

In science, it is possible to be precise but not accurate. *Accuracy* depends on the difference between a measurement and an actual value. The smaller the difference, the more accurate the measurement.

Example

Suppose you look at a stream and estimate that it is about 1 meter wide at a particular place. You decide to check your estimate by measuring the stream with a meter stick, and you determine that the stream is 1.32 meters wide. However, because it is difficult to measure the width of a stream with a meter stick, it turns out that your measurement was not very accurate. The stream is actually 1.14 meters wide. Therefore, even though your estimate of about 1 meter was less precise than your measurement, your estimate was actually more accurate.

Graduated Cylinders

How to Measure the Volume of a Liquid with a Graduated Cylinder

- Be sure that the graduated cylinder is on a flat surface so that your measurement will be accurate.
- When reading the scale on a graduated cylinder, be sure to have your eyes at the level of the surface of the liquid.
- The surface of the liquid will be curved in the graduated cylinder. Read the volume of the liquid at the bottom of the curve, or meniscus (muh-NIHS-kuhs).
- You can use a graduated cylinder to find the volume of a solid object by measuring the increase in a liquid's level after you add the object to the cylinder.

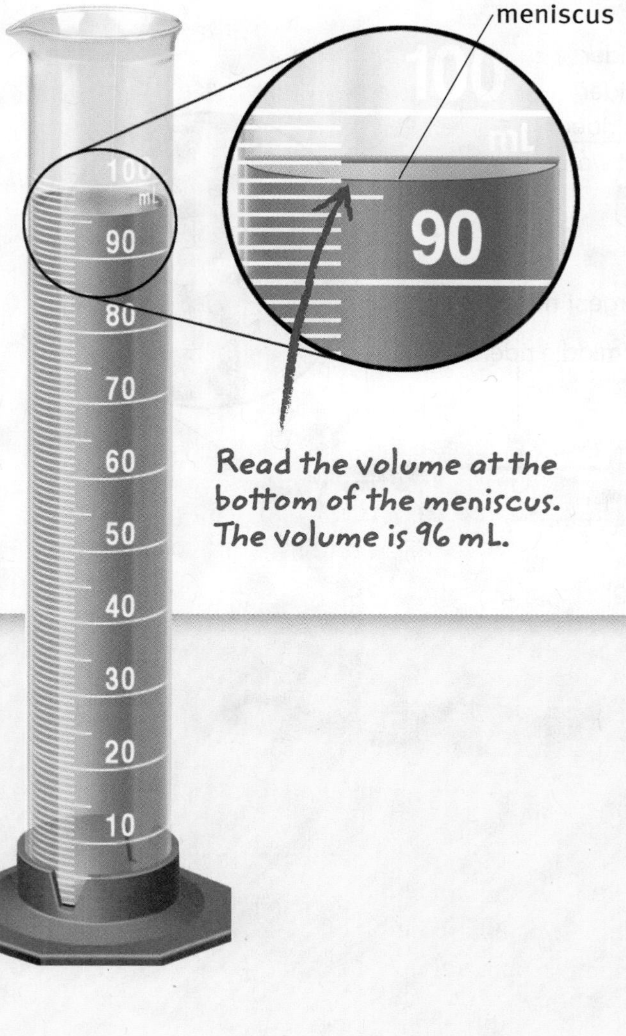
meniscus
100
mL
90
80
70
60
50
40
30
20
10
Read the volume at the bottom of the meniscus. The volume is 96 mL.

Metric Rulers

How to Measure the Length of a Leaf with a Metric Ruler

1 Lay a ruler flat on top of the leaf so that the 1-centimeter mark lines up with one end. Make sure the ruler and the leaf do not move between the time you line them up and the time you take the measurement.

2 Look straight down on the ruler so that you can see exactly how the marks line up with the other end of the leaf.

3 Estimate the length by which the leaf extends beyond a marking. For example, the leaf below extends about halfway between the 4.2-centimeter and 4.3-centimeter marks, so the apparent measurement is about 4.25 centimeters.

4 Remember to subtract 1 centimeter from your apparent measurement, since you started at the 1-centimeter mark on the ruler and not at the end. The leaf is about 3.25 centimeters long (4.25 cm − 1 cm = 3.25 cm).

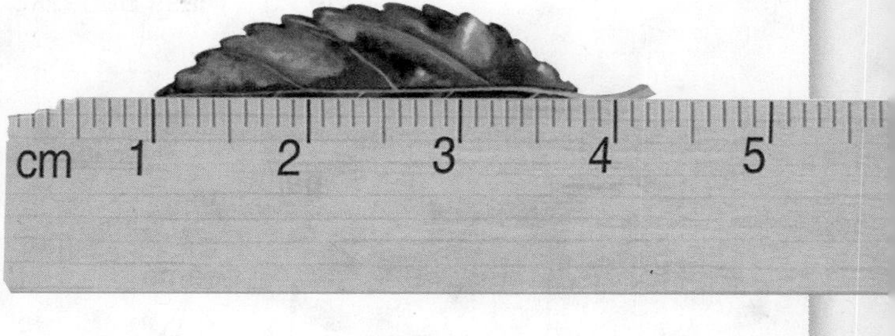
cm
1
2
3
4
5

Triple Beam Balance

This balance has a pan and three beams with sliding masses, called riders. At one end of the beams is a pointer that indicates whether the mass on the pan is equal to the masses shown on the beams.

How to Measure the Mass of an Object

1. Make sure the balance is zeroed before measuring the mass of an object. The balance is zeroed if the pointer is at zero when nothing is on the pan and the riders are at their zero points. Use the adjustment knob at the base of the balance to zero it.
2. Place the object to be measured on the pan.
3. Move the riders one notch at a time away from the pan. Begin with the largest rider. If moving the largest rider one notch brings the pointer below zero, begin measuring the mass of the object with the next smaller rider.
4. Change the positions of the riders until they balance the mass on the pan and the pointer is at zero. Then add the readings from the three beams to determine the mass of the object.

300 g	position of largest rider
90 g	position of middle rider
+ 3 g	position of smallest rider
393 g	mass of beaker and water

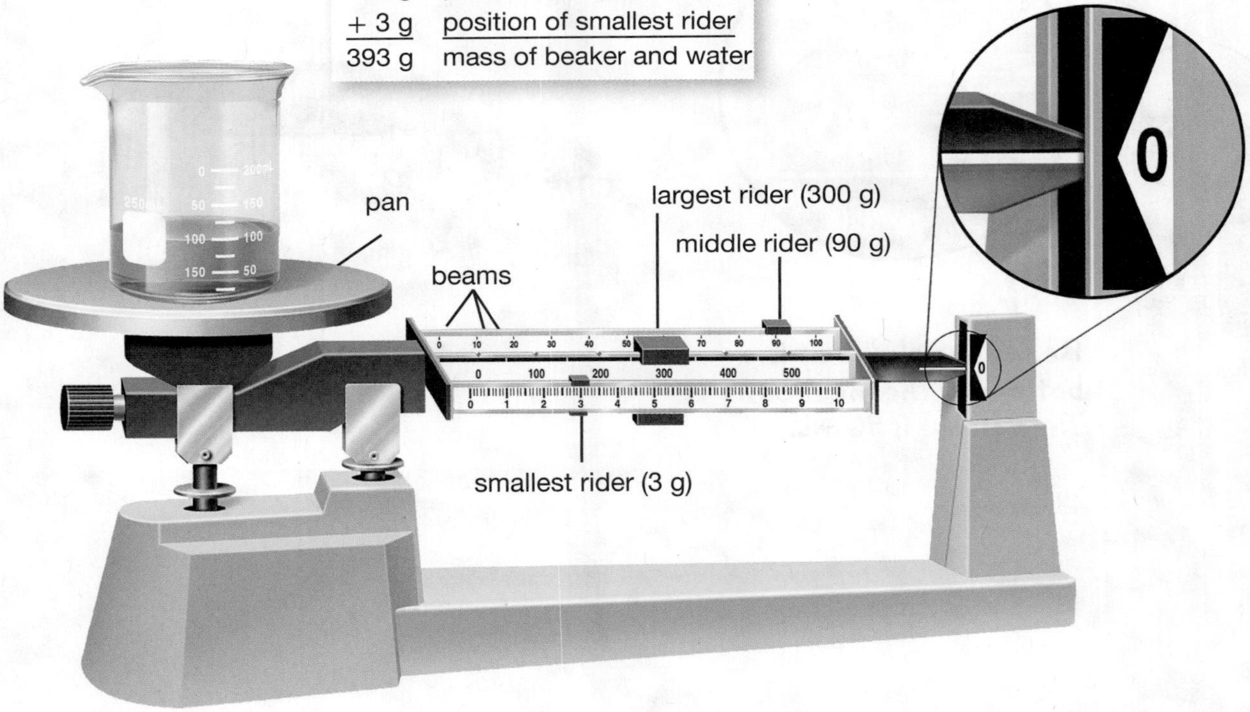
pan
beams
largest rider (300 g)
middle rider (90 g)
smallest rider (3 g)
0

Using the Metric System and SI Units

Scientists use International System (SI) units for measurements of distance, volume, mass, and temperature. The International System is based on powers of ten and the metric system of measurement.

Basic SI Units		
Quantity	**Name**	**Symbol**
length	meter	m
volume	liter	L
mass	gram	g
temperature	kelvin	K

SI Prefixes		
Prefix	**Symbol**	**Power of 10**
kilo-	k	1000
hecto-	h	100
deca-	da	10
deci-	d	0.1 or $\frac{1}{10}$
centi-	c	0.01 or $\frac{1}{100}$
milli-	m	0.001 or $\frac{1}{1000}$

Changing Metric Units

You can change from one unit to another in the metric system by multiplying or dividing by a power of 10.

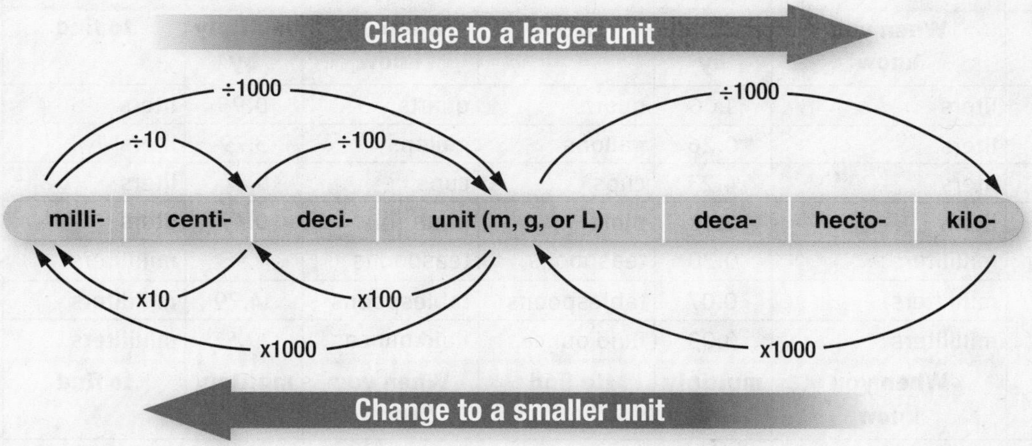
Change to a larger unit
÷1000
÷10
÷100
÷1000
milli-
centi-
deci-
unit (m, g, or L)
deca-
hecto-
kilo-
x10
x100
x1000
x1000
Change to a smaller unit

Example

Change 0.64 liters to milliliters.

1 Decide whether to multiply or divide.

2 Select the power of 10.

Change to a smaller unit by multiplying

mL ← x 1000 — L

0.64 x 1000 = 640.

ANSWER *0.64 L = 640 mL*

Example

Change 23.6 grams to kilograms.

1 Decide whether to multiply or divide.

2 Select the power of 10.

Change to a larger unit by dividing

g — ÷ 1000 → kg

26.3 ÷ 1000 = 0.0263

ANSWER *23.6 g = 0.0236 kg*

Converting Between SI and U.S. Customary Units

Use the chart below when you need to convert between SI units and U.S. customary units.

SI Unit	From SI to U.S. Customary			From U.S. Customary to SI		
Length	**When you know**	**multiply by**	**to find**	**When you know**	**multiply by**	**to find**
kilometer (km) = 1000 m	kilometers	0.62	miles	miles	1.61	kilometers
meter (m) = 100 cm	meters	3.28	feet	feet	0.3048	meters
centimeter (cm) = 10 mm	centimeters	0.39	inches	inches	2.54	centimeters
millimeter (mm) = 0.1 cm	millimeters	0.04	inches	inches	25.4	millimeters
Area	**When you know**	**multiply by**	**to find**	**When you know**	**multiply by**	**to find**
square kilometer (km^2)	square kilometers	0.39	square miles	square miles	2.59	square kilometers
square meter (m^2)	square meters	1.2	square yards	square yards	0.84	square meters
square centimeter (cm^2)	square centimeters	0.155	square inches	square inches	6.45	square centimeters
Volume	**When you know**	**multiply by**	**to find**	**When you know**	**multiply by**	**to find**
liter (L) = 1000 mL	liters	1.06	quarts	quarts	0.95	liters
	liters	0.26	gallons	gallons	3.79	liters
	liters	4.23	cups	cups	0.24	liters
	liters	2.12	pints	pints	0.47	liters
milliliter (mL) = 0.001 L	milliliters	0.20	teaspoons	teaspoons	4.93	milliliters
	milliliters	0.07	tablespoons	tablespoons	14.79	milliliters
	milliliters	0.03	fluid ounces	fluid ounces	29.57	milliliters
Mass	**When you know**	**multiply by**	**to find**	**When you know**	**multiply by**	**to find**
kilogram (kg) = 1000 g	kilograms	2.2	pounds	pounds	0.45	kilograms
gram (g) = 1000 mg	grams	0.035	ounces	ounces	28.35	grams

Temperature Conversions

Even though the kelvin is the SI base unit of temperature, the degree Celsius will be the unit you use most often in your science studies. The formulas below show the relationships between temperatures in degrees Fahrenheit (°F), degrees Celsius (°C), and kelvins (K).

$$°C = \frac{5}{9}(°F - 32) \qquad °F = \frac{9}{5}°C + 32 \qquad K = °C + 273$$

Examples of Temperature Conversions

Condition	Degrees Celsius	Degrees Fahrenheit
Freezing point of water	0	32
Cool day	10	50
Mild day	20	68
Warm day	30	86
Normal body temperature	37	98.6
Very hot day	40	104
Boiling point of water	100	212

Math Refresher

Performing Calculations

Science requires an understanding of many math concepts. The following pages will help you review some important math skills.

Mean

The mean is the sum of all values in a data set divided by the total number of values in the data set. The mean is also called the *average*.

Example

Find the mean of the following set of numbers: 5, 4, 7, and 8.

Step 1 Find the sum.

$5 + 4 + 7 + 8 = 24$

Step 2 Divide the sum by the number of numbers in your set. Because there are four numbers in this example, divide the sum by 4.

$24 \div 4 = 6$

Answer The average, or mean, is 6.

Median

The median of a data set is the middle value when the values are written in numerical order. If a data set has an even number of values, the median is the mean of the two middle values.

Example

To find the median of a set of measurements, arrange the values in order from least to greatest. The median is the middle value.

13 mm 14 mm 16 mm 21 mm 23 mm

Answer The median is 16 mm.

Mode

The mode of a data set is the value that occurs most often.

Example

To find the mode of a set of measurements, arrange the values in order from least to greatest and determine the value that occurs most often.

13 mm, 14 mm, 14 mm, 16 mm,
21 mm, 23 mm, 25 mm

Answer The mode is 14 mm.

A data set can have more than one mode or no mode. For example, the following data set has modes of 2 mm and 4 mm:

2 mm 2 mm 3 mm 4 mm 4 mm

The data set below has no mode, because no value occurs more often than any other.

2 mm 3 mm 4 mm 5 mm

Math Refresher

Ratios

A **ratio** is a comparison between numbers, and it is usually written as a fraction.

Example

Find the ratio of thermometers to students if you have 36 thermometers and 48 students in your class.

Step 1 Write the ratio.

$$\frac{36 \text{ thermometers}}{48 \text{ students}}$$

Step 2 Simplify the fraction to its simplest form.

$$\frac{36}{48} = \frac{36 \div 12}{48 \div 12} = \frac{3}{4}$$

The ratio of thermometers to students is 3 to 4 or 3:4.

Proportions

A **proportion** is an equation that states that two ratios are equal.

$$\frac{3}{1} = \frac{12}{4}$$

To solve a proportion, you can use cross-multiplication. If you know three of the quantities in a proportion, you can use cross-multiplication to find the fourth.

Example

Imagine that you are making a scale model of the solar system for your science project. The diameter of Jupiter is 11.2 times the diameter of the Earth. If you are using a plastic-foam ball that has a diameter of 2 cm to represent the Earth, what must the diameter of the ball representing Jupiter be?

$$\frac{11.2}{1} = \frac{x}{2 \text{ cm}}$$

Step 1 Cross-multiply.

$$\frac{11.2}{1} = \frac{x}{2}$$

$$11.2 \times 2 = x \times 1$$

Step 2 Multiply.

$$22.4 = x \times 1$$

$$x = 22.4 \text{ cm}$$

You will need to use a ball that has a diameter of 22.4 cm to represent Jupiter.

Rates

A **rate** is a ratio of two values expressed in different units. A unit rate is a rate with a denominator of 1 unit.

Example

A plant grew 6 centimeters in 2 days. The plant's rate of growth was $\frac{6 \text{ cm}}{2 \text{ days}}$.

To describe the plant's growth in centimeters per day, write a unit rate.

Divide numerator and denominator by 2:

$$\frac{6 \text{ cm}}{2 \text{ days}} = \frac{6 \text{ cm} \div 2}{2 \text{ days} \div 2}$$

Simplify:

$$= \frac{3 \text{ cm}}{1 \text{ day}}$$

Answer The plant's rate of growth is 3 centimeters per day.

Percent

A **percent** is a ratio of a given number to 100. For example, 85% = 85/100. You can use percent to find part of a whole.

Example

What is 85% of 40?

Step 1 **Rewrite the percent as a decimal by moving the decimal point two places to the left.**

$$0.85$$

Step 2 **Multiply the decimal by the number that you are calculating the percentage of.**

$$0.85 \times 40 = 34$$

85% of 40 is 34.

Decimals

To **add** or **subtract decimals**, line up the digits vertically so that the decimal points line up. Then, add or subtract the columns from right to left. Carry or borrow numbers as necessary.

Example

Add the following numbers: 3.1415 and 2.96.

Step 1 **Line up the digits vertically so that the decimal points line up.**

$$\begin{array}{r} 3.1415 \\ +\,2.96 \\ \hline \end{array}$$

Step 2 **Add the columns from right to left, and carry when necessary.**

$$\begin{array}{r} 3.1415 \\ +\,2.96 \\ \hline 6.1015 \end{array}$$

The sum is 6.1015.

Fractions

A **fraction** is a ratio of two nonzero whole numbers.

Example

Your class has 24 plants. Your teacher instructs you to put 5 plants in a shady spot. What fraction of the plants in your class will you put in a shady spot?

Step 1 **In the denominator, write the total number of parts in the whole.**

$$\frac{?}{24}$$

Step 2 **In the numerator, write the number of parts of the whole that are being considered.**

$$\frac{5}{24}$$

So, $\frac{5}{24}$ of the plants will be in the shade.

Math Refresher

Simplifying Fractions

It is usually best to express a fraction in its simplest form. Expressing a fraction in its simplest form is called **simplifying a fraction.**

Example

Simplify the fraction $\frac{30}{45}$ to its simplest form.

Step 1 Find the largest whole number that will divide evenly into both the numerator and denominator. This number is called the greatest common factor (GCF).

Factors of the numerator 30:
1, 2, 3, 5, 6, 10, **15**, 30

Factors of the denominator 45:
1, 3, 5, 9, **15**, 45

Step 2 Divide both the numerator and the denominator by the GCF, which in this case is 15.

$$\frac{30}{45} = \frac{30 \div 15}{45 \div 15} = \frac{2}{3}$$

Thus, $\frac{30}{45}$ written in its simplest form is $\frac{2}{3}$.

Adding and Subtracting Fractions

To **add** or **subtract fractions** that have the same denominator, simply add or subtract the numerators.

Examples

$\frac{3}{5} + \frac{1}{5} = ?$ and $\frac{3}{4} - \frac{1}{4} = ?$

Step 1 Add or subtract the numerators.

$\frac{3}{5} + \frac{1}{5} = \frac{4}{}$ and $\frac{3}{4} - \frac{1}{4} = \frac{2}{}$

Step 2 Write in the common denominator, which remains the same.

$\frac{3}{5} + \frac{1}{5} = \frac{4}{5}$ and $\frac{3}{4} - \frac{1}{4} = \frac{2}{4}$

Step 3 If necessary, write the fraction in its simplest form.

$\frac{4}{5}$ cannot be simplified, and $\frac{2}{4} = \frac{1}{2}$.

To **add** or **subtract** fractions that have **different denominators**, first find the least common denominator (LCD).

Examples

$\frac{1}{2} + \frac{1}{6} = ?$ and $\frac{3}{4} - \frac{2}{3} = ?$

Step 1 Write the equivalent fractions that have a common denominator.

$\frac{3}{6} + \frac{1}{6} = ?$ and $\frac{9}{12} - \frac{8}{12} = ?$

Step 2 Add or subtract the fractions.

$\frac{3}{6} + \frac{1}{6} = \frac{4}{6}$ and $\frac{9}{12} - \frac{8}{12} = \frac{1}{12}$

Step 3 If necessary, write the fraction in its simplest form.

$\frac{4}{6} = \frac{2}{3}$, and $\frac{1}{12}$ cannot be simplifed.

Multiplying Fractions

To **multiply fractions,** multiply the numerators and the denominators together, and then simplify the fraction to its simplest form.

Example

$\frac{5}{9} \times \frac{7}{10} = ?$

Step 1 Multiply the numerators and denominators.

$$\frac{5}{9} \times \frac{7}{10} = \frac{5 \times 7}{9 \times 10} = \frac{35}{90}$$

Step 2 Simplify the fraction.

$$\frac{35}{90} = \frac{35 \div 5}{90 \div 5} = \frac{7}{18}$$

Dividing Fractions

To **divide fractions**, first rewrite the divisor (the number you divide by) upside down. This number is called the reciprocal of the divisor. Then multiply and simplify if necessary.

Example

$\frac{5}{8} \div \frac{3}{2} = ?$

Step 1 **Rewrite the divisor as its reciprocal.**

$\frac{3}{2} \rightarrow \frac{2}{3}$

Step 2 **Multiply the fractions.**

$\frac{5}{8} \times \frac{2}{3} = \frac{5 \times 2}{8 \times 3} = \frac{10}{24}$

Step 3 **Simplify the fraction.**

$\frac{10}{24} = \frac{10 \div 2}{24 \div 2} = \frac{5}{12}$

Using Significant Figures

The **significant figures** in a decimal are the digits that are warranted by the accuracy of a measuring device.

When you perform a calculation with measurements, the number of significant figures to include in the result depends in part on the number of significant figures in the measurements. When you multiply or divide measurements, your answer should have only as many significant figures as the measurement with the fewest significant figures.

Examples

Using a balance and a graduated cylinder filled with water, you determined that a marble has a mass of 8.0 grams and a volume of 3.5 cubic centimeters. To calculate the density of the marble, divide the mass by the volume.

Write the formula for density: Density $= \frac{\text{mass}}{\text{volume}}$

Substitute measurements: $= \frac{8.0\text{ g}}{3.5\text{ cm}^3}$

Use a calculator to divide: $\approx 2.285714286\text{ g/cm}^3$

Answer Because the mass and the volume have two significant figures each, give the density to two significant figures. The marble has a density of 2.3 grams per cubic centimeter.

Using Scientific Notation

Scientific notation is a shorthand way to write very large or very small numbers. For example, 73,500,000,000,000,000,000,000 kg is the mass of the moon. In scientific notation, it is 7.35×10^{22} kg. A value written as a number between 1 and 10, times a power of 10, is in scientific notation.

Examples

You can convert from standard form to scientific notation.

Standard Form	Scientific Notation
720,000 5 decimal places left	7.2×10^5 Exponent is 5.
0.000291 4 decimal places right	2.91×10^{-4} Exponent is –4.

You can convert from scientific notation to standard form.

Scientific Notation	Standard Form
4.63×10^7 Exponent is 7.	46,300,000 7 decimal places right
1.08×10^{-6} Exponent is –6.	0.00000108 6 decimal places left

Making and Interpreting Graphs

Circle Graph

A circle graph, or pie chart, shows how each group of data relates to all of the data. Each part of the circle represents a category of the data. The entire circle represents all of the data. For example, a biologist studying a hardwood forest in Wisconsin found that there were five different types of trees. The data table at right summarizes the biologist's findings.

Wisconsin Hardwood Trees	
Type of tree	**Number found**
Oak	600
Maple	750
Beech	300
Birch	1,200
Hickory	150
Total	3,000

How to Make a Circle Graph

1 To make a circle graph of these data, first find the percentage of each type of tree. Divide the number of trees of each type by the total number of trees, and multiply by 100%.

$$\frac{600 \text{ oak}}{3{,}000 \text{ trees}} \times 100\% = 20\%$$

$$\frac{750 \text{ maple}}{3{,}000 \text{ trees}} \times 100\% = 25\%$$

$$\frac{300 \text{ beech}}{3{,}000 \text{ trees}} \times 100\% = 10\%$$

$$\frac{1{,}200 \text{ birch}}{3{,}000 \text{ trees}} \times 100\% = 40\%$$

$$\frac{150 \text{ hickory}}{3{,}000 \text{ trees}} \times 100\% = 5\%$$

A Community of Wisconsin Hardwood Trees

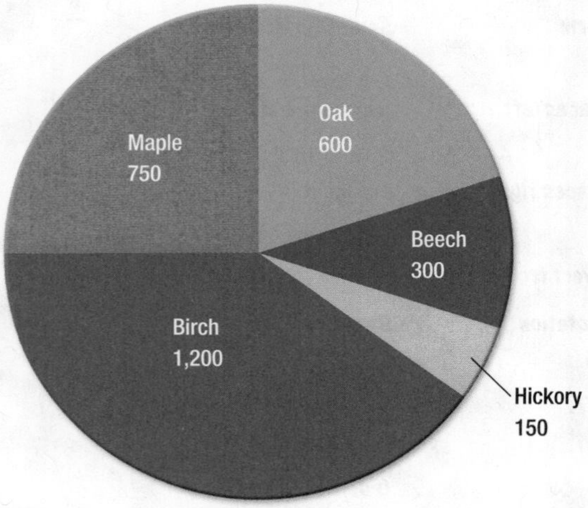
Oak
600
Maple
750
Beech
300
Birch
1,200
Hickory
150

2 Now, determine the size of the wedges that make up the graph. Multiply each percentage by 360°. Remember that a circle contains 360°.

$20\% \times 360° = 72°$ $\quad$ $25\% \times 360° = 90°$

$10\% \times 360° = 36°$ $\quad$ $40\% \times 360° = 144°$

$5\% \times 360° = 18°$

3 Check that the sum of the percentages is 100 and the sum of the degrees is 360.

$20\% + 25\% + 10\% + 40\% + 5\% = 100\%$

$72° + 90° + 36° + 144° + 18° = 360°$

4 Use a compass to draw a circle and mark the center of the circle.

5 Then, use a protractor to draw angles of 72°, 90°, 36°, 144°, and 18° in the circle.

6 Finally, label each part of the graph, and choose an appropriate title.

Line Graphs

Population of Appleton, 1910–2010	
Year	**Population**
1910	1,800
1930	2,500
1950	3,200
1970	3,900
1990	4,600
2010	5,300

Line graphs are most often used to demonstrate continuous change. For example, Mr. Smith's students analyzed the population records for their hometown, Appleton, between 1910 and 2010. Examine the data at right.

Because the year and the population change, they are the variables. The population is determined by, or dependent on, the year. Therefore, the population is called the **dependent variable,** and the year is called the **independent variable.** Each year and its population make a **data pair.** To prepare a line graph, you must first organize data pairs into a table like the one at right.

How to Make a Line Graph

1 Place the independent variable along the horizontal (x) axis. Place the dependent variable along the vertical (y) axis.

2 Label the x-axis "Year" and the y-axis "Population." Look at your greatest and least values for the population. For the y-axis, determine a scale that will provide enough space to show these values. You must use the same scale for the entire length of the axis. Next, find an appropriate scale for the x-axis.

3 Choose reasonable starting points for each axis.

4 Plot the data pairs as accurately as possible.

5 Choose a title that accurately represents the data.

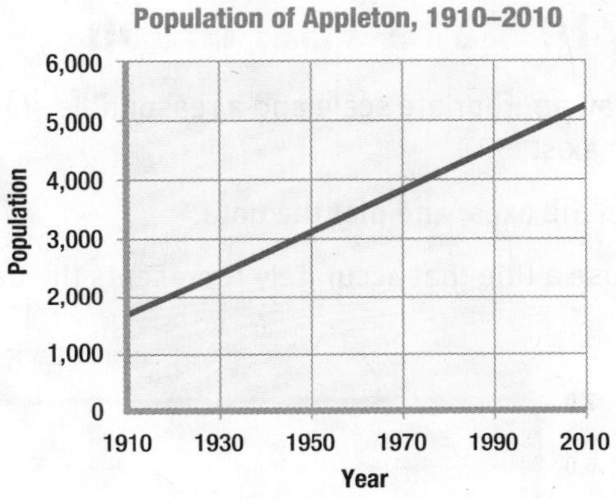

Population of Appleton, 1910–2010
6,000
5,000
4,000
3,000
2,000
1,000
0
Population
1910
1930
1950
1970
1990
2010
Year

How to Determine Slope

Slope is the ratio of the change in the y-value to the change in the x-value, or "rise over run."

1 Choose two points on the line graph. For example, the population of Appleton in 2010 was 5,300 people. Therefore, you can define point A as (2010, 5,300). In 1910, the population was 1,800 people. You can define point B as (1910, 1,800).

2 Find the change in the y-value.
(y at point A) $-$ (y at point B) $=$
5,300 people $-$ 1,800 people $=$
3,500 people

3 Find the change in the x-value.
(x at point A) $-$ (x at point B) $=$
2010 $-$ 1910 $=$ 100 years

4 Calculate the slope of the graph by dividing the change in y by the change in x.

$$slope = \frac{change\ in\ y}{change\ in\ x}$$

$$slope = \frac{3{,}500\ \text{people}}{100\ \text{years}}$$

$$slope = 35\ \text{people per year}$$

In this example, the population in Appleton increased by a fixed amount each year. The graph of these data is a straight line. Therefore, the relationship is **linear.** When the graph of a set of data is not a straight line, the relationship is **nonlinear.**

Bar Graphs

Bar graphs can be used to demonstrate change that is not continuous. These graphs can be used to indicate trends when the data cover a long period of time. A meteorologist gathered the precipitation data shown here for Summerville for April 1–15 and used a bar graph to represent the data.

Precipitation in Summerville, April 1–15			
Date	**Precipitation (cm)**	**Date**	**Precipitation (cm)**
April 1	0.5	April 9	0.25
April 2	1.25	April 10	0.0
April 3	0.0	April 11	1.0
April 4	0.0	April 12	0.0
April 5	0.0	April 13	0.25
April 6	0.0	April 14	0.0
April 7	0.0	April 15	6.50
April 8	1.75		

How to Make a Bar Graph

1 Use an appropriate scale and a reasonable starting point for each axis.

2 Label the axes, and plot the data.

3 Choose a title that accurately represents the data.

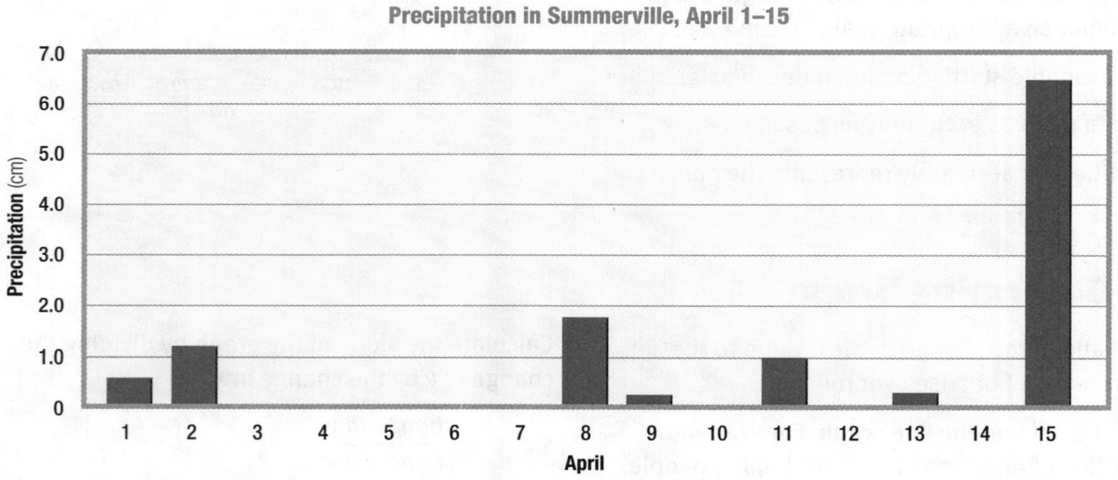

Precipitation in Summerville, April 1–15
7.0
6.0
5.0
4.0
3.0
2.0
1.0
0
Precipitation (cm)
1
2
3
4
5
6
7
8
9
10
11
12
13
14
15
April

Glossary

Pronunciation Key

Sound	Symbol	Example	Respelling
ă	a	pat	PAT
ā	ay	pay	PAY
âr	air	care	KAIR
ä	ah	father	FAH•ther
är	ar	argue	AR•gyoo
ch	ch	chase	CHAYS
ĕ	e	pet	PET
ĕ (at end of a syllable)	eh	settee lessee	seh•TEE leh•SEE
ĕr	ehr	merry	MEHR•ee
ē	ee	beach	BEECH
g	g	gas	GAS
ĭ	i	pit	PIT
ĭ (at end of a syllable)	ih	guitar	gih•TAR
ī	y eye (only for a complete syllable)	pie island	PY EYE•luhnd
îr	ir	hear	HIR
j	j	germ	JERM
k	k	kick	KIK
ng	ng	thing	THING
ngk	ngk	bank	BANGK

Sound	Symbol	Example	Respelling
ŏ	ah	bottle	BAHT'l
ō	oh	toe	TOH
ô	aw	caught	KAWT
ôr	ohr	roar	ROHR
oi	oy	noisy	NOYZ•ee
ŏŏ	u	book	BUK
ōō	oo	boot	BOOT
ou	ow	pound	POWND
s	s	center	SEN•ter
sh	sh	cache	CASH
ŭ	uh	flood	FLUHD
ûr	er	bird	BERD
z	z	xylophone	ZY•luh•fohn
z	z	bags	BAGZ
zh	zh	decision	dih•SIZH•uhn
ə	uh	around broken focus	uh•ROWND BROH•kuhn FOH•kuhs
ər	er	winner	WIN•er
th	th	thin they	THIN THAY
w	w	one	WUHN
wh	hw	whether	HWETH•er

A

acceleration (ak·sel·uh·RAY·shuhn) the rate at which velocity changes over time; an object accelerates if its speed, direction, or both change (22)
aceleración la tasa a la que la velocidad cambia con el tiempo; un objeto acelera si su rapidez cambia, si su dirección cambia, o si tanto su rapidez como su dirección cambian

analog signal (AN·uh·lawg SIG·nuhl) a signal whose properties can change continuously in a given range (187)
señal análoga una señal cuyas propiedades cambian continuamente en un rango determinado

Archimedes' principle (ar·kuh·MEE·deez PRIN·suh·puhl) the principle that states that the buoyant force on an object in a fluid is an upward force equal to the weight of the volume of fluid that the object displaces (62)
principio de Arquímedes el principio que establece que la fuerza flotante de un objeto que está en un fluido es una fuerza ascendente cuya magnitud es igual al peso del volumen del fluido que el objeto desplaza

atmospheric pressure (at·muh·SFIR·ik PRESH·er) the pressure caused by the weight of the atmosphere (58)
presión atmosférica la presión producida por el peso de la atmósfera

B

buoyant force (BOY·uhnt FOHRS) the upward force that keeps an object immersed in or floating on a liquid (62)
fuerza boyante la fuerza ascendente que hace que un objeto se mantenga sumergido en un líquido o flotando en él

C

centripetal acceleration (sen·TRIP·ih·tl ak·sel·uh·RAY·shuhn) the acceleration directed toward the center of a circular path (25)
aceleración centrípeta la aceleración que se dirige hacia el centro de un camino circular

computer (kuhm·PYOO·ter) an electronic device that can accept data and instructions, follow the instructions, and output the results (190)
computadora un aparato electrónico que acepta información e instrucciones, sigue instrucciones, y produce una salida para los resultados

D

digital signal (DIJ·ih·tl SIG·nuhl) a signal that can be represented as a sequence of discrete values (188)
señal digital una señal que se puede representar como una secuencia de valores discretos

E

electric charge (ee·LEK·trik CHARJ) a fundamental property that leads to the electromagnetic interactions among particles that make up matter (128)
carga eléctrica una propiedad fundamental que determina las interacciones electromagnéticas entre las partículas que forman la materia

electric circuit (ee·LEK·trik SER·kit) a set of electrical components connected such that they provide one or more complete paths for the movement of charges (146)
circuito eléctrico un conjunto de componentes eléctricos conectados de modo que proporcionen una o más rutas completas para el movimiento de las cargas

electric current (ee·LEK·trik KER·uhnt) the rate at which electric charges pass a given point (138)
corriente eléctrica la tasa a la que las cargas eléctricas pasan por un punto dado

electric generator (ee·LEK·trik JEN·uh·ray·ter) a device that converts mechanical energy into electrical energy (180)
generador eléctrico un aparato que transforma la energía mecánica en energía eléctrica

electric motor (ee·LEK·trik MO·ter) a device that converts electrical energy into mechanical energy (176)
motor eléctrico un aparato que transforma la energía eléctrica en energía mecánica

electrical conductor (ee·LEK·trik·kuhl kuhn·DUHK·ter) a material in which charges can move freely (132)
conductor eléctrico un material en el que las cargas se mueven libremente

electrical insulator (ee·LEK·trih·kuhl IN·suh·lay·ter) a material in which charges cannot move freely (132)
aislante eléctrico un material en el que las cargas no pueden moverse libremente

electromagnet (ee·lek·troh·MAG·nit) a coil that has a soft iron core and that acts as a magnet when an electric current is in the coil (173)
electroimán una bobina que tiene un centro de hierro suave y que funciona como un imán cuando hay una corriente eléctrica en la bobina

electromagnetic induction (ee·lek·troh·mag·NET·ik in·DUHK·shuhn) the process of creating a current in a circuit by changing a magnetic field (178)
inducción electromagnética el proceso de crear una corriente en un circuito por medio de un cambio en el campo magnético

electromagnetism (ee·lek·troh·MAG·nih·tiz·uhm) the interaction between electricity and magnetism (172)
electromagnetismo la interacción entre la electricidad y el magnetismo

electronic device (ee·lek·TRAHN·ik dih·VYS) a device that produces or is powered by a flow of electrons and contains an integrated circuit (186)
dispositivo electrónico dispositivo con un circuito integrado, que produce o cuyo funcionamiento depende de un flujo de electrones

energy (EN·er·jee) the ability to cause change (82)
energía la capacidad de producir un cambio

F

fluid (FLOO·id) a nonsolid state of matter in which the atoms or molecules are free to move past each other, as in a gas or liquid (56)
fluido un estado no sólido de la materia en el que los átomos o moléculas tienen libertad de movimiento, como en el caso de un gas o un líquido

force (FOHRS) a push or a pull exerted on an object in order to change the motion of the object; force has size and direction (30)
fuerza una acción de empuje o atracción que se ejerce sobre un objeto con el fin de cambiar su movimiento; la fuerza tiene magnitud y dirección

free fall (FREE FAWL) the motion of a body when only the force of gravity is acting on the body (48)
caída libre el movimiento de un cuerpo cuando la única fuerza que actúa sobre él es la fuerza de gravedad

fulcrum (FUL·kruhm) the point on which a lever pivots (108)
fulcro el punto sobre el que pivota una palanca

G-H

gravity (GRAV·ih·tee) a force of attraction between objects that is due to their masses (44)
gravedad una fuerza de atracción entre dos objetos debido a sus masas

I-J

inclined plane (in·KLYND PLAYN) a simple machine that is a straight, slanted surface, which facilitates the raising of loads; a ramp (112)
plano inclinado una máquina simple que es una superficie recta e inclinada, que facilita el levantamiento de cargas; una rampa

inertia (ih·NER·shuh) the tendency of an object to resist a change in motion unless an outside force acts on the object (34)
inercia la tendencia de un objeto a resistir un cambio en el movimiento a menos que actúe una fuerza externa sobre el objeto

integrated circuit (in·tih·GRAY·tid SER·kit) a circuit whose components are formed on a single semiconductor (186)
circuito integrado un circuito cuyos componentes están formados en un solo semiconductor

K

kinetic energy (kih·NET·ik EN·er·jee) the energy of an object that is due to the object's motion (90)
energía cinética la energía de un objeto debido al movimiento del objeto

L

lever (LEV·er) a simple machine that consists of a bar that pivots at a fixed point called a fulcrum (108)
palanca una máquina simple formada por una barra que gira en un punto fijo llamado fulcro

M

machine (muh·SHEEN) a device that helps do work by changing the magnitude and/or direction of an applied force (104)
máquina un dispositivo que ayuda a realizar trabajos cambiando la magnitud y/o la dirección de una fuerza aplicada

magnet (MAG·nit) any material that attracts iron or materials containing iron (158)
imán cualquier material que atrae hierro o materiales que contienen hierro

magnetic field (MAG·net·ik FEELD) a region where a magnetic force can be detected (159)
campo magnético una región donde puede detectarse una fuerza magnética

magnetic force (MAG·net·ik FOHRS) the force of attraction or repulsion generated by moving or spinning electric charges (158)
fuerza magnética la fuerza de atracción o repulsión generadas por cargas eléctricas en movimiento o que giran

magnetic pole (MAG·net·ik POHL) one of two points, such as the ends of a magnet, that have opposing magnetic qualities (159)
polo magnético uno de dos puntos, tales como los extremos de un imán, que tienen cualidades magnéticas opuestas

mechanical advantage (mih·KAN·ih·kuhl ad·VAN·tij) a number that tells how many times a machine multiplies input force (106)
ventaja mecánica un número que indica cuántas veces una máquina multiplica su fuerza de entrada

mechanical efficiency (mih·KAN·ih·kuhl ih·FISH·uhn·see) a quantity, usually expressed as a percentage, that measures the ratio of work output to work input in a machine (107)
eficiencia mecánica una cantidad, generalmente expresada como un porcentaje, que mide la relación entre el trabajo de entrada y el trabajo de salida en una máquina

mechanical energy (mih·KAN·ih·kuhl EN·er·jee) the sum of an object's kinetic energy and potential energy due to gravity or elastic deformation; does not include chemical energy or nuclear energy (94)
energía mecánica la suma de las energías cinética y potencial de un objeto debido a la gravedad o a la deformación elástica; no incluye la energía química ni nuclear

motion (MOH·shuhn) an object's change in position relative to a reference point (8)
movimiento el cambio en la posición de un objeto respecto a un punto de referencia

N

net force (NET FOHRS) the combination of all of the forces acting on an object (32)
fuerza neta la combinación de todas las fuerzas que actúan sobre un objeto

O

orbit (OHR·bit) the path that a body follows as it travels around another body in space (48)
órbita la trayectoria que sigue un cuerpo al desplazarse alrededor de otro cuerpo en el espacio

P-Q

parallel circuit (PAIR·uh·lel SER·kit) a circuit in which the parts are joined in branches such that the voltage across each part is the same (151)
circuito paralelo un circuito en el que las partes están unidas en ramas de manera tal que el voltaje entre cada parte es la misma

pascal (pa·SKAL) the SI unit of pressure (symbol, Pa) (57)
pascal la unidad de presión del sistema internacional de unidades (símbolo: Pa)

position (puh·ZISH·uhn) the location of an object (6)
posición la ubicación de un objeto

potential energy (puh·TEN·shuhl EN·er·jee) the energy that an object has because of the position, condition, or chemical composition of the object (92)
energía potencial la energía que tiene un objeto debido a su posición, condición, o composición química

power (POW·er) the rate at which work is done or energy is transformed (84)
potencia la tasa a la que se realiza un trabajo o a la que se transforma la energía

pressure (PRESH·er) the amount of force exerted per unit area of a surface (56)
presión la cantidad de fuerza ejercida en una superficie por unidad de área

pulley (PUL·ee) a simple machine that consists of a wheel over which a rope, chain, or wire passes (111)
polea una máquina simple formada por una rueda sobre la cual pasa una cuerda, cadena, o cable

R

reference point (REF·er·uhns POYNT) a location to which another location is compared (6)
punto de referencia una ubicación con la que se compara otra ubicación

resistance (rih·ZIS·tuhns) in physical science, the opposition presented to the current by a material or device (140)
resistencia en ciencias físicas, la oposición que un material o aparato presenta a la corriente

S

semiconductor (sem·ee·kuhn·DUHK·ter) an element or compound that conducts electric current better than an insulator does but not as well as a conductor does (133)
semiconductor un elemento o compuesto que conduce la corriente eléctrica mejor que un aislante, pero no tan bien como un conductor

series circuit (SIR·eez SER·kit) a circuit in which the parts are joined one after another such that the current in each part is the same (150)
circuito en serie un circuito en el que las partes están unidas una después de la otra de manera tal que la corriente en cada parte es la misma

solenoid (SOH·luh·noyd) a coil of wire with an electric current in it (173)
solenoide una bobina de alambre que tiene una corriente eléctrica

speed (SPEED) the distance traveled divided by the time interval during which the motion occurred (9)
rapidez la distancia que un objeto se desplaza dividida entre el intervalo de tiempo durante el cual ocurrió el movimiento

static electricity (STAT·ik ee·lek·TRIS·ih·tee) electric charge at rest; generally produced by friction or induction (131)
electricidad estática carga eléctrica en reposo; por lo general se produce por fricción o inducción

T-U

transformer (trans·FOHR·mer) a device that increases or decreases the voltage of alternating current (179)
transformador un aparato que aumenta o disminuye el voltaje de la corriente alterna

V

vector (VEK·ter) a quantity that has both size and direction (15)
vector una cantidad que tiene tanto magnitud como dirección

velocity (vuh·LAHS·ih·tee) the speed of an object in a particular direction (15)
velocidad la rapidez de un objeto en una dirección dada

voltage (VOHL·tij) the amount of work to move a unit electric charge between two points; expressed in volts (140)
voltaje la cantidad de trabajo necesario para transportar una unidad de carga eléctrica entre dos puntos; se expresa en voltios

W-Z

wheel and axle (WEEL AND AK·suhl) a simple machine consisting of two circular objects of different sizes; the wheel is the larger of the two circular objects, and the axle is attached to the center of the wheel (110)
rueda y eje una máquina simple formada por dos objetos circulares de diferentes tamaños; la rueda es el más grande de los dos objetos circulares, y el eje está sujeto al centro de la rueda

work (WERK) the transfer of energy to an object by using a force that causes the object to move in the direction of the force (80)
trabajo la transferencia de energía a un objeto mediante una fuerza que hace que el objeto se mueva en la dirección de la fuerza

Index

Page numbers for definitions are printed in **boldface** type.
Page numbers for illustrations, maps, and charts are printed in *italics*.

A

B

C

D

E

F

N

O

P-Q

R

S

T

U

V

W-Z